THE FORTIES

Edmund Wilson

EDMUND WILSON

The Forties

From Notebooks and Diaries of the Period

Edited with an Introduction by
Leon Edel

FARRAR, STRAUS AND GIROUX

NEW YORK

Library of Congress Cataloging in Publication Data
Wilson, Edmund, 1895–1972. The forties.
Includes index.
1. Wilson, Edmund, 1895–1972—Diaries.
2. Authors American—20th century—Biography.
I. Edel, Leon, 1907–   II. Title.
PS3545.I6245Z465   1983   818'.5203 [B]   82–21028

B

WILSON

MMLL

CONTENTS

1946–1949

ILLUSTRATIONS

EDITOR'S FOREWORD

Edmund Wilson's *The Twenties* and *The Thirties* were printed from typescripts he prepared and partially edited before his death. *The Forties* does not have the benefit of his editing; it is a wholly posthumous book and lacks the retrospective passages Wilson would have written had he been able to put it together. Certain portions are fragmentary; others are very full and require little gloss. A few sections existed in typed form: the European notes, which were extracted from the author's notebooks in the preparation of *Europe Without Baedeker*; and the account of the Zuñi, amplified for EW's later book *Red, Black, Blond and Olive*. The Haiti portion has been assembled from almost illegibly scrawled notes—put down on the spot in a kind of semi-shorthand, like a reporter's notes. Wilson usually clear-copied such notes into his journals, but in this instance he seems to have expanded them directly into the three articles he wrote for *The Reporter*, the New York liberal magazine.

The other portions of this volume came from the large-sized ledgers in which he kept his journals. The years from 1940 to 1945 are the scrappiest of all his journal-keeping, and had to be assembled from loose pages and sporadic entries in the back covers of his notebooks. To these I have added the undated scenario for a novel, "The Story of the Three Wishes" or "The Red Bank and Moscow Novel." I also found a few tentative retrospective notes, which I have included. The meagerness of the entries of 1940–45 results not so much from Wilson's malaise over the war as from the fact (as he said) that he did little journal-keeping during his third marriage, which culminated in divorce.

As before, I have edited the texts with a light hand, in accordance with Wilson's instructions, correcting slips, deleting repetitions, and touching up the punctuation—all that he would have done were he preparing the book for his publisher. He did not want to be edited in the academic manner, as if he were a classical text, but insisted that his journals—written often in haste, and rough at best—should be treated as any manuscript is treated in a publisher's office: tidied up and made ready for the printer. We know that Wilson kept these notebook-journals originally for his own use. They were written hurriedly and he had no intention of checking names or historical facts as he wrote. The result is that we encounter in the manuscript at certain points a question mark in parentheses—Wilson's interrogations of himself. The reader must recognize these as part of the tentativeness of the journal; everything was to be set right and verified later, if he should need to use the passage. Readers must take these queries as meaning "Was it *di* or *de* in that name?" or "Have I got my spelling right?" There are some passages which were clear enough to Wilson, for he would set down some word to jog his memory, but which are a mystery to us. I have left these occasional little mysteries: only Wilson could have explained them, but they suggest the nature of this kind of journal-keeping. Wilson was

never afraid to correct his errors: he pretended to none of
the omniscience which he saw and deplored in academe.
Certain books which he autographed for me contain, beyond the inscription, references to pages where he corrects
his own and the printer's errors and sometimes writes in
an explanatory footnote.

The Forties has benefited from an earlier grant given
me by the National Endowment for the Humanities. The
death of Edmund's widow, Elena Wilson, occurred just as
I was beginning work on this volume and deprived me of
a valuable source of information and help. But I am grateful for the continued assistance of EW's older daughter,
Rosalind, and his younger, Helen Miranda. Phyllis
Stenger, a lecturer at the University of Hawaii, helped
with identifications and footnotes, Ella Wiswell with the
Russian allusions, Kathleen Falvey with the Italian, and
Ines Kinnell checked the typescript against the holograph
text. Finally, I want to thank my wife, Marjorie, for reading the entire manuscript when it was completed.

L.E.

EDMUND WILSON IN MIDDLE AGE
"The Bit Between My Teeth"

In his earlier decades, Edmund Wilson was too busy "living" to reckon the mounting years. He turned thirty-five at the end of the 1920s but continued into the economic depression with all the energy of his youth. He assayed "the American jitters" as we have seen in *The Thirties*. He went to Russia when he turned forty in 1935 and on his return spent five years writing *To the Finland Station*. But at the end of 1940—when he was forty-five— he suddenly found himself reckoning with his mortality. F. Scott Fitzgerald died in December of that year of a heart attack. Fitzgerald was a year younger than Wilson. At that moment—the moment when he grieved for a writer who had always seemed so much younger—the aging writer awoke with a shock to the fact of his middle age.

"I have felt Scott's death very much," he wrote to his Princeton friend John Peale Bishop (who would also die soon). "Men who start writing together write for one another more than they realize till somebody else dies." And then, Wilson observed, "it's extremely depressing to me that Joyce should have died, too—even though I suppose his work was finished. Yeats, Freud, Trotsky and Joyce have all gone in so short a time—it is almost like the death of one's father."

Wilson had indeed lost a series of literary and political fathers; they had been important characters in his books *Axel's Castle* and *To the Finland Station*. But Fitzgerald had hardly been fatherly; he was a kind of younger brother who looked up to Wilson and called him his "intellectual conscience." And now, in one brief moment, he had been deprived of his entire future. It was this abrupt termination that deeply upset Wilson: it could so easily happen to him. Gathering Fitzgerald's literary remains into a volume, which included his painful record of his decline into apathy, Wilson used his title *The Crack-Up*—and felt as if he himself was cracking up. His elegiac verses in the opening pages mourn more than the loss of a friend:

> Those eyes struck dark, dissolving in a wrecked
> And darkened world, that gleam of intellect
> That spilled into the spectrum of tune, taste,
> Scent, color, living speech, is gone, is lost
> And we must dwell among the ragged stumps . . .

Gone . . . lost . . . But neither could Wilson face the thought of a sudden disconnection from all the books he felt still inside him and from his growing children. He was plunged into a middle-age crisis—quite of the text-book variety.

Wilson had for too long cultivated the carefree irresponsibilities of his earlier time—hard work, hard drinking, endless love affairs and promiscuities, and a kind of devil-may-care attitude. He had for years scrambled from small furnished rooms to cheap apartments, or the little shabby frame house at 314 East 53rd Street which he had rented for fifty dollars a month. And then he had made unhappy marriages—his first wife, an actress, always had to be at the theater; his second, a lively companion, spent much time in California taking care of a young son by an earlier marriage. His life now, with Mary McCarthy, was stormy—she was ambitious and devoted to her writing. And his children needed him, his daughter, soon to come of age, his young son, born at the end of the 1930s.

Edmund Wilson did not, however, give way to depression. He hated uncertainties. He liked to act, and to act decisively. In 1941 he bought a commodious house on Cape Cod, at Wellfleet, the corner of America he loved best. In 1943 he went to work for *The New Yorker*. In July 1946 he and Mary McCarthy were legally separated. In December 1946 they were divorced, and he then married an aristocratic woman of considerable beauty and grace named Elena Mumm Thornton. She was half Russian and half German (her family had given its name to a famous champagne). She had been married to a stockbroker and lived in the suburbs with one son and her husband. Wilson first met Elena through mutual friends on the Cape, but had gotten to know her better at *Town and Country*, where she was an editor, when the journal published one of his *Hecate County* tales.

"A great relief after a year of rocky households," Wilson wrote in his journal. "I remarried when, in spite of my difficulties with Mary, I began to function normally again."

Things had not been normal for a long time. Deeper feelings stirred in him than he could describe. In the journals we read fugitive sentences and phrases that tell us of the crystallization of Wilson's middle-age emotions. He visits the Spectacle Ponds on the Cape, describes the place with Thoreau-like care, examines the water plants, and listens to the chorale of the bullfrogs—"as if the frogs and the orchids flourished and perfected themselves, had their lives, for their own satisfaction." Wilson was ready now to have his life for his own satisfaction: he had spent two decades dealing with historical philosophy, theories of revolution, utopias, while struggling for some kind of self-realization. Now he felt an affinity between the self-sufficiency of the biological life in the ponds "and my life at this time—and a darkness into which I sink and a clear round single lens, well guarded and hidden away." That single lens was the lens of selfhood—independence and a desire to write as he pleased instead of shaping reviews and occasional pieces to earn a living. Looking into the pond of himself, he saw "many things nourished and lurking at the bottom that have not yet been brought to light."

At the beginning of the 1940s Wilson lived a kind of hand-to-mouth existence. He was using up money as fast as he earned it. His $1,700 advance for *To the Finland Station* evaporated long before the book was finished. He postponed other important work in order to review current books. He was always in debt to publishers. However, he did not hesitate to borrow $1,500 from the bank to buy the spacious old-fashioned Wellfleet house that would serve as his base for the rest of his life. He paid what now seems a very modest $4,000 for it and spent another $1,000 renovating it. Before he went to work for *The New Yorker,* he outlined to Harold Ross what his needs were: $10,000 a year with perhaps another $3,000 in perquisites and a considerable degree of independence to call his time his own. The enlightened policies of this journal made such luxuries possible.

His marital life had had a destructive pattern from the time he first married in the 1920s. Wilson's fourth marriage, and his last, was dictated, as the journals show, by an intense passion, but it marked a significant change—perhaps because Elena Wilson was European and therefore clearly conscious of her husband's needs. In his fiction he had always regarded the "exhilarating Western girl, laughing her open-air laugh," as ideal—but it was a European woman of much greater sophistication who (with a great deal of laughter and liveliness) provided the understanding and domestication he sought.

In the final pages of Wilson's *Memoirs of Hecate County* we can read what possessing a house and a settled way of life meant to him. The narrator writes, "How stabilizing to drive up beside my buried stone house—a lodge that was almost a castle—and put my car in my own garage, to open my own front door, to find everything just as I had left it . . . It had the dignity, that rude yet snug little house, of everything in my life that was good . . . I could rejoin my old solitary self, the self for which I really lived and which kept up its austere virtue, the self which had survived through these trashy years."

I can recall my own glimpse of the well-organized house in Wellfleet and the ways in which Elena protected Wilson's privacy. During a visit in the late 1950s I was put into comfortable quarters in a little separate guest house. Wilson occasionally appeared during the day, uncombed, unshaven, in his pajamas and bathrobe—the daylong uniform of his work; he would pat the dogs, talk to the marmalade Persian cats, exchange a few words, munch a sandwich, and disappear into the recesses of his study. His social day began around 5 p.m., when he descended freshly shaved, with a cherubic glow on his Roman features, fully dressed, wearing a jacket and a tie set into a crisp shirt ironed by his wife, ready for the evening bottle of whiskey in the parlor. Louise Bogan, who had known Wilson from the time of his casual Village life, charm-

ingly describes the new mode of life. Elena, she writes, in
a letter to May Sarton, "has really effected a tremendous
change in Edmund's way of living." She had "evidently
put real elbow grease into decorating: scraping floors and
walls and making curtains." There was the parlor upholstered in yellow with a good deal of Federal mahogany
—Wilson's mother's; a dining room with more mahogany
against the blue walls and "lovely blue Staffordshire and
silver." A middle room had blue walls and blue chintz and
good linen. And then at the back, Wilson's study, with a
bathroom attached and a stairway to attic rooms filled with
books. "For the first time," Bogan wrote, "poor Edmund
has attention, space and effectively arranged paraphernalia
of all kinds—Mary never really helped in the more practical ways; and Edmund has had a very scrappy kind of
life down the years. Now all moves smoothly; tea on a
tray for his 'elevenses,' absolute silence in his working
hours and good meals at appropriate intervals." Elena also
helped with his proofs and showed a constant interest in
his literary pursuits. I remember friendly talk in the evenings with neighbors and old-timers when on occasion
Wilson was capable of polishing off the remains of the
bottle of whiskey which he had begun before dinner—a
dinner during which a good number of glasses of wine
were also consumed.

Wilson himself records in his journals his delight in his
new life. He had from his earliest years lived in country
houses, and on this day in 1948, coming back from walking the dogs, he was happy to find himself in full possession, a member of the local gentry, like his father and all
his relatives "enjoying its brightness and pleasantness—
bow window in the dining room, gleam of candlesticks,
comfortable pink and blue of Elena's middle room." The
dogs seemed to him to share his "joyful excitement" and

"I let them out, then came back for another drink, and enjoyed the look of the house some more."

In some way he thought himself Shakespeare's Prospero. He was putting the affairs of his life in order, straightening out his relation to his children and friends and relatives on his bit of enchanted ground at Cape Cod. The daughter born to Edmund and Elena in 1948 was given the name Helen for Wilson's mother and for one of Elena's aunts, but her middle name was Miranda, a recall of *The Tempest,* even as his older daughter had been named Rosalind, after the heroine of *As You Like It.* With the birth of Helen Miranda Wilson the author of *To the Finland Station* and *Memoirs of Hecate County* (which had recently earned him $60,000) could feel that the time of tempest was over. He had reached a calm sea —and he had endured, among the mirror ponds and the thick woods of New England.

It was after his fourth marriage, when Edmund Wilson had acquired many of the creature comforts he needed and enjoyed, and was making himself into an important man of letters, that he had occasion to revisit his love of the old bohemian time, Edna St. Vincent Millay. They had last met nineteen years before. This visit of 1947 is documented both in the journals and in his memoir of Millay that was first published in *The Nation,* and later in *The Shores of Light.* The journal record is more direct; it reflects with great vividness Wilson's immediate feelings, which he later filtered into polished recollections. He and Elena had gone to Tanglewood to attend the summer concerts. One day they drove to Austerlitz, about an hour away, to call on Millay and her husband, Eugen Boissevain, in their big house, Steepletop, set deeply into the woods. Seeing Edna again was more difficult than

Wilson had been ready to expect, but it seems to have helped him come to grips with what he had been in the 1920s—in contrast with his present domestication. In his old memories, Edna was still a *gamine,* a sprite who dashed around the corners of Greenwich Village—a friend remembered her running there one day, pursued by Floyd Dell. But the woman he now faced was incapable of moving quickly; he might not have recognized her. She had ceased to be a sprite. He used words like "heavy," "dumpy," "ruddy," "overblown," to describe her—she might have used similar words to describe him. He found it awkward and uncomfortable to face her. Later he remembered how much he kept looking away out of the window. Behind their casual talk and the martinis they sipped, terror crept into the conversation. Or, as Wilson put it, "the visit was like the desires and fears, the revived emotions, of sleep: old images exaggerated, deformed, swollen with longing or horror." They discussed one of Catullus' poems which Edna was trying to translate. It was about the death of love. It spoke of "an end to this despair." Reaching for ways of bridging awkwardness, Wilson asked her to read some of her poetry. He wanted Elena to hear her. She always had read beautifully, pronouncing every syllable and giving every sound its value, with a mastery of tempo and tone. He chose "The Poet and His Book" from *Second April.* It had been one of his favorites, but Wilson's romantic memories apparently screened out what these verses really said. Unconsciously, he knew they expressed exactly what had been troubling him ever since Scott Fitzgerald's death—and more recently that of his old friend John Peale Bishop. Wilson recalled the poem as having homely and magical images and he had liked its "urgent and hurried movement." But that urgent movement now caused a kind of consternation in him. He had allowed aesthetic and nostalgic appeal to cover up his memory that the poem was a cry for survival.

> Stranger, pause and look;
>   From the dust of ages
> Lift this little book,
>   Turn the tattered pages,
> Read me, do not let me die!

That *cri du coeur* was repeated in several of the stanzas with all the passion of Millay's voice: it filled the room with sadness and memory. Wilson found himself on the verge of tears. He was not usually given to such display of emotion. "I began to find it difficult to hear. I could not weep. I did not want her to weep, and though Elena thought we ought to have stayed, I soon insisted on leaving."

Later, in his journal, he could say to himself how strong was the tug of his emotions within his aging body. "I was being sucked into her narrow and noble world, where all that mattered was herself and her poetry." Edna was still, he wrote, "almost as disconcerting as she had ever been in the twenties, to which she had completely belonged—for she was not a part of the present, and my relation to her . . . exerted on me a sort of pressure as if to gouge me out, extirpate me, from my present personality." She had been among those who give themselves up "completely to art, to emotion, to enjoyment, without planning for the future or counting the cost." This, he said, produced "dreadful disabilities and bankruptcies later." Here the "reorganized" Edmund speaks for his own future—for his having chosen a comfortable middle-class way of life. The violence of the word "gouge," the sense of being dragged up by the roots, spoke for the way his old feelings were tearing at him. Millay seemed to be pulling him into a pocket of the past.

He finally admitted to himself that he had actually had a moment of fright. "What had desolated and frightened me was death." And what he had seen was that Millay was "making her last fierce struggle." He thought of death —but with it he was thinking of survival. In the midst of these intensities we find this sentence: "I felt a certain satisfaction in the idea that I was outlasting her." The cruel thought—as if he were in a competition with Millay to endure—was followed by the reiteration that he was "troubled and depressed at finding the metamorphosis she had undergone." But he, too, had changed. And he summarized the changes for himself: his life was now "organized and grounded"; he had children to worry and divert him. His work was leading him into new endeavor. All this made it profoundly disturbing to see Millay and her husband living in their big woodsy comfortable old house isolated from the world. He described them as looking like "deteriorated ghosts." And they were haunting their own home.

So much of Wilson's compelling drive toward an arranged future—domestication, endurance, survival—is to be found in the 1940s journals. Wilson's period of self-reorganization—his problems with Mary McCarthy, his pressing need for money, his quest for a permanent anchorage—made for less frequent journalizing during 1940–45. However, among his papers I found a plan for a novel reflecting his retrospective mood and his anxieties. These notes are undated. But their theme establishes them as belonging to this time, for they constitute a kind of stock-taking of his adult life. His fantasy shows a disillusionment and dissatisfaction with what he now called his "trashy years," and he seeks to vindicate his return to the solidities of existence and to a greater independence. The novel would have been autobiographical—in his notes he gives his characters the names of certain persons he knew and draws directly on both the twenties and the thirties. He called his proposed fiction (as if it were an old fairy tale) "The Story of the Three Wishes." The scenario he began to draw up is labeled "Red Bank and Moscow Novel"—thus bringing his place of birth and his Russian experience together.

The notes show that his narrator undergoes a series of transformations: first he becomes a man of the 1920s who lives out the jazz age and the "boom and bust." Then he is transformed into a Russian bureaucrat in Moscow, and finally he becomes a man of the contemporary world living on Cape Cod. In the end, the narrator becomes himself again, revisiting his old home in Red Bank and finding that his parents are gone but that a woman has waited for him. Solveig for his Peer Gynt. He is led in this way to the ultimate revelation: the three different Edmund Wilsons have all been the same—the romantic Wilson, the Marxist Wilson, and the independent Wilson. To the actuality of his domestication, Edmund Wilson was adding a fantasy of "ego integration." This self-acceptance in the proposed novel was a summing up of his life to the middle of his middle age. He writes in the notes:

The principal effect of the book depends on making the three episodes appear to be quite different while they are going on. Each seems a different world in which he is hoping to find something new and distinct: first, the world of people with money during the Boom; then the revolutionary world of the Soviet Union; then the world of the independent man who has tried to get away from society, to accomplish something in which he believes. But now the reader

is to find out for the first time that they have all been
the same thing—the modern world . . . the three men
are the same man.

And that same man was the man of letters, now ready to
"accomplish something in which he believes." What remains, Wilson adds, is "a residue of wisdom from experience, a different moral from any he had been aiming to
illustrate in any of his three exploits." That difference was
middle-class enough, if measured by bohemianism and
revolution: assuming responsibilities of parenthood and
trying to lead some kind of regular existence to provide
more money. What wasn't middle-class was his quest for
independence.

During the 1940s Wilson published seven books and
more than a hundred essays and articles—sufficient evidence that his domestication and life at Wellfleet chan-
neled his resources. The books included one work of
fiction, his *Memoirs of Hecate County,* which for a while
was a best seller, until the self-appointed censors brought
it into court for its candid sexuality. His most important
critical work was *The Wound and the Bow,* in which
Wilson, in a highly original way, dealt with what he
called "the literature of trauma" and used Freudian in-
sights with much greater skill than his predecessors. This
was what literature meant to him—as he would later
explain—"narrative and drama as well as discussion of
comparative values." The journals of the time tell us little
about these works; but they include the notes for the three
travelogues of the decade that resulted in *Europe Without
Baedeker* and two of the essays in the later book *Red,
Black, Blond and Olive:* the trip to Zuñi with his remarkable description of the Indian dances and his account of
the new republic of Haiti, soon to become a dictatorship.

Distinctly absent from the 1940 journals are the events of the war, except for some brief thoughts about the bombings of cities set down in 1944 and the 1945 journey to Europe. The journal records, rather, his walks beside the New England ponds, his love affair with Elena, his period in Reno waiting for his divorce, and his usual notes on talking and drinking with friends and acquaintances. And yet in certain ways the fragmented forties have a greater solidity than his two earlier volumes of the preceding decades. There is a maturity and self-confidence, the sense of authority of a man who has found his course and knows where he is going. As always, there is much routine and even turgid material; but with this there are many felicities of observation and feeling.

In the 1914–18 war Wilson had been a wound-dresser and a medic in the tradition of Walt Whitman. In the 1939–45 war he resisted military pressures and refused to use his pen for the war effort. He viewed the conflict passively and chose instead to continue in his role as writer and interpreter who moved from the imaginative in literature to the concrete in society. He felt, as he would say, that there was "a certain irreconcilability between the ideals of ordinary life and the special hazards of art," and his curiosity led him to range within "ordinary life" while risking the hazards of his artistic conscience. His work on *To the Finland Station* had made him aware of "that great international department of thought" called Marxism, and without being a member of that faith he nevertheless felt that it gave him a breadth of vision denied to those who closed their minds to it. He had acquired, in a word, a grasp of the revolutionary origins of modern life—the struggle of the masses against exploitation by industry and technology and their defeat sometimes by the Right and sometimes by the Left—as if human inadequacy can overturn systems and then create new systems that need in turn to be overthrown, inadequacy and ignorance being the common factor in all governments. Wilson hated Stalinism; he hated imperialism, especially of the British kind, and America's corporate imperialism. He didn't want to use the word "God," he said at the end of his *Europe Without Baedeker*, but added that if it had to be identified with anything, he would identify God with "a vigorous physical persistence, a rectitude in relation to others and to one's work in the world and a faith in the endurance of the human mind."

This seems to be the faith he had reached in his settled life at Wellfleet, where the nipping Atlantic breezes helped ventilate his mind and clear away the rubble of the war. He had taken the bit between his teeth and set his feet on the firm path that would direct his talent and his skill into making him America's outstanding man of letters.

LEON EDEL

CHRONOLOGY

The Forties

1940   Publishes *To the Finland Station*. Plans a novel tentatively titled "The Story of the Three Wishes." Death of F. Scott Fitzgerald. Friendship with Vladimir Nabokov.

1941   Buys house in Wellfleet, Cape Cod. Plans memorial volume, *The Crack-Up,* for Fitzgerald; *The Boys in the Back Room* and *The Wound and the Bow.*

1942   *Notebooks of the Night;* lectures at Smith College; critical studies of Russian writers.

1943   *The Shock of Recognition,* anthology of American literature—"first rate figures on other first rate figures." Accepts position as book critic for *The New Yorker.*

1944   Death of John Peale Bishop. Summer on Cape. In New York for winter.

1945   War reportage in England, Italy, Greece, and Crete for *The New Yorker.*

1946   Separates from Mary McCarthy. *Memoirs of Hecate County* a *succès de scandale*. Divorces Mary McCarthy and marries Elena Mumm Thornton.

1947   *Europe Without Baedeker*. Visits Zuñi in New Mexico.

1948   Birth of third child, Helen Miranda. Papers on Beerbohm, Edith Wharton, Tolstoy, Swift, and Faulkner.

1949   To Haiti for *The Reporter*.

1940–1945

NOTES FOR
THE WOUND AND THE BOW

[EW's early journals of the 1940s contain miscellaneous jottings which show him groping for the contents of his volume of essays *The Wound and the Bow,* published in 1941. He seems also to have been thinking of a play and a volume of his shorter fictions and was reading again in Poe and Henry James.]

Studies in the Literature of Trauma?
The Wound and the Bow
   1. Sophocles: The Wound and the Bow
   2. Dickens
   3. Casanova
   4. Kipling
   5. Justice to Edith Wharton
   6. Ernest Hemingway: Bourdon of Literature
   7. Peggy Bacon, the Poet[1]
   8. Kafka
   9. Rhapsody on Returning to Provincetown.
Joyce?

---

[1] Peggy Bacon, EW's artist friend. See p. 305.

Octave Mirbeau?[2]

Woodrow Wilson

Goethe: more light

Nazis: Gilles de Retz, Joan of Arc, and late Roman emperor

[Notes for a play]

Inquisition of Joan: first ordinary third degree, then psychological—her cigarettes.

End of First Act: burst of hysteria?

Scene between man and woman: only thing we have to depend on in the world each other; movements, hystorical forces (*hysterical* forces), nothing; the relationship between individual human beings. —This must later go to pieces?

The Abstract Man—should he be a character?

Comedy scenes with Broadway characters?—breaking up the grim tensity of the First Act.

[EW seems to have sketched at this time a volume of his shorter fictions, as the following list shows:]

Landscape with Variations

Galahad

After the Game

The Death of a Soldier

The Road to Greenwich Village

The Beach Street Players

Return from Louisiana

[2] Octave Henri Marie Mirbeau (1850–1917), French playwright and novelist, one of the earliest defenders of the Impressionists. See "In Memory of Octave Mirbeau," *Classics and Commercials*, pp. 471–85.

Lobsters for Supper
At Laurelwood

Philoctetes' Wound—The Wound and the Bow
Octave Mirbeau
Stephen Crane
Rilke
Woodrow Wilson

[EW repeated his list for *The Wound and the Bow* on another page in another form:]
Casanova
The Mystery of Edwin Drood
Tolstoy
The Last Phase of Kipling
Justice to Edith Wharton
Peggy Bacon, the Poet
Bourdon Gauge of Morale: Ernest Hemingway
Sophocles: The Wound and the Bow
Kafka?

[EW finally chose seven essays for this book: "Dickens: The Two Scrooges," "The Kipling That Nobody Read," "Uncomfortable Casanova," "Justice to Edith Wharton," "Hemingway: Gauge of Morale," "The Dream of H. C. Earwicker" (Joyce), and "Philoctetes: The Wound and the Bow." He did not use the formulation "Studies in the Literature of Trauma" but simply "Seven Studies in Literature." The book was published in 1941. This volume, perhaps more than any of his other works, defined for his generation the nature of the artist who nurses a particular wound, and struggles with the traumas of "conditioning" that enable a man or woman to be an artist. The artist becomes thus a creature of his sufferings: at odds with society and often an outcast from that society.

[EW describes the conflicts arising out of Dickens' childhood, or Edith Wharton's defiance of a society that rejected her, or Hemingway's "Bourdon"—his ability to pull himself together at the very moment that he seems to be going to pieces. He is alluding to the "Bourdon gauge" used to measure the pressure of liquids—"a tube which has been curved into a coil will tend to straighten out in proportion as the liquid inside is subjected to an increasing pressure." In the tensions, the coiling, the tight-drawn bow, EW sees the parable of the artist: out of inner disequilibrium and tensions unique qualities emerge, and create the unique entity in society—the artist.

[EW's unused formulation, "the literature of trauma," can be applied to this century's long discussions of art and neurosis and the psychological biographies that have been written since EW's pioneer critical work employing the Freudian discoveries of our time. To the modern reader the absence of Virginia Woolf and the questioning of Kafka's inclusion might seem curious omissions of two of the most "wounded." But EW was not at home with the deeper soundings of the unconscious. He resisted these soundings in his own life. Yet he showed awareness of them—as in his remark while visiting the Spectacle Ponds: "many things nourished and lurking at the bottom that have not yet been brought to light." Some would never be brought to light. EW preferred the literary extroverts—Dickens, Kipling, Hemingway—rather than the subjectivists; and he chose, as we can see, those "cases" which provided him with the possibility of a dramatic narrative.]

Notes on American Literature

Henry James— Distance from audience—however good he keeps up, communications lapse: talking to himself. A few vivid scenes which seem more vivid after you have read the story and afterwards think about it; but he doesn't

really think he is talking to anybody: dreary books published by Harper's in the '80s: *Terminations* and *The
Altar of the Dead* never before published elsewhere. Tries
to get back to America and after *Awkward Age,* etc., I
must read *The Ivory Tower.*

[James's volume *Terminations* had appeared elsewhere
—first in London, published by Heinemann in May 1895,
and by Harper in the United States in June 1895. "The
Altar of the Dead" was a story included in *Terminations.*
The Awkward Age was published in 1899. The posthumous *Ivory Tower* in 1917. EW read this unfinished
novel when it came out. See *The Twenties,* p. xxxv.]

Poe's earlier poems—better than Baudelaire—next
thing after Keats—unhappy capitulation to Chivers[3]—better in a way, but less like Chivers, in Mallarmé's prose
translation.

"Love Poems": Comparison to English, pre-eighteenth-
century anthologies, p. 110: Half Lives— They limit
themselves to their tight little island—not even the Con-
tinent impinges on them much—and less so since the
Russian Revolution.

Night Thought: Reading late at night after work I
found myself correcting the sentences of the author to
make them read the way I wanted mine to. To stretch
them tauter than the vibrant bow.

Word Fetishism. —crawling like ants through the
mind! I trace initiatives, resemblances.

D[os] P[assos]: Bolsters up the wish of mediocre by
taking a higher view of their importance—from the point
of view of Europe and the First World War. Time when
America was farther from it than it had been at the be-

[3] Thomas Holley Chivers (1809–58), a Georgia poet principally remembered for his association with Poe.

ginning of the republic and when Europe, including
Russia, was going in for the most inflamed and hysterical
nationalism—so that we meant more to Europe too!

Thursday night of March 23, 1940. Full moon, on night
of terrific wind, we looked at it through the panes of the
upper story of Polly Boyden's[4] house, and saw the inky
clouds driven rapidly across it, showing their silver hems
as they passed, and then the bright complete white
(blinding) moon showing through the dark gauze fringe
and swimming clear, complete and bright again, with the
wind all the time, the wind of March that meant, after all,
that winter was over, blowing past us, no longer pounding
at the walls. The moon remained fixed and supreme. Mary
said she always thought it was moving—I always thought
it was standing still.

April 1940. Here at the top of the house I lie alone—
glad to hear only the wind in the window frame—or
silence, silence—of the dullness of neighbors who do not
know one another—of friends who have slid away down
the other side of the mountain while still, if a little
estranged, we seemed within calling distance—of death,
of a person who never again can reach one, that one never
again can reach—you cannot hear her voice because it is
no longer there—she is not somewhere far away now,
even sitting alone, writing you a letter—she is no part of
this house, of these houses, of any houses of people—she
cannot make, cannot hear, a sound—all around there is
nothing and I lie alone with silence sloping on every side,
slipping (sliding) away to nothing, and I, as it were, content. If I cannot hear or hold that person, I would rather
have silence alone.

July 5, 1940. Those blocks of New York neutral yellow,

---

[4] Polly Boyden, wife of a Chicago lawyer, had written one
novel and lived on the Cape. See *The Thirties*, p. 162.

if even that, traveling above the neutral water of the river, neither gray nor blue, slowly on the summer afternoon, when most people must have left town—contrasting through the window of the boat, a plain-enough but flesh-bodied girl fixes her hair by the reflection in the window, with her tanned and reddish-glowing arms contrasting with those neutral walls, plain but still flesh and blood; black curly Jewish-looking hair—

[An undated description of his room at the old Princeton Club in New York.]

Room 33 at the Princeton Club. —a bathroom next door with no shower but a big white-enameled old-fashioned bath on claw feet—room very nice, looking out on Park Avenue—two sets of shelves, one high in an alcove against a door, the other, next to it, in a small recess made by a protruding window frame—they were obviously dusty—on the hearth was a dirty rag which had been left there by whosoever cleaned the room; a fireplace of little white tiles with a mantelpiece supported by Ionic columns and decorated by classic wreaths—tiny high-hatted well-bred andirons, each with one foot set out (the whole thing the imperfectly disguised remnants of the original house) —the hearth dark with dirt, not ashes—a long tumbler turned upside down and pushed back on the bureau. A fairly strong new note struck by a greenish-blue-covered chair—striped red and brown, with dark-crossed-white pins; not-so-new faded curtains. A floor light with a clipper ship in the middle of a steering wheel, to which was attached an anchor. The neutral checked green carpet all torn up, as if by rats, around the radiators. The folding old-fashioned cream-colored blinds.

Another time: no towels: the unexpected youngish Negro girl. The bath was greenish and opaque, like well-watered pea soup.

NOTES FOR A NOVEL

[During the early days of the war when he was staying with Mary McCarthy at Truro or Stamford, EW wrote some notes for a novel of "transformations." He thought of the proposed fiction as containing three phases of his life—his 1920s experiences in the period of "boom and bust"; the subsequent economic depression and his flirtation with Communism; and then the period of his life in Provincetown.

[The story would have been a kind of H. G. Wells "time machine" story or would use some of the ghostliness of Henry James's *Sense of the Past,* in which a character goes back in time. EW's notes variously call the project "The Story of the Three Wishes" and "The Red Bank and Moscow Novel."

[Portions of it were written, but the work was never completed. He wrote instead *Memoirs of Hecate County.* We may speculate that EW preferred, in the end, to deal with more immediate experience rather than what he came to regard as his dead past.]

The time is about fifteen years ago. A youngish man who works in New York, an architect, is on his way down to a town near the Jersey coast to spend a weekend with his parents. It is spring; he is stale on his work and New York—not making as much money as he would like; he is sleepy and suffering slightly from a hangover. A man and a woman sit down in the seat opposite him. The girl is attractive; they talk in low tones, evidently understanding each other at a word. The other man—who tells the whole story—is not conscious of envying the young man, because he believes himself to be very well satisfied with a love affair he is having in New York. But he presently becomes aware of symptoms which have visited him on several occasions before at times of nervous exhaustion. He finds that he is identifying himself with the young man: imagines that he looks like him, is wearing his clothes, etc. (This is a real psychiatric phenomenon.) At last the train stops between stations and both men go out to see what is the matter. When the narrator comes back and sits down in his place, the girl says something to him, to which he finds himself replying quite naturally, as if he knew her well. Then the train pulls into the station and he finds himself getting out with her at a stop that comes before his own.

He is now actually the other man. Rapidly his former past fades into vagueness, vanishes; other memories are there instead. He and the girl (she is divorced) have gone off to spend the weekend at a summer hotel on the shore. They are not married; but presently they do marry, and you have their life in New York. He is a broker, who is not very good at his job, not really caring very much about it. She has some money and makes possible for him a more or less fashionable life. You have the period of the Boom, becoming more and more hysterical; then the stock market crash—disillusion on the part of the husband. The

marriage ends tragically with a divorce. The man becomes hipped about Communism, turns against his past
work and former social world.

A second episode now begins—there are three such
elaborate episodes, which take up most of the book—each
of them a story in itself, realistically presented while it is
going on. We see the ex-broker in Moscow, to which he
has come as a convinced Communist sympathizer. He is
trying to get one of the innumerable permits that you
have to have to do anything in Russia: a passport or a
permit to take valuta out of the country. He has been sent
from office to office, referred from official to official. At
last he interviews a man who seems likely to do something
for him, a small official, not a Communist, who has to wait
for the decision of his Communist chief. The American
waits interminably in the office, while the official goes on
with his work. The American feels a certain sympathy
toward him: he speaks French, is evidently one of those
Russians educated under the old regime, who has stayed
on to work for the Revolution. Again, without quite being
conscious of it, he is envying another man. The official
gets up and leaves the room; and while he is absent, his
chief comes in. The American gets up to meet him, with
an instinctive feeling of deference. He finds himself talking to the Communist about business which, after a
moment or two of fumbling, seems perfectly familiar to
him. When the chief is gone, he takes his place at the
desk, only for a moment feels a little that it is strange that
he should be able to read Russian.

He has now turned into the Russian official, and for
five years he lives his life. You have Moscow during the
years when the Leninist revolution is turning into the
Stalinist tyranny. The man (still telling his own story,
though, with each of his transformations, his personality

undergoes a change) has stayed on in the Soviet Union when the rest of his family have gone abroad, to work for socialism in Russia. You have two or three of his love affairs—the most important with a brilliant woman lawyer, who is always vacillating between enthusiasm for and rebellion against the regime. He himself remains consistently loyal, though he becomes worried as the reaction sets in after the Kirov affair. Finally he is given a diplomatic post in Western Europe. The purge goes on; the Red Army generals are shot; the old diplomatic staff begin to disappear. He realizes at last with a shock that the Revolution is definitely washed up, and that the GPU are after him, not because he has committed any offense [but] simply because he belongs to this old apparatus and was a friend of one of the generals who were shot. He runs away and goes to Paris.

Third episode. He has come to the United States and is visiting some writers' and artists' colony of the type of Provincetown, where he has come to see some writer of the type of Max Eastman who is interested in hearing about Russia. His host takes him to the house of a friend —a former lawyer from Philadelphia, who some years ago created a scandal by running away from his wife with a young girl, to whom he is now married. He has several children by this second wife and is living in more or less of a state of easygoing bohemian squalor. But the Russian has been much thrilled by Provincetown (to call it that). These people are splendidly free, he thinks: what a relief after the life of the Soviet Union with its espionage, fear, and constraint! These people can say what they please, devote themselves to literature and art. Would he have chosen, after all, the better part if he had gone with the émigrés to Paris? He finds himself alone for a moment in a bedroom on the bottom floor of the rather amorphous

household, where he sees the silver-backed military
brushes and other items of an expensive toilet set on the
bureau of his host's friend. So such things would have
appeared in Paris on the bureaux of white Russians who
had fled, before they would have been obliged to sell
them! But the man in this house has still a life—with the
beautiful autumn weather, the water, his children, his
young wife, the memoirs he has settled down to write.
Glancing at himself in the mirror, he is hardly surprised to
see a face which was not his own a moment ago. When he
comes out of the bedroom, the children appeal to him
about some difficulty they have got into. He is their father;
he lives in the house.

You now have five years of Provincetown. This experience is a disillusion like the others. As time goes on, the
penalties of making one's life outside the regular social
groups become more and more nagging and painful. One
pays principally through the disadvantages that one finds
one has inflicted on one's children. The narrator in this
new transformation has himself had the benefit of the
training of the society he had desired to escape from; but
he finds that, with little money, he is now in no position
to give his children this. He and his companions, having
broken away, find themselves in a void. His serious purposes have lapsed; his life turns into a kind of comedy,
which, agreeable at first, becomes later, as his children
grow up and he himself grows older, more and more futile
and heartbreaking.

What makes his situation peculiarly difficult is the fact
that he has a son by his former wife, who has married a
rich man and is living at some place in New Jersey of the
type of Morristown or Bernardsville. He is obliged to go
down to see them and arrange about the boy's schooling.
He dreads it, because by this time he is nearly penniless,
and he can't bear his former wife's second husband. Hav-

ing the money, she is in a position to decide what the boy is to do, and she is going to send him to a school of which he disapproves. He is going down to try to talk her out of it; but he knows that she is still resentful against him and is glad to do something he doesn't want. His reluctance to make the trip is so great that he can hardly bring himself to take the train. He broods, staring out the window; it is a warm day in late May. He fixes his attention on passing objects to the exclusion of what is most on his mind, as one does on the way to an operation. The train stops at a station which is several stops before his destination. He finds himself getting up and getting out. He takes a taxi and expects the chauffeur to drive him to the right place; but the man does not understand and asks him where he wants to go. He explains. It is the house of his parents; he is back in his original character. He is surprised that, even after he has mentioned the name, the driver does not know what he means.

The house, when they get there, seems shut up. The driver says that nobody lives there. Our narrator lets him go; finds that the grass and hedges have not been cut, all the doors are locked. At last, however, he gets in by a window. The place is empty. From a word of the driver's which he had not grasped at the time, he realizes that his parents are dead. Terror seizes him: he seems to be falling down the elevator shaft of a nightmare—the empty house, his past that isn't there (the last fifteen years are a frightening blank), the life which he has apparently never lived! He should have filled this house with something; and now his parents are dead, and there is nothing! It is one of those big cupola'ed and piazza'd piles that people used to build in the eighties. He goes from room to room sweating with horror, as if its deadness were a crime of which he was guilty.

Then he hears a "Hello" from outside. He looks out
and sees a woman, whom he soon recognizes as a girl he
had known all his life. She has just happened to stop in
her car and come in to take a look at the old place. She
tells him that she had lost touch with him completely—
what has he been doing all these years? He finds himself
replying naturally enough that he was married and lived
in New York; then worked for several years in the Soviet
Union; then came back and lived in Provincetown.
Hitherto, he had been unable to remember the episodes
of the last fifteen years; but they come back into his mind
very strangely as three separate lives. Now, as they are
talking, he finds that she reminds him first of one and
then of another of the three women who were central to
these experiences, and he sees that there has been a constant element: a feminine type who has always appeared
and with whom he has always had to deal. The well-to-do
divorcée, the woman lawyer in the Soviet Union, the
young girl just out of school with whom he had eloped to
Provincetown—they are in some way the same woman.
And he has his identity, too!—he realizes now with relief.
He has been the same man all along—he has grown
middle-aged through three lives which were really a con-
secutive development.

The principal effect of the book depends on making the
three episodes appear to be quite different and distinct
while they are going on. Each seems a different world in
which he is hoping to find something new: first, the world
of people with money during the Boom; then the revolutionary world of the Soviet Union; then the world of the
independent man who has tried to get away from society
to accomplish something in which he believes. But now
the reader is to find out for the first time that they have all
been the same thing—the modern world for any of these

three men has everywhere presented the same problems; the three men are still the same man.

And what he has left is not merely the empty house in which he has never lived, but a residue of wisdom from experience, a different moral from any he had been aiming to illustrate in any of his three exploits. What his point of view is will have to be shown concretely in his attitude toward a family situation—still brought out in this scene with his old friend—which he had been thinking about how to handle on his first trip down to New Jersey on the train. —In the end, the old man-and-woman relationship, with its mixture of understanding and antagonism, will already have been resumed between himself and this fourth woman, who—though less interesting than any of the others (she has simply been living in the country all the time)—is, as it were, the pure type of them all.

[Having written out his preliminary general statement for his proposed novel, EW tried to work out some particulars of his story.]

The Three Wishes: Constant Factors The Soviet careerist in various forms? —difficulties about love affairs and children.

In every case of a transformation, there must be strong motive for his wanting to be the other person, for his not wanting to be himself—and/or . . .

Names for Characters:

Kay Burke { Dillon   Constance, Fenshard, Nicolls,
             Frost   Fenton, Seymour, Celia,
                         Paula, Terry

Nick Carter

Fritz Dietrich—works for Payne and Keller, went to school at Kendall's, had gone round with girl named

Evelyn Manning, lives at the Tavistock
Caroline Glover—Carrie
Caroline's Uncle Teddy—girlfriend is named Agnes Harris
    (Chestnut Hill)
Irving (Irv) Freeman
Ellis

Phil Dewitt   Friends of theirs: Joe Lovett,
                                Bertha Runkel
Claire
Julie } Powell   Fred Lagrange
Henry   They live in Crolskill in
                             Dutchess County
Jehuda Janowitz
Ben Furstmann   Miriam Nicolls and Tony
                             Goresen of the League for
                             New Music

Eddie Frink
Martha Gannett
Lefanu
Elizabeth Danziger
Joe Frijanza   } Nightclub
Dixie McCann
Sam and Lyddie Burnet   They must live on Park Ave.
                             and this uses up a lot of their
                             income
Bill Chippen
The Train That Took Fifteen Years
A trip to Monmontaburg
Fish   Myra, etc. Mina Cain, Kane, Keogh, Myrna
Carr, Mina Clary Foley

[EW is searching for a name for his Mary McCarthy
character (see page 21) and comes close to the original
when he proposes Myrna Carr. He then adds:]

. . . seen trying as a matter of course to live up to the moral code of the Middle Western town she had come from and of the convent—she had some Irish blood—where she had been sent for a few years in her girlhood. Caroline at that time, whom she knew through me, was the only woman of the world of her acquaintance and . . .

Mina McCoy

Red Bank and Moscow Novel

Prelude: He is going down to Red Bank on train on weekend trip to see family: what he expects to find, his attitude toward them. —Thinks about living in the house after his parents are dead?—carrying on the same life. —Dissatisfaction with his life—as a lawyer or what?—in New York. He has still the remains of a hangover—it is about noon—and the staleness of year's work in the city —it is spring, early summer? —Man and girl, train being crowded, sit down opposite him: girl small, attractive and smart, man rather sensitive and good-looking: he envies him, though under the impression that he has had all that and is resigned to his life: the man and girl smile at each other, exchange intimate words in a low voice. He leans his head against the corner by the window and looks as if to go to sleep, but half opens his eyes occasionally to look at the couple. He has noticed a tendency in himself be-fore to identify himself, at moments of nervous disorder and exhaustion, with people he has casually met (my experience with Ed. Seaver in the *New Republic* office) and he now feels something of the kind about this man. —Is it because he thinks him an ass?—this tendency has usually manifested itself in connection with monstrosities, evidently betraying self-contempt or self-doubt—with his Brooks shirt and natty light-brown suit, his brown mus-

tache and quite finely intelligent brown eyes, and clean
gray soft hat—because he would like to be in his place?
—He gets up to go after newsseller and buy paper and
when he comes back sits down beside the girl—looks out
the window, yet feels more or less natural—she speaks to
him in her low quick slightly flurried way and he finds
himself answering her with a word or two (about what is
in newspaper)—they pass Red Bank, go on to Elberon,
Spring Lake, Ocean Grove (imaginary seaside summer
hotel), and get out—

First Episode

—swimming, lovemaking, gin

Second Episode

—difficulties of getting some kind of permit—finally
sent to official who is obviously well educated, derives
from old upper classes—speaks French, attitude rather
light and humorous—Oh la la!—sympathetic—he sits
watching him as he studies the paper slips (it is a question of getting a passport to stay longer)—chief of department who has been sitting up all night, that is the reason
he is so late—visitor puts himself in official place. Official
asks him to wait a few minutes, goes on to other business
—visitor sits watching him and thinking about him.
Higher official comes into room and both spring to their
feet and face him. Visitor as official finds himself talking
to superior, who sends him after something that causes
him to forget American, who only vaguely recurs to his
mind after that—

Great spaces of Russia contrasted with political nar-
rowness. —They stand on the steppe and think about
Russia—then they knuckle down, but the hero doesn't.

—Chavchavadze's[1] story about man who spent night in monastery, put glass eye in tumbler of water, and when monk came in in the morning, he thought it was something miraculous—that the traveler was some sort of saint, and had put his eye on watch while he slept.

Third Episode

After his escape from the diplomatic service, he comes to U.S.A. and goes up to see [Max] Eastman, John Dos Passos at Provincetown. Enjoys the writers' and artists' freedom, thinks of living in such a place, sitting down and writing about what has happened to him, trying to get to the bottom of it and find out what it really means. (Thinks about how C. must look at himself in mirror, seeing himself still as gentleman. He almost sees the image of C. when he looks in the mirror himself.) Provincetown Harbor—the quiet, the leisure, the sea. —Chauncey Hackett's[2] military hairbrushes: he understood him so well—mightn't he have been like that, too, if he had been an American?—if he had been a White Russian exile, he would have been such a slightly ridiculous figure with his monogrammed silver hairbrushes laid out like that in his bathroom. When he comes out of the bathroom, he finds that Chauncey has gone and that he is there with the children, to whom he begins to talk quite naturally. Presently Mary[3] comes back.

---

[1] The Chavchavadzes were Russian friends of Elena Wilson and Wellfleet neighbors.

[2] EW's old Provincetown drinking companion, reported on variously in *The Thirties*, e.g., pp. 204–5.

[3] Mary McCarthy.

Emptiness that he feels at first on coming back, has made nothing of his life—as the result of his three lives, he has nothing: there he is in the empty old shell of the family. —But presently he sees that he fills it.

—Just before he goes down to Morristown, he takes pity on Brownie L'Engle,[4] whose face is ravaged, whose daughters have disappointed her. Bill [her husband] has given up so completely that it is hard for people to say any more that it is all her fault; but he is also kind to Bill. —The next day, when he is traveling down, it all seems easy enough to him to have been kind to somebody who has been giving you drinks when it has cost you nothing. —He gets sicker and sicker.

Coda

He thought of Pushkin's *Nopa, non dpuz, nopa*—and wished he could say that to Irene, who would perhaps respond better than Mrs. Pushkin—but would she? Chauncey goes down to New Jersey—on his way to some place like Morristown to see his first wife about his first children!—has memories of Rumson in his childhood?—sleepy memories of summer lawns—gets into a musing dreaming state of mind which has been shown to be characteristic of him, gets off in that mood at Red Bank, gets into a taxi at station and asks to be taken to house of family of original character—is surprised that driver doesn't seem to know it right away, must be new, from out of town. —Oh, yes: that's on Wallace Street, isn't it? —Yes—in short businesslike way as if he were still of the commanding classes, that he has brought over from his

---

[4] Reported on variously and critically in *The Thirties*; see also p. 29 in this volume.

life as a lawyer (both characters lawyers?—this would come in handy here). Hedge untrimmed, grown to great height; house shut up, has a hard time getting in. Wanders around it and the place all uncared for—realized he had been away for years, had almost forgotten that—had been trying to get back to this home of his youth, to fill it with something of his own, and now that he had found it again, it was nothing but an empty shell—and he, what had he brought to it?—nothing but the incoherent memories of years, already grown very vague, when he seemed to have lived the lives of other men.

—The lady—cousin or friend of his youth—appears. She asks him about himself: he tells her—years of his marriage at Montecito, years in the Soviet Union, years at P'town—it all comes out perfectly naturally. As they talk, she reminds him successively of all the three women he has known in his three various incarnations. She is the same as all of them, and he sees that there are qualities that they all have in common, that there *has been* something constant in his experience. And if this is true of her, he now reflects, why not also of him? In the course of their further conversation, he realizes what he is, what he has learned, what he represents now as a type of the thinking human being, independent of class (?) or nationality, at this point of man's progress.

At the end, it is apparent that he is falling into a relationship with this woman similar to those which have gone before—the same satisfactions and attractions, but also already the same difficulties, the same antagonisms— the same world with the same problems before them (but must allow for more resigned and experienced point of view of middle age).

—The fourth woman, who has stayed there and never quite had what she wanted, is a little bit envious and

hardened—laughs sharply—Dorothy Stilwell, Helen
Vinton.[5]

[Undated fragment] —[con]ceivably say. Franz Höllering,[6] being German, didn't know the difference. The
Englishman—who was a little tight—was also tempera-
mental and always stopping and saying he couldn't go on
and having to be coaxed back to reading. He had one set
of names in the first set and a different set in the second
set, and complained that he couldn't keep the characters
straight himself and couldn't read his own handwriting.
The English actress had a silly little dog which kept running around and getting on his nerves, but wouldn't do
anything to keep the dog quiet. I had been having a cold
in the head and was alternately afflicted with coughing
spells and nosebleeds. The guy from Dwight Wyman's
was one of those smart young New York theatrical Jews,
who sat in ominous silence figuring out the set with a
pencil. When the author paused at the end of a scene, the
Wyman representative would make no comment. It lasted
till after midnight. —When I said I had enjoyed *The
Women*,[7] the theatrical guy and his girlfriend flew into
perfect convulsions. I imagine that a good many producers
turned it down, so that it is quite a sore spot on Broadway.

Bee McFee paid me a whirlwind surprise visit one night
last week. I had gone to bed early, not feeling well, and
didn't know what was going on; but Bee, who was apparently a little exhilarated, insisted on coming in and was
charging right for my bedroom when Hatty headed her

[5] Dorothy Stilwell, a first cousin of EW, and Helen Vinton
Augur, a second cousin.
[6] The Austrian-born novelist (b. 1896), who lived in New
York.
[7] The play by Clare Boothe Luce.

off. She left a note saying that I was just like a character in Dostoevsky. Please don't tell her I told you this. I wrote her a note afterwards: "Well, my dear: you'll soon be out of that old hospital. Write to me when you can. Best regards to Connie. Best love, *Bunny*."

Carnegie Hall: Steps go up steeply from street to heavy glass door that is hard to open and swings out so as to embarrass your entrance and press back those who are coming behind you—you go up more stone steps inside and, through the excessively uninviting outer lobby where people rarely go to smoke, into the narrow and rubber-lined inner lobby.

—The dreary hall with its faded gilt and its shabby cream and bisque—its old curtains that seemed to need dusting—its wide squat proscenium arch that framed the musicians in their dark clothes (matinee) and the backs of the music racks, the podium with the brown double basses on one side and the gold harp and brass kettle-drums on the other, balancing each other, with the serried ranks of violins bristling with their bows between them. The imitation bas-relief pillars and the doors with their jutting angular architraves.(?)

—Blond woman violinist with Portia-like yellow hair—Ruth Posselt—long full black dress and arms bare almost to the shoulders—played Barber concerto, and as I watched the sawing motion of her pretty round arm always held away from her body and saw the bow moving straight across the bridge and eliciting the sweet and tender and rather sentimental strains of the alleged first movement, I realized that violin music was intensely sexual and feminine, even when produced by a man, in the sense that it represents the feeling for a woman of the underpart of the penis lingeringly passing in and out and eliciting exquisite music.

GULL POND, 1942

Gull Pond, May 21, 1942. —The lady's slippers were
out, sprinkled so sparsely around the brink of their solitary
flowers—deepening in a couple of days from flimsy stoop-
ing ghosts as pale as Indian pipe to a fleshy veined purplish pink swollen between pigtails and curling topknot
that also suggested Indians; and along the white sand of
one side, where the bowl of the pond shelved so gradually,
the little white violets with their lower lips finely lined as
if with beards in purplish indelible ink, their long slim
rhubarb-purplish stalks and their faint slightly acrid pansy
smell, grew with thready roots in the damp sand; they were
yellowish like ivory here, but on the opposite, more marshy
bank (with its round stones, its patches of red irony water,
its shooting box with a flock of square black-and-white de-
coys, its steeper banks, its dead gulls and fishes) their effect was not quite so dry and they showed a vivid white
like trillium where they bloomed against the deeper and
the more luxuriant green. As one walked in the water one
encountered pines putting out their soft straw-colored (?)
bunches of cones and smelling with a special almost sweet-

fern fragrance. The baby cones seemed almost embar-
rassingly soft, almost like a woman's nipples. —When we
got to the shallow channel between Gull Pond and the
next one, I found a mother herring trying to get through
from the latter by gliding and flapping on her side. She
was silvery with purple-silver along the upper part of her
length. At the mouth of the channel there were several of
them splashing and when I came close I saw that the
water was all dark with a whole crowd of them—from
above they are just roundish muddy streaks under water.
The sand here, flat and more marshy and grown with
green rushes, was all tracked with the trefoil (?) of gulls'
feet, where they had come to get the fish.

On the other side of the pond, the stretch where there
was a screen of tall pines, a new and grander note, almost
theatrical—and then the little screen of scent-pines that
left a little strip of sand between it and the thick tangled
jungle of bushes and shrubs and briars that covered the
hill behind. . . . Today we cleared a place under the low
branches of the pines so that we could get a little shade,
and the light openwork shadows rippled on Mary's white
skin . . . as the breeze stirred the branches; also fish
splashing . . .

—For lunch we had had from the brown picnic basket
the classical boiled eggs, bean salad in glass jars, cucumber
sandwiches, and sandwiches filled with some mixture of
green chopped herbs and white cottage cheese (and there
were bananas, tomatoes, and sliced sweetish green cucumber pickles which we didn't get around to eating); and
had iced lemonade out of the thermos bottle and white
California wine out of a glass jar that had been cooled in
the refrigerator and that we tried to keep from getting
tepid by standing it in the water. —Before lunch, we had
gone in for a dip: not too cold to be uncomfortable . . .

Mary looked very pretty and white. But she was ripened
by the summer sun where her face and neck and arms had
been exposed while working on her garden, and the tan
of her forearms and the reddening tints brought out in her
rather pale skin were in harmony with her blue suit of
overalls . . .

—I had a sense of adventure in exploring the other bank
of the pond and walking all the way around. At one point,
the bottom was stony; in one place, there were little fish;
at another, there were water bugs featherily and (elu-
sively) flawing (scrawling?) the surface. (Shooting box,
etc.) Further on, a light and slow ripple gave the illusion,
as you walked in the water, that it was the sand of the
bottom, with its rare stones and sticks, that was rippling
like some thin and light sheet slowly and lightly shaken
out as one might shake out a long carpet.

—When we had first come, between one and two, the
lake had not looked so attractive—a little roughened and
opaque from a distance (in the foreground along the water
were forts and walls and moated castles built by and for
Reuel from several days before); but when we came back
from our walk around it, there were dark and soft-looking
clouds, which did not look as if they were really going to
rain, hanging over the pond from the opposite bank, and
yet leaving above us, among white shreds (?)—more like
bits of cotton pulled out from the roll—of cloud, a fresh
and bright and (rarified, not dense) blue; and the water
had a leaden look that was at the same time perfectly
limpid—and lovely.

—When I went back to get the towels, on which Mary
had been lying, I saw a little orange-and-black bird, like a
finch, hopping around in those scrub pines just where we
had been.

Mary McCarthy and Edmund Wilson, Wellfleet, 1942

—The little yellow buds of the pines are not the cones, neither these nor "the candles," with bristly conelike scales, that rise from the middle of the cluster. The cones are little round green cones that grow underneath on the branch. When you shake the soft things, they give out a lemon-yellow dust that looks like lemon-colored smoke.

—The deer dung and sharp deep divided hoofprints just opposite where we lay—the yellow-and-black butterfly (monarch?) that was flying out over the pond . . .

Brownie L'Engle during War: Prodding people to do things.

Signed up Harl Cook for something when he was already signed up for something else.

Makes life a burden to Bill, who was now definitely fighting back by making fun of her among friends and even being rather disagreeable, as I had never known him to do before. I can say it better in French (apropos of her violent concern about somebody who was not doing anything about the war effort): *Ce n'est pas votre affaire.*

Had just read a biography of Churchill and thought he had had the most wonderful life.

Then she would go South after Christmas as usual. If we told her we did not know how the war effort would get along without her, she would say that she hoped to be able to go on with her work down there.

Later on (1942) she told us that they were going South because they didn't want to use the oil, which was by that time being rationed.

—Margaret Bishop:[1] I just go around with a stick and make people do things they don't want to. Very congenial work!

[1] John Peale Bishop's wife.

Brownie pretty unbearable the night Edie Shay[2] called up to tell her that the Americans had invaded North Africa (October '42)—singing the *Marseillaise*—told Norman Matson[3] afterwards that she would have said a little while ago that he shouldn't be writing a light fantasy, but that now she thought it was all right.

[2] Wife of Frank Shay. Provincetown friend of EW and Dos Passos.

[3] Norman Matson had apparently lived with Susan Glaspell. See *The Thirties*, pp. 194–95.

WILMINGTON

Wilmington, Jan. 16, 1943. Delaware has a quality quite special: it has something of the Main Line and something of the Deep South. The Biggses[1] and the Ruperts (Anna's family).[2] —I found John Biggs in the Federal Building, more than ever solidly pear-shaped, sitting in a swivel chair among his legal books, with his feet up on the ashtray. His nice bright thinnish secretary, who was obviously indispensable to him: "Mrs. G." We drove out through the sordid end of Wilmington. Big old yellow Rupert house (plastered), square but made complicated and rambling by a built-on part and an irregular internal design. Unkempt estate, hardly delimited from the road and the neighboring fields, hardly a hedge or a fence. The first thing I saw as I went in was the expanse of white wall of the hallway, on which some child had been

[1] John Biggs, Jr., who had been at Princeton with EW and Scott Fitzgerald, was now a federal judge on the Third Circuit bench in Philadelphia. He was Fitzgerald's executor and EW, now engaged in editing Fitzgerald's literary remains, had a number of questions to discuss with him.

[2] Anna Swift Rupert Biggs, wife of Judge Biggs.

scratching words, aimless lines and faces as if it were the wall of a school lavatory. John said without surprise, "Somebody has been decorating the wall." The front room where we found Anna's mother—looking very much like Anna (John's wife), head bent and shoulders humped up with arthritis or something, she was seventy-five—looked almost like the living room–dining room of a farmhouse where people sit and sew as well as eat. Old footstool covered with silk (?) completely worn through, a great torn hole; a bowl of stockings on the table which she had been darning; a small radio; a glass bookcase, with the books rather conscientiously arranged according to authors: a shelf of Edith Wharton. Two large piles of new French books (Maurois, Romains, books about the fall of France), and the paper jacket of [Arthur Hobson] Quinn's life of Poe. I [showed] Anna something Rupert [had] written in one in rather an uncertain hand; and asked if she had a granddaughter who read all those French books. She answered that she and her daughter read a good deal of French; there was a local branch of the Alliance Française. I wondered whether this interest in French was inspired by the Du Ponts. —She had read French two hours a day (I think it was) for thirty-five years—you could cover a great deal of ground in that time. She had pale blue sharp German eyes. She served excellent Chinese tea and toasted English muffins and jam in the big glass jar in which it had been put up. They simply sat down in a row on the chairs pushed back along the wall—I took one of the chairs from the dining table and moved it to face them and make something like a social circle. There was a light brown dog, very white around the paws and muzzle—I asked what its name was: Belinda. Mrs. Rupert asked whether I thought it was a beagle—I thought it was half dachshund. It turned out that they had simply found it in the road a few days before—had taken it in as a matter of

course—it was gentle, seemed depressed in a resigned way
—had only a little nameless ropelike leather collar—had
come perhaps from a slightly sordid environment. The
dining room was full of old silver (they had one of the
finest collections of apostle spoons in the country—this
was kept in a safe—they wanted to sell it, John told me,
and couldn't get their price) and blue and other china
(some of it, it seemed to me, not particularly beautiful)
crammed into china closets or lined up, without arrangement, along the plate rack. Large fine mahogany table;
row of glass decanters with silver bases, set out in a similar
random manner, containing sherry and other things. I
wandered into a little conservatory behind, similarly informal and improvised in a hallway: curious things like
bulbs fastened to a section of bark: Mrs. Rupert said that
this was a wild orchid from the South—they had told her
she couldn't make it bloom in captivity in the North—but
it *had* bloomed—little green flowers like the big ones you
buy. While Mrs. Rupert was out of the room getting the
tea, John said, "Here's a nice room," and took me through
the conservatory to a library which was a later addition to
the house. This room was up to the standard of splendor
which belonged to the Ruperts' status and it was kept up:
arranged and neat—but not lived in: family portraits,
good furniture, low glassed-in bookcases with their varied
assortment of objects on top of them: a fine standing can-
delabrum of lusters.

I walked over to the Biggs house with John III—shy
and lacking in chin (fifteen), made swinging and bear-
like movements with his head when uncertain how to act
as we were talking about New York [while] walking over
there, but talked to me on the way about his preoccupa-
tions. (John probably babied him too much, would [not]
send him away to school, kept on kissing him at fifteen.)
Beagling a terrible sport—you had to bring in jackrabbits

for them, cottontails would just run into their holes—
they couldn't catch the jackrabbits—the only time he had
ever seen them catch one was when they got him up
against a wall—and when they got the rabbits, they didn't
do anything with them, except the dogs killed them. The
gray day, the muddy road, the hills were covered with a
reddish grass that was just the color of a fox—one of them
was called Fox Hill because somebody had seen a fox
there. Anna's sister and a slightly pansy art student from
Philadelphia who was visiting her came along to pick us
up when we were nearly there. —Anna's sister collected
modern paintings and painters, but she did not paint herself. She had a way of saying "Uh-uh" in assent in a
matter-of-fact way which was somehow rather damping to
conversation, as it made one feel that in matters of art she
was really not very well posted. John's house was at the
top of a pretty steep hill—it was the same general kind of
thing as the Ruperts', only smaller—all the houses seemed
to belong to this group of families in common, as it were
—when anybody got married, they moved into one that
happened to be vacant. —Thus the town house in which
John's sister had gone to live when she married had just
been vacated by Anna's sister, who had just divorced her
husband. You crossed a little stream called Clay Creek,
where the fish, John III told me, had all been killed by
the dye factory further up, on a curious old wooden
bridge, all enclosed like a tunnel, with a large cross-
hatching of beams inside—gray and unpainted, would
only bear three tons. John asked me what I thought of it
and said that he was going to get a ship's figurehead for it.
That evening he told about a truck which had fallen into
an insufficiently roofed-in old cistern underneath their
drive—the driver had come in with his nose flattened and
phoned the company that he had fallen into a well, "Yes, a
well." In the Biggs house, even more disorder and an

omnipresent whimsical element. They had installed a
billiard table in what had apparently been the main living
room—it filled the whole room—not very good portraits
painted by Hal Roosevelt's daughter, who couldn't paint
hands—Anna had suggested that she do them in gloves
(fancy portrait of John's sister as a young witch in one of
the bedrooms upstairs). In another room, there were
whiskey and rum bottles alternating with vases on the
mantel; a large oriental elephant made of different kinds
of wood. I went over to look at something which I fancied
was a rare book in a glass case—it turned out to be a
cheap green boys' book in a small empty aquarium. Fine
old dark English bed (fifty years before reign of Elizabeth) with bulging columns in which John slept. John's
study, into which the family had moved, turning the old
living room into a billiard room. Fine view from the hill—
venetian blinds—walls covered to the top with law books,
and a stepladder to get at them. An armchair made of
moose horns which John had brought from Wyoming; on
the mantel an eagle. John was fond of eagles: Mrs. Rupert
had given him from her place an iron one with spread
wings, which was poised over one of his outbuildings, and
a large clay caricature made by the Indians of the Southwest. Cocktail trays, with, under the glass of the bottom,
wild ducks by Audubon and a hideous Rowlandson drawing, called *The Taming of the Shrew*, in which a horrible-
looking woman had been fastened on her back to the bed
by her husband, by means of stocks in the headboard and
footboard. He had something like a gag in his hand, and
she was snarling like an English bulldog. In one corner
was a little iron spiral staircase, the white wall around it
covered with photographs of distinguished members of the
bench simply nailed or pasted to the wall. Up above was
a double sleeping porch, looking out in two directions,
with a partition between, which had rows of little army

cots, so that it rather resembled a flophouse, where the family slept in summer.

Mrs. Biggs, at the time of my visit, had a stroke in the street; she fell in front of a car but was not run over. Though she was seventy-two or three, and had already had one stroke, she had insisted on still going around alone and doing things for herself. Anna, however, invited me to stay, said that everything was "frozen" till Monday anyway. She had been busy all day checking airplane instruments and had got to know a lot about planes. John couldn't drive on Sunday on account of being a federal judge and pleasure driving being forbidden.

He was at special pains to bring his sister in Wilmington a large box of Whitman's chocolates—she shared his morbid passion for chocolate. Her house was quite smart, well ordered and modern. Her husband, who was Dutch, spoke half a dozen languages, and was foreign representative and a vice-president of the Hercules Powder Company. Genial and well mannered but naturally rather brutal big-industrial face. Rachel had written for *The New Yorker*—also novels which hadn't been published, one highly sophisticated about a wedding. She was quite different from John, dark, wiry, nervously intent, manner either imitated from Katharine Hepburn in *The Philadelphia Story* or an example of some original that Hepburn was imitating—semi-passionate semi-ironic way of emphasizing certain words—bringing down upper eyelids in a spasmodic way—that gave her enthusiasms a kind of virulence. "Peter, on your feet!" to her husband, when it was time for a new old-fashioned. Her writing was *all* she cared about. A row of blue-patterned white Delft china cows on the mantel. Prevalent lack of certainty and elegance in taste on the part of all these people: inferior colored landscape on the wall. Butler in a white coat, probably refugee, who put one hand to his back with the palm out and bent over very low when he offered us the hors d'oeuvre. Conversation at dinner between John and Peter about getting—Peter's idea—some representation of labor on the "planning board"—John suggested the editor of the local *Labor Herald,* an A.F. of L. organ: evidently harmless, wrote rather literary editorials that had little to do with labor. There was another man he said, no doubt rightly, who was quite crooked.

I paid a visit in Wilmington to Frank and Lily Herzog[3] (whom I had known in Moscow). The apartment was bright and clean like their apartment in Moscow—some of the same Russian paintings on wood, etc., little china figures doing Russian dances. Her mother-in-law and sister had been with them a year—and this had been too much for Lily, who had had spells of collapse—they thought they could treat her like a maid because she was a little Russian. She missed the theater—aside from a few books, the only cultural entertainment they seemed to have was listening to concerts on the radio—one was going when I arrived. Frank's progress as a photographer—he was more artistic than I realized. On the other hand, as he had got older, he had grown rather soft and flabby. He still more or less believed in the socialism of the Stalinist Soviet Union—thought that it would stand behind any working-class revolution in the West and rescue the postwar situation. Lily had a shrewd disillusioned smile: she knew that the industrial working class was being exploited and that the Soviet Constitution was a mockery. Frank said that the Du Ponts had refused to do anything whatever for the government: they would have to send their own men, put

[3] EW had met the Herzogs in Moscow in 1935. See *The Thirties,* pp. 552–54.

up their own plants, etc. Pretty little girl; she seemed to me quite Russian though not short, round, and plump like Lily.

Haverford: The Main Line. —The neat clean smug uninteresting Philadelphia people—as the Sargents said, they all had awfully good teeth, you were sure.

THOUGHTS, 1943–1944

Mid-August 1943. It was as if the life of the year were struggling against the death-force of autumn: the growth of the vegetation against the powers of decay that were trying to get their teeth in. Then three days or more when it seemed to be "trying to storm" without being able to, people got nervous in the muggy overcast weather with its remote subdued claps of thunder and flickers of lightning that never worked up to anything. This would go on all night and keep you from sleeping: you kept waiting for the climax that never came with its relief and purgation. In the meantime the house became stuffy and sticky —everything one did seemed messy. Then one day you would unexpectedly wake to what seemed a clear and bright September day of the best vintage of the autumns up here—the quality of September one felt in the light, though you could hardly say this was different from the earlier days of August—steady sun and yet a little cool— just the day for the ponds. Then next day it would be muggy again.

[Once he had settled into the Wellfleet house, EW began to cast about for some kind of employment that would leave him sufficiently free to carry on his own work. He had been struck by the way Cyril Connolly was editing *Horizon* in England in the midst of the war and it occurred to him that a similar journal could—if modestly organized—be successful in the United States. In April 1942 he wrote to Harold Ross, editor of *The New Yorker*: "Why don't you start a literary magazine and make me editor?" He said he was convinced such a magazine could be a success; there were no magazines in the country that published serious writing—the subsidized magazines had gone under because of economic strain during the war, *Harper's* and *The Atlantic* "are so stuffy and second-rate that nobody interested in literature reads them," and except for the *Partisan Review* "in its small way" there was no literary journal worthy of the name. "I am convinced such a magazine could be a success." Wilson added that *The New Yorker* was the only magazine outside the Luce group which "shows any imagination, and the only one that has any real distinction—so I thought I would suggest the idea to you."

[Ross seems to have replied that he was only an editor and not a publisher and that he would explore the matter with *The New Yorker*'s publisher. By the end of May he had told EW that there were various kinds of difficulties in starting the kind of literary journal he envisaged. EW wrote back: "Aside from the magazine question, I'm looking for some kind of regular—preferably part-time job" and he inquired whether there was anything that would fit him at *The New Yorker*. As it turned out, Clifton Fadiman, taken up with other activities, had decided to leave his job as head of the book section and Ross some months later offered the job to Wilson. In October 1943 EW suggested that he be given $10,000 a year for this job with $3,000 in perquisites and he made a great many practical suggestions for improving the book reviews. Thus began an association that endured for the next thirty years—to the time of EW's death.

[With his wide reading, his long experience at *The New Republic*, his love of satire and wit, his way of beginning in a sober fact-filled manner and building up a drama of literary achievement or failure, EW seemed ideally suited for the kind of writing *The New Yorker* published. And then he could range among the Europeans as well as the Americans. *Classics and Commercials*, the first of his "literary chronicles," published at the end of the decade, was largely composed of *New Yorker* pieces, and they range from "A Toast and a Tear for Dorothy Parker" to his penetrating analysis of Evelyn Waugh in "Never Apologize, Never Explain." He reviews Dover Wilson on Falstaff, discusses the origin of Tolstoy's Natasha, writes in his best scholarly manner out of his saturation with the Victorians on Thackeray, or examines with great liveliness a book of etiquette or the idiosyncrasies of detective fiction ("Who Cares Who Killed Roger Ackroyd?"), and in a few brief paragraphs captures the innermost essence of Katherine Anne Porter or explains the then-new Jean-Paul Sartre, both the novelist and the existentialist. His anglophobia doesn't prevent him from offering a just appreciation of Cyril Connolly, the particular talents of Harold Nicolson, "the rich, shy and fastidious" Ronald Firbank, and the particular magic of Max Beerbohm. For Wilson, reviewing a book was never a matter simply of praise or condemnation. The act was translated into a peculiar kind of exhilaration—that of inquiry, curiosity, analysis, criticism, in a measured, serious, and fair-minded way. His tendency was to be generous but he was also exigent. His pieces, week after week, were never jaded and never perfunctory—and in their quiet low-keyed prose never tedious. Occasionally he would amuse himself and his readers by writing about "pop" works—like his attempt to "ambush" a best seller, a page-turner of the time such as Anya Seton's *The Turquoise,* which fulfilled his prediction by selling a million copies, "a typical American novel written by a woman for women. The great thing about this kind of fiction is that the heroine must combine, in one lifetime, as many enjoyable kinds of roles as possible . . . A bait is laid for masculine readers, also, by periodically disrobing the heroine . . . And the whole book is written in that tone and prose of the women's magazines which is now so much a standard commodity." Readers of Judith Krantz and her many sisters will recognize that Wilson's definition of the modern blockbuster is classical, perhaps the last word on the subject.

[These are the qualities which now established a larger reputation for Wilson than he could ever have enjoyed in *The New Republic.* But the readers of *The New Yorker* got to know him also as a lively and observant reporter. He had been a very short time with the magazine when Ross sent him abroad to capture that singular moment when the war was ending and certain of the European countries found themselves in a state of emptiness—when the great tumult of disaster has ceased but its echoes are still in the ears of the populace, and the bewilderments of peace, grief, mourning, and reconstruction all must be faced amid a search for food in empty stores and warmth in houses without coal. Wilson went to England, Italy, Greece, and Crete, and out of the notes that follow emerged his book *Europe Without Baedeker.*]

Thoughts, January 1944: Magic Flute at the Metropolitan: Berlin had just been bombed, the Russians were cleaning up on the Germans. I felt pleasant when I went

The house at Wellfleet

to the opera, and sat in my excellent seat down front before the performance began. I thought, this is probably all wrong—is there an element of sadism in my satisfaction: to sit peaceful, well fed, and secure while the Germans were being exterminated. But then, when the performance began, I realized that it was impossible to enjoy there the masterpieces of musical art in the teeth of what was happening in Europe. The whole performance was terrible: bad scenery, terrible acting, even the voices not always good, long waits between the scenes, when the conductor would stand with his hand on his eyes. The only person who made the faintest pretense at acting was the man who played Papageno, and almost the only laugh he drew was with some line about "fellow travelers." The old supernatural machinery of the Met: the snake, the unfolding flower with Papageno inside, like the dragon that gave out clouds of dust when Siegfried struck it with his sword and the ravens in *Götterdämmerung* that used to fly across the stage afterwards; but now everything else was bad, too.

We have arrived now at the same state in which the Germans have been. We are bombing Berlin to cinders, but nobody talks about it. We meet it mainly with a mixture of competitive satisfaction and a mental evasion of the matter. —The phrase "softening up" process—a wonderful euphemism.

I have always thought André Gide overrated, but I must, in writing these notes, be profiting by his example of independent thought. Subjunctives in Proust balanced by admission that the mute *e* in French verse should perhaps be obsolete. Preoccupation in his journal with the literary world of Paris.

Mr. Nizer would have to get hold of Cain, etc.

We are already involved with the Germans and Japs in contests of killing and hatred, and at the moment that is all there is going on. Report on the cruelties of the Japs to American prisoners. I have felt for the first time that we were sucked into the spiral of our society going, as Dos [Passos] says, down the drain. Importance of not giving in to bloodthirsty impulses in regard to the Germans: this would carry us straight down into the darkness.

Conflict in our minds between humane and reasonable instinct and satisfaction at seeing the Germans get the same kind of punishment they inflicted on the English and the Dutch. Daytime fantasies like following a game.

Behavior of Franz Höllering:[1] vague about whether or not people—even Stalinists—thought the Russians could not do anything in Europe, dependent on us for supplies. Bert Wolfe[2] told me later that the Stalinists were getting a hold on the whole German emigration—because it would be only the Russians who would make it possible for the radicals to get back to Germany—maybe they thought that they could then do something different.

Evening at the Wolfes' in Brooklyn: bad habit of Marxists of trying to win an argument by talking one's opponent down. Parliamentary procedure, such as we learn at school, a better training. Dwight Macdonald has learned this bad habit, too. Talk so loud and fast that the opponent can hardly get a word in, and when he does it

---

[1] See p. 24.
[2] Bertram D. Wolfe (1896–1977) helped found the American Communist Party in 1919 and wrote *Three Who Made a Revolution* (1948).

is picked and distorted at once into an expression of some pretended opinion, which the opponent does not hold but the absurdity of which the Marxist is easily able to show. This is all particularly unfortunate since the Marxists pretend to depend on rational demonstration. If the opponent is not overcome, he is simply left with the conviction that the Marxist feels his own case to be weak and is trying to protect its fallacies, to avoid having its fundamental problems even brought into sight.

It may be that one thing which is responsible for the war is simply the desire to use aviation destructively. It must be a temptation to humanity to blow up whole cities from the air without getting hit or burnt oneself, and while soaring serenely above them. Many must feel vicariously as I do the thrill of doing this—I felt it when the Germans were bombing London before we had begun bombing them. It is the thrill of the liberation of some impulse to wreck and to kill on a gigantic scale without caring and while remaining invulnerable oneself. Boy with a slingshot shooting birds—can't help trying it out. This is true of mechanical warfare in general: the guns batter down at long distance, the tanks flatten out without feeling, the planes wipe out whole cities without one's having to picture what has happened. It is the gratification of the destructive spirit, as it were in a pure abstract form: if the enemy does not get you, you are free as a bird of the consequences. You are further removed from your object by the intervention of the mechanical bombsight: your end of the process is mathematical, the machinery sends the bomb to its target. Constraints of the conventions and codes that we live under, and that we are glad to see smashed. —There was an element of exhilaration about the whole Nazi exploit: the same thing was true of their backing diplomatic promises and the code of international law, and scrapping all the apparatus of justice. Malaquais[3] on the admiration which the French displayed for the German equipment. Admiration for naked power.

Stalin and Uban (?). See article in *Books Abroad*.

Marxism is the opium of the intellectuals.

Southerners: Benefit to the literature of a people to have suffered defeat in a war or otherwise to be struggling against the oppression of an unfriendly power: Ireland, Russia, France after 1870, the American South. At the same time it frees people from responsibility to do anything about the problems on the hands of the dominant group. I sympathize with the Southerners in their reaction against the standards brought in after the Civil War, their indignation against industrial slavery; but I don't see that, apart from art, they have any way of meeting these evils: imitative religion, Thomist Aristotelianism, regionalism in life (cultivating one's garden and studying one's part of the country). The important role, however, that they have played in our literature, much more important than any which they had ever played before (though the effect of the Civil War was to work, in the general prospective, a certain amount of injustice to the Southerners: [Paul Hamilton] Hayne, [Henry] Timrod and [William Cullen] Bryant, [William Gilmore] Simms and [James Fenimore] Cooper, G. W. Cable.[4]

Feeling of emptiness, Dec. 14, 1944, Gramercy Park Hotel apartment.

[3] Jean Paul Malaquais (b. 1908), Polish-born French novelist, author of *Le Gaffeur* (1953). EW probably refers here to his *Journal de guerre* (1943).

[4] EW here contrasts Southerners with Northerners: Timrod with Bryant and Simms with Cooper; he would ultimately write an entire book on this subject, *Patriotic Gore*.

—Effect of airplanes on dignity of human habitations. Palaces and courts and railway stations, cathedrals and churches used to be solemn places: men had built roofs higher than themselves and were impressed when they entered these edifices. They had constructed a habitation which substituted itself for the earth—they lived in the buildings and could forget about the outside setting which did not reckon with them. But from above, from a plane, these habitations are like wasp-cells stuck in the slit of a blind, they are mere shells which men have knocked together in order to crawl inside them and which a bomb dropped casually from above can shatter or annihilate in a moment. Difference in this connection between Mary's point of view and mine—she has never known a time when there weren't planes. —We are probably on the brink of a new construction by man of a conventional world for himself—the network of air travel and radio, instead of a precarious extension, will be part of the self-contained human house. Already "ceiling" means not only any more the roofs a few feet above our heads but also the cloud formation above our heads under which our airplanes range.

—Soon the globe will be known and a bore.

Thoughts—Newsreel I saw, just after the publication of the Jap atrocities in which you were shown dead or writhing Chinamen executed by the Japs. One of the American officers who had brought back the stories said, in what was obviously a prepared dialogue, "No, I think that the Japanese are animals." The Announcer: You hear what Captain US says. He thinks that the J's are animals. And now we must fight these *animals!* We must buy bonds to defeat these *animals!* etc. This is precisely the kind of thing that Goebbels used to instill into the Germans, the idea that they could exterminate the Poles: the

Poles were an inferior race—the blacks are not people, but animals. —See anecdote from Sigrid Schultz.[5] —This should be followed by the section on anthropoids.

Bombing of the Cassino monastery: pleasant way of reporting it in the papers—the Germans ran out of it like ants, etc.

Red Bank, July 18, 1944. —Walking down and looking at the Shrewsbury and going into the woods on the road past our old house to the Rumson, where I used to go as a child. *America:* It still seems even to us a country strange and wild. It is as if we had just sailed into this estuary and found the quiet little harbor with its pale opaque blue-gray waters, half brackish and half salt, tranquilly rippled with evening and the little white moored launches, with the birds flying over the water and the grassy and wooded banks—as if the little white sailing boats against the gold sun had just found themselves there themselves. What a good place to build a house—among the trees by the tranquil water. And so in the woods with its big old trees and its towering seed-tufted ailanthus, its blackberry bushes and its carpet of vines—in the swamp below we used to find skunk cabbage. There was a little white farmhouse and a neat plowed field where the land had been cleared right beside it, but the tangle loomed all around right beside, the uncouth and yet comfortable tangle of that one spot of earth that had never been cleared among estates richly landscaped-gardened—the wonderful solitude and space and peace—the country which we still found so wild and to which we were still new.

[5] Sigrid Schultz (b. 1893), broadcaster for the Mutual Broadcasting System and war correspondent for the Chicago *Tribune*.

ITALY, 1945

[EW's journals which follow record his trip to Europe in the spring of 1945 for *The New Yorker* when the war was nearing its end.

[A note by EW at the beginning of the passage reads: "I first went to London, where I remained longer than I expected, because my orders to go to Germany as a war correspondent for *The New Yorker* failed to come through. *The New Yorker* had two correspondents in Germany, which was all they were allowed; but Ring Lardner's son had been killed, and they wanted to have me replace him. The permission was, however, not granted, so I finally went instead to Italy."

[EW not only went to Italy but proceeded to Greece, and he had two visits to England in his shuttling back and forth. He also paid a visit to Crete, where he stayed with the United Nations relief organization. He seems to have kept no regular journals in Crete—at least, none have been found. But the details of this visit, and the record of his British, Italian, and Greek experiences recorded here, were expanded and sometimes utilized directly from the

49

journals in his book *Europe Without Baedeker*, published in 1947.]

April 28, '45: Flight from London to Naples: Marvelous to see, in a few hours, the maps of England, France, and Italy unrolled underneath the plane, one thing succeeding another so quickly—Paris in one hour forty minutes; Paris–Marseille, two hours; Marseille–Naples, three hours. All shapes and textures of green and brown fields, in Italy some that were reddish pink; little winding English rivers, red roofs; French red roofs, longer less compact strips of fields, straight canals—soon dries up toward the south, Maritime Alps, empty riverbeds, lichenlike dark green bushes—fields (not necessarily in Midi) that looked like corrugated brown sweet crockery—round white puffs of cloud with the landscape of parqueted pieces underneath, and then, further south, the large cloud-shadows that made the earth look like a river in which the ice is thawing, with the lighted spots looking like the ice; vineyards, then olive groves; Anzio with its battered earth and buildings and L-trenches, shaped like boomerangs and now overgrown with grass. Patches of thick rich green carpetlike nap.

The Italian sea near Naples: Wonderful colors at once delicate and varied—bluing green jade on the shore where the little white waves were breaking, shading, in the sky where a storm was fading, to the indigo of ink that has been dropped into water and is being diluted. There had been a rainbow after the shower, and we flew past the upper part of the arc: a strange and attractive sensation.

Finding oneself in the world of the army after the world of the English in London: transported everywhere in Europe by American facilities, given American food at all stops, handed recent American magazines and even New York papers on the plane. Officer from Westchester

County, with Scotch terrier puppy, which, as he said, had done the right thing in peeing immediately on the soil of France; his story about American captain arriving in Naples: "I want the harbor master." "I get you nice woman—two nice women—three," etc. Captain repeats request: "All right—I try to feex!"

American signs; overlaid on the German, which are overlaid on the French: *"Schweisseraum"* in Paris, *"Rauchen verboten," "Defense de fumer"* at Marseille.

Naples: I took a walk in the streets before it became too dark—ruined streets, with fragments of walls rising like crumbled sand castles out of mounds of pulverized plaster or battered tenements—paper panes, cracked-off pink paint—rising fairly high over streets with no real pavements, but filthy children playing among the garbage, the butcher shops with gruesome cuts of meat and an occasional half-obliterated shrine—women in doorways with babies, one of them showed her baby to me, and I waved and smiled. Depressing return to misery. No police, no traffic except an occasional cart drawn by a donkey (those silver religious things they have and a tiny little tramway), no streetlamps. It seems that they have had streetlights only within the last few days.

April 29: The next day the two American soldiers told me that things were better—at first the people had worn rags and had no shoes. —I decided to go to Pompeii—got on a little electric train and waited about two hours for it to start—people kept getting on and finally coming in through the windows, squeezing in over a metal bar in a way that was painful to see—at last there were so many that the people inside began to expostulate indignantly and try to keep any more from coming—I finally wanted to give up and get off but we were jammed so tight that I couldn't. The two American soldiers were getting off at Herculaneum, and I decided to, too, in order to escape the "torture train," as a Scotch soldier on board called it. We plunged through saying *"Permesso! permesso!"*—a device which the soldiers had learned—the Italians said *"Permesso!"* too. Afterwards, I caught a motor lorry back to Naples, along with blue-clad men in the Canadian flying corps. It was exhilarating—I stood up in the lorry and took off my hat in the cool wind—Vesuvius, its top obscure in smoke and cloud, the water on the other side—we whizzed through the main streets of Naples—where the bomb damage was by no means so bad.

The Americans said that we got on badly with the English—they came to our shows and our bars and then made themselves disagreeable: we got paid so much better than they did. They wouldn't pick us up when we were hitchhiking, and so we had stopped picking them up. —The Italians "had no use for us"—just wanted to grab everything—though an American officer at dinner said that we were now getting along with them better.

The attractions of Naples, such of them as are left, are at the same time frivolous and a little sinister—unbroken tradition of pleasure—Pompeii and Capri, along with Ferdinand and his Queen as described by the Marquis de Sade; Leopardi imprisoned by his father; that Russian case history in the French edition of Havelock Ellis, with the little girls in Naples that are so mad about sex that one of them would masturbate madly while he was in the next room with the other; Vico writing his book, looking straight back through the ancient world, and nobody's knowing about it. Now the factories are destroyed, and the people are all driven out on the streets pimping and peddling things—annoying ape-chatter of competing cabmen, kids that hang around the station waiting to make a little money doing something for you. —What is Naples but a few old antiquities (something about the way the man said *"Antichite"* when he was showing us the right train at the station), and a groveling population that ought to be prevented from breeding in filth. —I have had moments when I have felt, "Let the Americans take it over and make it into something which will be much better if it is only as good as Stamford, Conn."! All the little sections of Europe, like Italy—why should anyone take them seriously as countries: Italy and Greece might be kept on as quaint and picturesque old places, as New Orleans is with us. The great mistake about Europe is taking the countries seriously and letting them quarrel and drop bombs on one another.

On the train, I had read in the Italian papers that Hitler had offered to surrender, that Goebbels had committed suicide after killing his five daughters or, alternately, that Hitler had told him to commit suicide and that he had refused and been shot, and that Mussolini had been captured by the *patrioti*. Later, a kid told me at the lemonade stand that Hitler had killed himself and that the war was finished, and an American officer told me that Mussolini was supposed to have been executed. The man at SHAEF said that the Italians, though not an emotional people, were a very excitable people and that they were continually repeating rumors, had had the war finished several times.

Lili Marlene is really touching—that we should have picked it up from the Germans and that the troops on both sides should sing it—it is also quite a good song, enough variety and both simple and not too obvious. There is not a trace of nationalism or political nonsense in it—it is just about a girl waiting by a lamppost at the barracks gate in the rain for her man to come back from the war.

April 30 [Rome]: Shelled farmhouses outside Rome— from air, like broken-in barnacle shells—cattle in the fields like lice. A man from Massachusetts drove me into Rome;

talked about chances of frost killing the cranberry crop on the Cape on account of the early spring having been so warm. I asked him about some ruins which looked small and brown and a little bit sordid. He said he guessed it was the old "water line." —Business of filling up with gas at a gas station in the regular American way—very strange on the beautiful clear fresh day in sight of the old stumps of ruins. —He said that the English and the Americans didn't get on together—we'd have to fight them next.

Rome[1] astonished me: cleanness and brilliance—I had remembered a rather ignoble modern city with ancient monuments embedded in it; but the Rome I found was smart and delightful. —Fine to see self-respecting Italians after Naples—women handsome—girls in smartly cut short skirts, with the bare feet and legs that were clean, walking on raised pattens with a strap at the heel that managed to be attractive in spite of the poverty of the materials. Hoepli, ices and cakes pretty good—though I ate the latter at a shop which had tables on the sidewalk and where I was right opposite a crowd of tattered people who were waiting to get into some place where the Americans were giving them a handout—the kids kept hovering near the cakes like flies, and the waiter would shoo them away like flies—I pretended not to see them. Opera pretty lousy. A certain atmosphere of freedom and exhilaration that I hadn't expected to find, quite different from London —posters all over the walls—war bonds, *partigiani,* end of the war—elegance and abundance of books—Communist and socialist literature—*Tobacco Road* and *Lady Chatterley*—picture no longer seemed dominated by the catacombs, the Cappuccini, etc., as I remembered it from

[1] See *Europe Without Baedeker* (1947), pp. 39–55 (hereafter given as *EWB*).

my youth: old brown bones—Umberto monument and
Mussolini's balcony—monument all white frosting—wonderful open squares with monuments and arcades.

Bright handlebars and spokes of bicycles—all seemed
new. *La Via del Tabacco, L'Amante di Lady Chatterley.
In Due si canta meglio* (Serenade?) by J. M. Cain.

Communist poster with hanged man all over: *"Ven-
dichiamoli."*

May 1: Newspaper account of the killing of Mussolini,
his mistress, and his supporters, much expurgated in the
report that was published in the *Stars and Stripes.* The
method left something to be desired from the point of
view of the best English public school standards. The
Pope later issued a rebuke.

Demonstration in Piazza del Popolo. I saw them coming away from it, with red neckerchiefs and red flowers
on their coats—one group had a banner that said *"Viva
la Monarchia,"* but others were tearing down the flags,
and I saw one with the cross cut out of the center.

VISIT TO SANTAYANA[1]

The Colosseum was terrific as I came upon it from
above and saw how big it was—it had looked smaller
from below and behind the immense dripping white wedding cake of the Vittorio Emanuele monument—it seemed
as gigantic as anything modern—I went round between it
on the one hand and the Arch of Titus and the Forum on
the other. It was almost a little scaring to be looking up
Santayana in that old quarter full of fragments of ancient
Rome and of more or less still living churches and con-
vents of the Rome of the Christian era. I found myself
entering the Via di Santo Stefano Rotondo as it curved
round an old orange-washed wall, behind which was evidently some sort of institution, with a gray wall in the
other side. Inside the gate of No. 6, trees and grass, a
drive that led round to the hospital proper. A little girl
sitting in the doorway of a sort of gatekeeper's house told
me that the *professore, dottore,* was at the hospital. The
Blue Nuns had blue headdresses that seemed to have been

[1] George Santayana (1863–1953) spent the war years in the
Roman convent of the Blue Nuns, where he received EW. See
EWB, pp. 41–55.

dyed with deep bluing. I tried Italian, then asked if they spoke English, and they answered that they were English. They said that the professor was always glad to see people. I waited in a little parlor, rather dark and nineteenth-century (British) with modern and rather dreary religious pictures. Santayana occupied a single room, with the bed concealed by a large screen (he had a toilet, he told me). He was slight and shrunken, wore a brown bathrobe which did make him look rather like a monk. He excused himself for lying down on a kind of little chaise longue, with a blanket over his legs.

It turned out that he had not sent me the book[2] with the inscription that had come just before I left New York. He was blank when I mentioned it—perhaps someone else had written in it, the publishers?—he had a poor memory for names, didn't remember writing my name in a book—then remembered that an American soldier had come and gotten him to write in a number of books for people he didn't know (this was undoubtedly the explanation). Though this was disappointing for me, he received me with great politeness and amiability and began at once to talk about his autobiography and himself. The first two volumes had a number of omissions which he hoped could be eventually restored—there had been something about some American friends which another friend had persuaded him to leave out, though he had proposed showing it to the people first—and the third volume, though already written, was not to be published till after his death —there was more about [Bertrand] Russell in it—Russell had not been jealous of Santayana's sympathy with one of

[2] Probably *The Middle Span* (1945), Vol. II of Santayana's autobiography, *Persons and Places*. Vols. I and III were *The Background of My Life* (1944) and *My Host the World* (1953). EW reviewed *The Middle Span* in *The New Yorker*, May 5, 1945.

his three wives, but had accused him of siding with her.
—He had written about the Wigglesworths in his novel,[3]
he said, with his little mischievous smile that screwed up
his mouth—a little as if he might have been a freshman
still at Harvard. —When I mentioned [Logan] Pearsall
Smith and Irwin Edman,[4] he said that he had known
them well, but characteristically did not ask how they
were or show the faintest interest in what they were doing.
He remarked that Smith had published a book of selec-
tions from his, Santayana's, works. —His face was a little
abîmé by age and, I suppose, his meager diet—and the
whole interview was a shade spooky—it began raining
outside, so that the room was dark—and on the Cappuccini side of Rome. (He said that he had been getting fat
before the war, and his friends had disapproved and
thought that he was doing some damage to his spiritual
side, that his condition was becoming quite "vicious"; now
the diet had made him thinner—the nuns were raising
their own vegetables in the garden just beyond the window, and he usually had an egg for dinner.) The convent
had had the advantage that they spoke English. —Even
the colds he used to have had disappeared since he had
been eating less and living with the nuns. But I was impressed by his readiness of the traditional philosopher
(Kemp Smith[5] had this, too) to receive anybody and start
talking—and he did talk very well.

[3] Santayana's only novel, titled *The Last Puritan* (1936).

[4] Logan Pearsall Smith (1865–1946), American essayist and
aphorist; he compiled *Little Essays Drawn from the Writings of
George Santayana* (1920). Irwin Edman (1896–1954), professor
of philosophy at Columbia University.

[5] Norman Kemp Smith (1872–1958), Scottish-born professor
who had taught EW at Princeton. Later, he held the chair of
moral philosophy at Edinburgh.

He had reread all of Dickens, became enthusiastic as he spoke—liked especially *David Copperfield* and *Great Expectations*—had always especially liked *Great Expectations* (I think it corresponded partly with his own experience). He said that his new book[6] about Jesus had been stimulated by living in the convent and reading so many religious books—had felt that he could now express better what he thought on this subject. He had read the whole Bible and a good deal of St. Thomas and a lot of religious novels (had been rather hard up for reading matter). He had read the six novels of Jane Austen and a novel by Charlotte M. Yonge,[7] which had made upon him a very strong impression (more so than Jane Austen, whom he had read before)—he recommended it to me for an ocean voyage or something of the sort—the villain was only a villain because he was too good. —He was now reading a translation of Aristophanes, which he had had around a long time, thinking it did not look very good, but to which he had finally resorted and which he was now enjoying, though Americanisms had been put in which jarred with the rest of the style. He had not spoken of the war in his third volume of reminiscences, because he was writing about it—and about the first war, too—in a book of which he indicated the MS. lying beside him on a table—a book about politics on which he had been working off and on for years.[8] He had been much concerned about the other war, had written books directly prompted by it, but he knew about the present one only as he knew about the

[6] Santayana's new book was *The Idea of Christ in the Gospels, or God in Man* (1946).

[7] Charlotte M. Yonge (1823–1901), the sentimental, moralistic Victorian novelist.

[8] *Dominations and Powers: Reflections on Liberty, Society and Government* (1951).

Battle of Cannae. He spoke several times of loving or
wanting "to write something," as if it were merely a way
of passing the time.

He wanted to go for a visit to Avila, and also, I think,
to Paris after the war. But if he went back to Spain, he
would have to speak Spanish, and he did not really speak
it well, could not express nuances as in English. The
Spanish they had spoken at home was mechanical—his
mother had not spoken any language really well. He
would never be able to come to the United States because
he would have to go out socially to some extent and put
on evening clothes. The war had prolonged his life—"not
that it matters now"—by keeping him there in Rome. He
had had something like a small stroke this year, so that he
had to be careful now. He used to walk all over Rome, but
he couldn't do so any more. At Avila he had friends and
near relations that he had to think about, so it was a relief
to be in Rome instead. —He had lived for two years without money—I think he rather fancied himself in the role
of a Franciscan monk. The nuns had given him credit—
though now he paid like any other inmate.

He wanted to get out an illustrated edition of his
memoirs, with photographs and pictures of paintings, but
his situation had made this impossible. The reviewers in
the United States, he said, were complaining that there
was too much about obscure figures—I said that this was
nonsense, that the part about Trumbull Stickney,[9] for
example, was interesting. He was one of the better known
ones. He had written about the others, not on account of
their importance, but because of their interest to him. —I

[9] Trumbull Stickney (1874–1904). EW wrote a foreword to
The Poems of Trumbull Stickney (1972).

spoke of his recent popularity in America. —He was evidently pleased by this—said that he had never been known at all in his earlier days. His point of view was entirely unfashionable—he dealt with things (*Realms of Being*) in the medieval categories, not in the modern ones —they were going back and reading even his older books. —Yes (apropos of nothing and, in fact, a complete shift of the topic of conversation, except that I had earlier spoken of his memoirs), his position had been very unusual —between two civilizations—and he had dealt with it in an unusual way—for he had not availed himself of any of the opportunities which were open to him in various ways.

I spoke of the antagonism of the English toward America. "You don't have to tell me!" he said. An English officer (a Colonel Perry, I think), who had spent two years in prison, had somehow escaped and had been hidden at the hospital there—it was courageous of the nuns. From talking to him, Santayana had been able to see that he was troubled about England's place in the world (I had said that they were irritable, felt insecure). He had liked the English, had been taken in by them in a very friendly way—if he had been given a chair at Oxford, which seemed possible at one time, he might have spent the rest of his life there. But—though he did not explicitly say so —I gathered that in some way they had frozen him, as they are so much in the habit of doing. He had given in England a successful lecture—one of the chapters of *Character and Opinion in the United States*—the people had found out that they were supposed to laugh (at the expense of the United States, of course) and had been in gales of laughter. But then he had later returned and given an unsuccessful lecture. There had been something

uncomfortable about the lights and he had been introduced by Rennell Rodd[10]—now (ironically) Sir Rennell
Rodd—who hadn't known anything about him. Santayana
imitated Rodd's "uh-uh—a writer"—the lecture had apparently fallen flat, and he had left England knowing that
he would never go back. (There had been also something
about the light which I didn't grasp at the time, but I
afterwards found an account of this in the posthumous
volume of his memoirs.) He went on to say that the
trouble was that the English were preoccupied with their
own interests—like the French: he liked France very
much, but the French cared only about their own interests
—all the rest was only politeness. "And the English," I
suggested, "are not polite." "They're not polite," he con-
firmed me.

He spoke with a good deal of intelligence of the role of
the United States—the United States and Russia now
were the important powers. His mother and father had
been more or less identified with the Philippines, and he
had never been sympathetic with the idea of Anglo-Saxon
domination. In showing appreciation by associating himself with England and the United States, he had really
been taking the side of the enemy—but he had never
been willing to "cooperate" with either the Spanish or the
American end. I said that the United States was now less
Anglo-Saxon, and he said that he knew that was true—he
could see from the literature that reached him from Harvard that the university was reaching out tentacles in a
way that was very unlike the old narrow Anglo-Saxon
conception of Harvard. He had lived in the United States
when the ideal of Anglo-Saxon conquest, etc., was at its
height. Now the United States was called upon to play a

[10] Sir Rennell Rodd (1858–1941), diplomat and Conservative
Member of Parliament, 1928–32.

great role in the world. People used to talk about Manifest Destiny. It wasn't Manifest Destiny but a demand that had arisen in the natural course of things, and he thought that people had to meet these demands that were made upon them—not to do so was to make *il gran rifiuto*. And now relations with South America were changed. We and not Spain were to become the dominant influence. He had always been against the idea of Spain's influencing South America, just as he had been against that of England's influencing the United States.

I said that the atmosphere of Rome seemed freer and more stimulating than I had expected—as if they had really gotten something out of getting rid of the regime. "Oh, the regime was splendid, I assure you!"—the city had been cleaned and improved—a lot had been done for the young people—and people were nicer: they did things for you like Americans—something that had been unknown in Europe. The regime had had its defects—like everything else—but his point of view was one of approval. He had received a letter one day asking him whether he didn't want to become a Roman citizen—he went to the bureau and explained that he was a Spanish subject and wanted to remain one. They said that being a Roman citizen would not interfere with this. He asked what the duties and obligations would be, and they told him so many lire. He declined and so, as he said, missed his opportunity of becoming a *civis Romanus*. I think that an important element in his approval of the Fascist regime was his admiration for virility and uniforms. I think it was Irwin Edman who told me that Santayana had responded to Mussolini's call for gold by sending in a supposed gold medal given him by a British philosophical society. It was returned with thanks but with the explanation that it [was] not made of gold but of gilded lead.

He thought that it had probably been due to the Pope

that Rome had not been bombed. The Pope had not been appointing new cardinals—there were only forty now where there should have been sixty-nine, the seventieth was never appointed. The Pope was waiting till after the war, so as to get them from both sides—some from Germany, [and] undoubtedly the Archbishop of Westminster. I said that in America the Catholic Church was playing a new and rather sinister role. He answered that it worked the other way, too—the United States was more important at the Vatican—they depended on American money, as everybody in the world now did.

A very great man was coming to see him—he said this with his nuance of irony—Jacques Maritain.[11] He was evidently not much impressed by Maritain—he said that he was unforgiving to his enemies, that there was something of the Calvinist about him—he liked better the Catholics who were charitable—he, Santayana, had said to someone that he was a Catholic in everything but faith.

He said that there had been in philosophy three important false steps—*faux pas*—made by Socrates, the Reformation, Kant. Socrates had tried to put the physical under the heel of the moral (and metaphysical?). He himself had strictly limited himself to the moral, but his followers had made things worse. The Reformation had taken and perpetuated all that was bad in paganism, instead of, like the Renaissance, reviving what was good. The German idealistic philosophers—not merely the German, but Locke, Berkeley, and Hume—had adopted the position that the order of discovery of objects comes before the order of genesis—as if some idea of our grandfather came before the fact of our grandfather (he laughed; he de-

[11] Jacques Maritain (1882–1973), the religious philosopher who was French Ambassador to the Holy See, 1945–48, and later taught at Princeton.

lighted in philosophical jokes)! For him, Santayana, our
conception of the flaming sun was a sensation of the same
order, an essence, as the older conception of Apollo with
his golden rays. Neither was an object that we knew, as
the idealistic philosophers believed. (When I repeated
this later to Irwin Edman, he said, "Did he really express
himself in such a polished literary way?" I found later,
when the last volume of his memoirs appeared, that he
had simply been reciting to me a paragraph he had recently written.)

He could not follow the German philosophers—not
that he criticized them on this account—he had always
felt that it was his fault and wished he could. Nietzsche
and Schopenhauer he had never had any difficulty in following. I felt that there was a light nuance of ironic
hypocrisy in all this.

There is a shade of the feminine and the feline about
him. I felt it when he was telling about the friend who
had persuaded him to omit the passage from his memoirs
—though he had only said that somebody was in love and
had married very happily (or something of the sort), and
when he told something at the expense of his nephew—
though, he explained, he perhaps shouldn't say it, since
the nephew had just died—even when, just as I was leaving and I tried again to clear up the mystery of the book
and asked him how he had known my name, he said, "Oh,
I didn't know it—the American gave it to me." I said that
I had heard he had read a book of mine, *Axel's Castle*.
"Oh, if you had told me that, I should have known who
you were." I noticed then, seeing his face three-quarters
for the first time, that his nose was more pointed—I suppose, more Spanish—than I had supposed from his photographs. What must have been the blondness and smooth-
ness of his face had been now somewhat decomposed. He
is much shrunken, of course, but he must always have

been rather a small, frail man, with a small man's slightly propitiatory and at the same time defiant attitude toward the world—the element of self-protectiveness and mockery. I felt also how much he must always have been on the fringes of the social organism—not really at home at Harvard, in England, or in Spain—and must feel better in Rome, where he could talk English with the nuns in the hospital. But he is a figure of remarkable dignity— just what a philosopher should be—and a writer of passionate vocation. It is really the writer who has survived everything else. He is not precisely narcissistic but interested in himself as a writer ought to be; and it is perhaps only now at the end of his life—since he has never realized himself as a poet—that his interest in himself is at last finding complete expression—with all the philosophies through which he has passed making an iridescent integument about him, the manners of all the societies in which he has lived supplying him with illustrations. I felt a sort of sacred awe at seeing him, in his little room: a shell of faded skin and frail bone, in which the power of intellect, the colors of imagination, still lived and gave out, through his books and through his gentle-voiced conversation, their vibrations and rays, of which the frequency seems to increase as the generator draws closer to dissolution—as if the spirit really worked more brightly and clearly, its communications were less interrupted, as the flesh became wasted. He wants to conserve himself, to realize himself as he never has done before—I don't imagine he is troubled by the thought of death—his present successful functioning absorbs, enchants, and satisfies him. The intellectual man must always tend to something of this sort —and the writer, when he ages, is in a better situation than the practitioner of some kind of work which requires more physical execution: he only has to sit and write, and he finds that he now knows his business better and is in full command of his forces. I have been feeling something of this as I have been coming closer to fifty.

A few days later, in my hotel room, the thought of his spending night after night, so far from Harvard and Spain, alone in that little bed, with its simple white pillow of which I could see a corner from behind the concealing screen, came back to me in my own solitude, my rather lonely evenings of writing and reading, actually to appall me. And was it a threat or a challenge? All alone there, he was still in the world of men, talking to them through his books, aware of what they were doing all around him —he was a microcosm, a monad, in which it was all reflected; he was a part of the human plasm. Others shuddered at the impact of its shocks, were uplifted by the excitement of its vibrations. So he had been, he said, at the time of the other war. Now his glass scarcely brightened or clouded; but the intelligence that persisted in him was the intelligence of the human race: he was thinking all their thoughts, taking part in all their points of view— so how could he be lonely? He had made it his business to spread himself through every human consciousness with which he had made any contact. He slept, in his plain single bed, in the consciousness of the whole human mind.

TRIP TO MILAN

May 3: Stove-in and broken barnacles of the clay-pink-roofed houses—intarsiatura of green and deep chocolate fields.

—Later, near Milan, fields under water that must have been rice fields

—pocked with shell craters (outside Rome) and boomerang-shaped L-trenches

—on way to airport, bits of old brown brick masonry, with weeds growing out of them, like warts

—planes taking off like fish surprised in shallows—sturgeon-snouted

—that morning before starting from Rome, at seven, at the end of the Via Sistina and looking out from the Pincian in the clear fresh morning air, where all the clay colors of the city, orange, red, gamboge, and the pale clayey color of old churches matched the pale straw of the morning clouds, which, along with the gray ones, lay under the pale fresh blue (surprise at finding that, in Italy, the air, the sky, and the light have not grown tarnished and greasy with the monuments)—on the further hills white villas (or what?)

—from the air, the Tiber with its earthwormlike windings

—where the coast makes a scoop, the waves of the blue-green sea are a white fringe like the edge of piecrust (approaching Genoa).

Milan. My first impression was that everybody was stunned—those colorless undernourished people dressed in threadbare clothes—children with looks of apprehension and indignation—trams running and people presumably going about their business, but general effect of deadness and stoppage. Public Relations hotel rather grisly—waiters and clerks who spoke English and who had probably also spoken German—white zinc numbers on the doors; *"occupato"* and *"libro"* on the W.C. doors; smell of hotel corridors—all of which reminded you of tourist travel (like the shopworn volumes of Tauchnitz that I saw later in the window of one of the bookstores) —elevator boy and other employees slightly afraid of the British and Americans. Lunch consisted of army bully beef and army greens, with a plate of very hard crackers, not unlike dog biscuits, that were the sole native contribution.

Posters of all the parties—Party of Action, Christian Democrats, Socialists, Communists, etc. An engineer I met, who had been in the United States, said that all they really needed were a party to govern and an opposition party. One good—probably Communist—poster of naked red farmerlike stripling, with his foot on the neck of Mussolini, lying crouched and dead: *"Il bestiale fascismo è vinto."* "Hurrah for the Anglo-Saxon Liberators."

GI's in dining room—one had been up in the mountains where it was cold, had a girl in Florence—had been working so hard since he had been in Milan that he hadn't seen the dead Mussolini or anything, didn't even know

where it had happened—getting bulletins out for Public
Relations. Another had found a record of an Italian song
he wanted—had found it unexpectedly (both the record
and the sheet music) in Milan and was going to try to
send it home if the censor would let him.

Little commandeered German cars that the *partigiani*
were riding around in—green with a kind of flocculent
black camouflaging.

Walk around the city with Philip Hamburger [who
was also there for *The New Yorker*]. Little hotel in which
the Germans had barricaded themselves with barbed wire
and a more solid barricade, a German truck still inside the
enclosure—for the rest, GI's—Italians standing around
outside. —The cathedral with the panes taken out and
the windows mostly blinded up, so that it was dark—the
Scala, where performances were suspended: excellent
repertoire, which included *Don Giovanni* and Stravinsky's
Mavra. Man in a bar who showed us snapshots of the
dead Mussolini and his mistress. —Girls with raised heels,
as in Rome, but this footwear, instead of being clogs, had
heels that gave the effect of French heels. I have noticed,
since coming back, that the women of Rome sometimes
have these, too. The whole city had the appearance of an
old brownish photograph such as one might look at
through a parlor stereopticon.

The excitement had been terrific, Hamburger said, and
now they were sobering up after the orgy, relapsing into
their former depressed and depleted state—awful looks of
chill, enmity, and tension on all the people's faces—none
of the correspondents with whom I had traveled seemed
to notice this—when we were back in the plane, and I
spoke of it, saying that Milan was a gloomy place, they
would say, "Yes, I didn't think much of it—didn't like it
as well as Rome."

Hotel men speaking perfect hotel English—had unquestionably just been speaking German—and, as Philip
Hamburger said, were expecting the Japs to come.

The whole visit affected me with horror—I was just as
glad not to stay. Hamburger, who had been present when
one of Mussolini's followers (Starace) had been shot and
strung up and had heard the partisans shooting Fascists
after dark, seemed to be getting a little nervous, as he
suspected, in the let-down mood of the Milanese, some
dissatisfaction with the Allies—perhaps they didn't like
these proclamations (announcing our taking over)—he
thought that we and British ought to clear out as quickly
as possible, though the British seemed opposed to the idea
of giving Italy back to the Italians. In his bedroom, just
before I left, he showed me photographs of the dead
Mussolini, etc., which made me rather sick. Nobody, however, that I talked to, including Hamburger, showed any
signs of disgust over the shooting and exposing of the body
of Mussolini's girlfriend, etc.—though somebody, coming
back in the plane, remarked that her sticking with him
showed her devotion, as she might very easily have left
him. Hamburger was about deciding that he would come
back to Rome the next day or even on the plane that
afternoon. The inhabitants had been enchanted by the
first jeep, but now might not like us so well when they
found that we weren't feeding them on a very big scale.

I walked from the Albergo Diana to the airport. The
mountains on the left, just beyond the town, a purified
and dimmed slate blue, with the snow along their tops,
designed in sharp lines but softened perspective, looked
like something that Stendhal might have seen as he went
out riding around Milan (I had just noticed in a bookstore a book called *Arrigo Beyle, Milanese*)—like an early-
nineteenth-century engraving or a sober and decorous

painting of that period. I walked a good part of the way
with a woman who was going home and who offered to
show me the way to the airport—she was terribly thin,
but not at all excitable, took everything now as a matter
of course. There was nothing to eat, no bread—she had
three children, showed with her hand the steps of their
ages—*"Povera Italia!"* she sighed. She had been so frightened these last days at all the firing—but they were glad
to have the Germans gone—they had come first, in 1940,
at the beginning of the war—and then *"più e più"* . . .
She was very pleasant, quite prosaic and dry, as I imagined the people are up here.

The man we met at the newsstand, who had spent eight
months in the United States, Camden and Pennsylvania,
and spoke English. He said his grandmother's name was
O'Brien, and he looked rather Irish. The Germans had
been after him, and he had taken to the *maquis* in the
hills. The factory where he worked as engineer was not
doing much now, and he would be glad to serve the
Americans for nothing. He wanted to do something after
these awful four years.

The stink of Mussolini's execution, etc., seemed to hang
over the whole place.

Hamburger told me the story of the British and American mess. The British mess sergeant was evidently smarter
than ours, and was managing to give them better food.
The Americans had finally said to them, "You're eating
our food—why don't you offer us some of it?" This had
given rise to a good deal of unpleasantness.

Wonderful blondes in Milan—though Hamburger says
they have them in Rome, too, and that they are dyed in
imitation of Veronica Lake, etc. Pictures of movie actresses

all over Italy. —So Mamaine [Paget] had asked me which
film actresses I liked in order to find out what type of
woman I liked.

They are still singing, in the streets at night, *Santa
Lucia* and *Oi Mari*. I first heard *Oi Mari,* as a child, when
a man, on the voyage to Naples, sang it to a guitar in the
steerage, while the first-class passengers listened on the
other side of the barrier and afterwards gave him some
money.

In 1922, they were writing "W Lenin"[1] on the walls—
twenty-three years later, they are doing the same thing:
Mussolini has come and gone.

One trouble about the Italians is probably partly the
discrepancy between their romantic classical rhetoric and
demonstrative feelings, on the one hand, and, on the
other, the conditions of modern life, with the exact and
sober modern point of view.

[1] The postwar double-V graffiti of the Left proclaiming victory.

ROME

Silone:[1] Silent and seemed *abattu,* would allow remarks
to pass without comment, but came to life occasionally to
say something rather brilliant: Thomas Mann had perfected his literary instrument so that he could say, "I will
do this or that"; but an artist did not choose in that way:
he did what he had to do. —I said that the Germans had
no literature of social observation, and he replied that they
had no real society—he had been in Germany and had
found that there were only official and proletariat—an
official was an official first and a man afterwards. Marxism
was the German novel. —He hadn't much cared for *La
Lutte avec l'ange,* objected to Malraux's[2] *"recherches de
style,"* which he considered unnecessary, and to its being
printed in red and black ink, for which he apparently
blamed Malraux himself, objected also, rather unfairly, in
view of Malraux's present point of view, to what he called
Malraux's nihilism. —He said that Italy would have a
"republic of the Left"—the Communists were strong, but

[1] Ignazio Silone (1900–78), Italian novelist, author of *Bread
and Wine* (1937). *EWB*, pp. 80–96, 170–73.

[2] André Malraux (1901–76), French novelist, philosopher of
art, and Minister of Culture under De Gaulle. *EWB*, pp. 80–96.

74

not strong enough to impose a dictatorship. —He talked about the role of the South vis-à-vis the North—in Italy, in France, in the United States, and I think, in Germany —it was always beaten by the North, but always had its *"revanche"* later. Explained the different characteristics and roles of the different Italian cities. The intellectuals from the various areas were now collected in Rome, but would eventually go back home.

Visit to Alvaro[3] *with [William] Barrett*[4] *[in our Embassy]:* Barrett told me that the *ragazzini* of the streets were the collectors for the black market; they would get food, clothes, and cigarettes from the soldiers and take them home to their parents, who would sell them at central exchanges. Once these kids had found a white GI with a black GI, who was dead drunk. The white soldier asked the kids if they wanted to buy a black man and sold him for 1,200 lire. The boys took him somewhere and stripped him and sold the clothes, doubtless for several thousand lire.

Alvaro had investigated the beggars for some paper. They came to work in a bus, which dropped them at their various posts. Some of the men would arrive briskly in the morning, pee against the wall, and then go into their act, becoming paralyzed and bent. But all were not frauds.

There was a crisis of prostitution. Hundreds of girls had been put out of work by the closing of the big Fascist offices, and many of them were now on the streets. Women had also come in from elsewhere on account of the Allied troops.

---

[3] Corrado Alvaro (1895–1956), Italian novelist, author of *L'Uomo è forte* (1938). The visit mentioned here is developed in *EWB*, pp. 70–71.

[4] William Barrett, American philosopher associated with *Partisan Review*.

Rome showed its poverty less than other places because people kept up appearances, making a point of looking respectable in public, when, actually, they were starving at home.

Mussolini as an actor: marvelous at a variety of roles—knew how to clap a soldier on the back as if he were an old comrade-in-arms, how to wink at an American journalist, talk to a Frenchman or a German. He had been extremely scared of Balbo.[5] Women used to come to offer themselves to him from all over Italy. A certain admiration showed through in these stories, like that of old union leaders when they talked about Lewis in spite of the fact that they had fought him, or that of Russian émigrés like Nicholas Nabokov[6] for Stalin. Foreigners, he said, ought not to be too much shocked over "the fury of the people" in the execution of Mussolini and his followers: after all, the Germans had been hanging people in public (verify) and leaving corpses around the streets. Alvaro's son was a partisan, and just back from Bologna—sunburnt, vigorous, good-looking (as Barrett said, rather like an American), evidently considerably stimulated—much more vitally than the older people—by what had been going on.

The Italians were disappointed with the WAACs, whom they had expected to look like American movie actresses.

Family orchestra, with mother and little tiny kids, including an infant in arms, that played on street corners—little instruments they tooted—*Lili Marlene*.

[5] Italo Balbo (1896–1940), Italian aviator and Fascist politician. See *The Thirties*, p. 374n.

[6] Nicholas Nabokov (1903–78), cousin of the novelist, was a composer and musicologist.

[William] Hughes, young Englishman, staff officer in charge of utilities. Story about Churchill at mess on the coast of England. Had asked Hughes, in his grunting spasmodic way, how many Germans he had killed with the revolver which he was carrying in a holster. Hughes had reminded him that, in modern war, people no longer shot the enemy with revolvers, and said that he hadn't seen three Germans in France. But Churchill then proceeded to tell them how he had killed people with a revolver in Egypt, and said he had thought Hughes's holster was rather high and wondered how he could reach for his gun in a hurry. Hughes explained that he was telling this to illustrate—not, as he might well have done, Churchill's romantic boyish out-of-date notion of war—but his love of face-to-face fighting.

He said that Italy had been like the frog in the fable which had blown itself up to be as big as a bull and burst —and he was now, as all British officials apparently had to be, rather contemptuous about the Italians: they were talking about their rights and ambitions, etc.

Works of Art—Dewald (a professor of art from Princeton, assigned to look after the works of art): Story about Duccio altarpiece at Siena. It had been put away in a villa outside the city—famous piece made in 1308, to which the Sienese had made their votive offerings. When the Allied commission had got it out, a British officer arranged to have it sent to Florence. The Sienese went crazy, and had all the church dignitaries aroused to intervene.

A Cranach Adam and Eve was among the things that the Germans were supposed to be moving out of their hiding places back into Uffizi, but they spirited it away in a Red Cross truck. It was afterwards found in the Tyrol.

Mantegnas at Padua destroyed by Americans, but not Giottos. Library at Naples with Hohenstaufen records destroyed by Germans—galley from Lake of Nemi.

He began by complaining about the people who took a contemptuous view of the Italians, but later went on to complain himself that they wanted us to baby them, take care of them, when they ought to be left alone and made to stand on their own feet. Prince Caetani[7] had told me that the Americans ought to stay here and sit on things awhile, so that they wouldn't be having all that awful trouble.

Dewald had been under fire in a villa in Florence when it was still being shelled by the Germans.

Count Morra[8] *and Mrs. Murray* told about the anti-Fascist press at Bari (devoted to printing Croce's works) which had been requisitioned by our armies.

Black Market

Newburgh (a Princeton classmate of mine, in the perfumery business): He had got to know a charming Italian family, used to go to their house, which was like a palace made of white soap. The father a splendid old figure with a great thick head of white hair and enormous *baffoni*. Everything was very pleasant until one day the old man broached the question of flints (for cigarette lighters)— proposed that Newburgh should supply him with them and take half the price he would get for selling them. So that was the end of that—he couldn't go there any more.

---

[7] Prince Caetani, an Italian nobleman, had married an American, Margaret Chapin, who became thus Principessa di Bassiano. She edited and published the international review *Botteghe Oscure*.

[8] Count Umberto Morra di Lavriano, well known in Italian literary and art circles. *EWB*, pp. 326–27.

The old man had the concession for making records of all the Vatican music—the Sistine Choir, the big organ—but no records were being made at the present time.

In Sicily, a British officer lived in a castle with a local countess, and they levied a personal tax on every load of wine that was shipped north (they had to send it by sea, too expensive to transport by land). He was now in northern Italy and they were supposed to have the goods on him—"but did you ever hear of an officer being convicted by a court-martial—especially if he's a British officer?"

An American officer had been offered a villa, which he could occupy after the war, if he would allow a shipment of supplies to be diverted to another destination.

At Civitavecchia, the carabinieri were allowing salt (a government monopoly) to be carried off by people if they left some with the carabinieri. Somebody had discovered that there was an account of the same thing in some history of ancient Rome.

No crops because the Germans had mined the fields and the more able-bodied men were mostly away with the army.

McBride of the Passaic News-Herald: He had been plastered in Italy for weeks—had disappeared for several days in Florence. He was lying around the Hôtel de la Ville practically inanimate. Philip Hamburger woke him up on one occasion and asked him whether he didn't want to go to bed. He said, "Where am I?" When Hamburger told him, he said: "Only two of us left!" He liked to tell of having been in the infantry in the last war, but Hamburger said he had never gotten further than Fort Dix, where he had edited a little army paper. He had spent his whole life on the Passaic *News-Herald.* —His crazy-driving habit of saying "Hm?" after everything.

Hamburger's story about the Borghese Gardens: He saw two Italians standing and looking with field glasses at something in the bushes. Hamburger stopped to see what it was and they said: "Fucking! Fucking!" A British officer came by and stopped and took the glasses and looked, and then said to Hamburger: "You see, they are an inferior race," and offered him the field glasses to look. He declined.

Roi Ottley[9] (colored correspondent for *PM*): He had been invited to the house of what seemed to be a respectable middle-class Italian family: but they produced an eighteen-year-old daughter and offered to let him sleep with her for $20. They kept saying they would make everything comfortable. When he declined, they thought he was haggling and offered her to him for $15. She looked tired and not too enthusiastic—she had a regular job during the day. Roi told them that they ought to be ashamed of themselves.[10]

Sunday (May 20) at Caetanis' at Ninfa:[11] Driving out in a car with Sir D'Arcy Osborne, British Minister to the Holy See, and Miss Cadogan, daughter of somebody in the Foreign Office [Sir Alexander Cadogan] then at the San Francisco conference. Fair hair, ruddy face, camera in brown leather case. Their conversation: hardly audible and, when audible, mainly unintelligible, was all about their friends—the usual story of some snub that somebody had administered to somebody. Sir D'Arcy commented on

---

[9] Roi Ottley (1906–60), author of *Black Odyssey* (1948), correspondent for *PM*, the New York daily of the 1930s and 1940s which specialized in news "focus" and summaries like *Time*. It carried no advertising.

[10] *EWB*, pp. 66–69.

[11] A village on the edge of the Pontine Marshes.

the smartness and excellent condition of everybody in Italy as compared to England. "Sad that that should be shattered"—of some church. He talked about how Winnie lay in bed in the afternoon—"which nobody else is able to do"—so came out "full of beans" at night, when the cabinet members were very tired. She told about her experience during the war, supervising, apparently, the firing of antiaircraft guns. The two ways they have of saying "Yes": the way they use it on the telephone, pushing you off and making a point of not establishing the faintest shade of a personal relation; and the more sententious way, when some expression of sympathy or concern is called for, which manages to remain quite hollow. They talked about quinine pills that turned you yellow—she said she'd rather have malaria.

The ruined towns between Rome and Ninfa: whole villages left as empty walls and rubble—pink houses—all the buildings looked soft, so that you thought of tearing the paper off a cardboard box and also tearing, by mistake, the gray underneath, or of slicing a part of the crust off a loaf of bread. In one place, a family of children were sitting in a room of which only two corners were left. They had little pots of flowers in the room, and seemed to be sitting around in their bright—black, green, and red— Sunday clothes. Children playing with an old gun that was camouflaged with green dappling—other guns were lying around, rusty, wrecked, and belly-up. Yet I saw "W Roosevelt" written on one wall. A town square with everything demolished around it—in the middle, a sort of rockery of brickwork with a white headless statue on the top. Women with jars on their heads.

Ninfa. Contadine passing along the road—oxen with long horns. Square brown brick medieval tower with little rectangular windows and M_M_M on top, with swifts and some kind of crows flying in and out of it—Caetani said that his ancestors had built it about 1300—Rienzi[12] had cut fourteen meters off the top to punish the nobles, who doubtless, he said, needed to be punished, as they had in other cases. Behind the town and the little low stone or brick houses rose the granite and dark shrub-green wall of the mountain, which seemed quite sheer, like a backdrop—because the flat wall of the town made it look flat—on the top of the hill to the right were the brown square houses of an unlikely-looking town, which the Princess never seemed to have got over regarding as rather quaint. There was a very swiftly flowing brook and a little river called the Ninfa, also rapid and incredibly clear, with great beds of green watercress and across on the opposite bank the elephant ears of some gigantic plant like mullein; queer and beautiful effect of the water, at once limpid and rather dark—there were trout in it. A little summerhouse with a brick base and straw–capped/covered/bonneted roof. The water was supposed to be filtered through the rock of the mountain.

The Caetanis had lost their son Camille in the war against Greece—he had been educated mainly in America. Poor Lelia, who had the Prince's profile, was too tall, too thin, and had little to say—but the brown spaniel, Honey, with his graying muzzle, was devoted to her. The Prince disappeared after lunch, as he had in Rome—he was preoccupied with his estate, which he was trying to get into shape again. He said he had to be there himself, and it would take him a long time—to excuse himself for not doing something or other that one of the Americans suggested his doing, in connection with some organization. He was worried about the four months' drought. He had stayed out at Ninfa all through the German occupation.

[12] Cola di Rienzi (1313–54), Roman patriot and popular leader.

—The Germans had brought in salt water to encourage the spread of malaria, and when German soldiers had pitched their tents on his property, he had not made any complaint, knowing they would catch malaria. Later on, he expressed surprise that they had decided not to do it again. "Oh, no," they had said. "Everybody had come down with malaria." "What a pity!" He is interested in music. His mother was English, one of his grandmothers was Polish.

My thoughts about the shortcomings of the British abroad; then Myron C. Taylor[13] and his wife, and the rest of the American Vatican set. Mrs. Taylor had a small navy-blue sailor hat on soft slightly curly hair that might have owed its yellow tint to dye, dark blue sun spectacles like horses' blinders, large rosette earrings, themselves rather pretty, in gold and blue, a rectangular face, a string of pearls or white beads, a wrinkled neck underneath her square jaw, a white dress with several plain large buttons down the front. She complained that I was being called Wilson when I had first been introduced to her as Warren; then at lunch she wrote Mr. Tittmann a note asking him what my name was, and after he had replied in the same way, addressed a remark to me as Mr. Wilson but soon relapsed into Warren. She said, at one point, that she didn't believe in international marriages. Lelia laughed and said she was the product of one. Mrs. Taylor said that she was an exception.

Mr. Tittmann (Taylor's assistant) talked at length about avocados, explaining to Caetani what they were.

Lunch began with some sort of salad of peas and other vegetables, exceptional ravioli, lettuce salad, sheep's-milk

[13] Myron C. Taylor (1874–1959), industrialist and the President's personal representative to the Vatican as ambassador without portfolio, 1939–50.

cheese, a sort of rice semi-dessert with honey, fruit compote, white wine. Food light and delicate. Caetani said he
thought that people always ought to be a little underfed
—had been reading about Byron's diet, had found that it
stimulated his mind.

Sir D'Arcy went off and took photographs. An Italian
representative of Morgan [bank?] talked to me about
Walter Lippmann. Tittmann's dog, a black spaniel, swam
in the river, then shook himself and jumped on people
and had to be shut up—a good deal of fuss and dramatiz-
ing of this in the tiresome American way. Caetani rather
droll, in the Nabokov way, about moving the table out of
the sun: "I think the air is a little cooler over here."

Count Morra had said, when I asked him whether the
Princess Bassiano were intelligent: "Not quite." (The
Princess Bassiano was Caetani's wife, Katherine Biddle's[14]
half sister.)

Caetani's grandfather had made the authoritative map
of Dante.

The hammer and sickle have been scratched on the
Caetani palazzo in Rome.

The whole occasion reminded me of the Soviet melo-
drama *Roar China!* in which caricatured representatives
of the various nationalities turn up in China, exhibiting
their national traits; but everybody here subdued and more
or less resigned to leftist developments.

Moravia:[15] He took a gloomy view of the future of
Europe. He said that there had been nothing like this
since Belisarius when the Goths and somebody else had
been fighting in Italy. He'd been in hiding in a barn just

---

[14] Katherine Biddle (1891–1978), poet and wife of Francis
Biddle, the U.S. Attorney General, 1941–45.

[15] Alberto Moravia (b. 1907), Italian novelist. *EWB*, p. 208.

on the line of battle, living on meat and bread and killing
the sheep, "veals," and goats very often himself, and he
was tired of being in danger of getting bombed or shot—
wanted to go away to somewhere like Greece, but Greece
was impossible now for an Italian. The partisans in the
North, though this had not yet been published, had killed
20,000 Fascists—in one small town, they had killed 800.
They had hoped that the Big Three would guarantee
peace for a period, but it didn't look like it now. Italy was
controlled now by England, but they might as well resign
themselves to this: if the English moved out, the Russians
would come in. Nationalism of the various nationalities
made it impossible to have a European federation—Russia
made it appear that you couldn't have socialism without
an intensification of nationalism.

Concentration camp film, with melodramatic music,
along with football, and Disney, malarial mosquitoes, dive-
bombing, and people that shriek and writhe in convulsions of agony. Leonor Fini's drawings for the Marquis de
Sade.

Palazzo in which Leonor Fini and Lepri[16] *live:* Going
in there at night *nel buio*—endless wide shallow marble
steps, great high-arched windows, gigantic Roman figure
like a surrealist object on landing—wrong door at which
we inquired, opened by a servant on a chain. I believe he
said that some prince lived there—he closed the door,
and we were again in the dark. They had a little duplex
apartment with fairly ample kitchen in one of the enormous rooms.

[16] Leonor Fini (b. 1918), Italian surrealist painter. *EWB*, pp.
184, 202–8. The Marchese Lepri, a young diplomat and artist.
EWB, pp. 205–7.

Palazzo of Mattei family,[17] in which American-Italian cultural meeting was held: sides of sarcophagi and other Roman fragments that had been found when the foundations were dug (c. 1600) embedded in the walls of the court; enormous and ugly busts of the Hapsburg emperors, each with some kind of more or less grotesque face or other symbol on its chest. Large painting of some battle in which the family had figured; the duchess's boudoir with its gilded and painted paneling; painted ceilings, and excellent frieze depicting processions of various kinds.

Chalked on a wall: "W anniversario di novembre 7 quando la libertà è stato data al popolo russo."

Morra's account of the insurrection at Naples: Like 1848: barricades in the street, boys with hand grenades strung around their waists. The Germans had announced that all the young men were to serve, then they had all disappeared. It was as if the spirit of the common purpose were communicated through the whole town by electricity.

Pessimistic views of the writers: Morra said that, in combating Italian rhetoric, as Papini[18] had done, they had simply developed a new type of rhetoric. —Antonio Russi [with whom EW took Italian lessons] thought that Italy would never now be anything: in the days of ancient Rome and the Renaissance, it had been in the way of the great trade routes; but it had not done much since, just as Greece had done nothing since the ancient world. They taught nothing but Greek and Latin, not enough modern

[17] Enrico Mattei (1906–62), leader of Italy's Christian Democratic resistance movement. He later became a powerful industrialist.

[18] Giovanni Papini (1881–1956), Italian writer and philosopher.

languages. —Moravia said that the Pope no longer means anything much in Italy. Both said that it was impossible for a writer to earn a living.

Moravia said that people were saying that Mussolini had shot Patacci[19] and himself in a suicide pact, since the bullet had gone in at the side of his head and blown out one eye.

Black Market: The price of cigarettes went up or down in proportion to the number of Americans in town on leave: once it sank from the normal 250 lire to 125 lire.

Silone's story about Prince Caetani: They had once been there for lunch when the stationmaster from Ninfa, whom the Caetanis knew well, arrived and sent to the Prince to ask whether he could give him some corn for his wife and ten children. He had said, No: he had had to give all his corn to the *ammassi*, the government pools. The Princess pled with him—and finally suggested that he might be able to get the man moved to another station where the trains were running, but the Prince said, No: that there was plenty of work for people to do on his place —that they wanted 300 lire a day but they would soon be forced to do it for 100.

Barrett told me that the *Italian companies* were organizing under the protection of the American firms so that it would be impossible for them to be nationalized. Myron Taylor had helped arrange this for one of them.

Fodor [an elderly foreign correspondent]: said that the younger generation of correspondents subsisted entirely

---

[19] Clara Patacci, Mussolini's mistress.

on handouts and didn't get things for themselves. He asked me how old I was, and told me he was fifty-five. It was a good thing to go out and move around. If you settled down, you aged much more, got habits you thought couldn't be upset. The only difficulty he found was getting up in the back of trucks, he had to be helped up. I had found the same difficulty myself.

[The passage which follows was amplified in *Europe Without Baedeker*, but EW disguised Sir Ronald Storrs as Sir Osmond Gower, presumably to avoid charges of libel or caricature. Sir Ronald, in his younger time, had been described by Lawrence of Arabia as "the most brilliant Englishman in the Near East" and he was now living on that reputation. Lawrence said, "Storrs sowed what we reaped, and was always first and the great man among us." EW was irritated by him and they played a game of upmanship in their quotations from Dante and other great books.]

Sir Ronald Storrs,[20] etc.: An English soldier who had taken him around said he was a pain in the neck. He had insisted on a big audience for his Lawrence of Arabia lecture in spite of the fact that it was VE day. Only fourteen people showed up, and he had arranged for a princess to be there (probably Bassiano). At first he had said he wouldn't lecture, but ?-Brown persuaded him that he would have to do something, so he gave them an informal talk. Finally, the next day, -? -? had to detail a lot of men to listen to him. He was quite impervious to suggestions that the subject was a little stale—"throwing his weight

[20] Sir Ronald Storrs (1881–1955), the early associate of T. E. Lawrence, gave lectures and broadcasts and wrote articles during the war years and also held various colonial governorships. *EWB*, pp. 163–69.

around," "*Was* he rude to you?" "It's shocking" (when I
said Storrs was very vain). Other man who had founded
Talbot House (?) and was now seventy and rather gaga.
Wrote to find out from his hotel whether he hadn't left
his pajamas there. The hotel said he had stolen two sheets.
He wrote explaining this and received another letter asking him to try the hotel in Florence. They said he had
also taken two sheets from them. He wrote the old man
this and got no answer.

My meeting with *Storrs* at dinner at Il Retrovo: (The
bad-smelling bachelor's buttons, etc., on which the water
hadn't been changed.) Storrs, fruitiness, his air of an old
ham—his assumption that it was a privilege to listen to
him; incomparable condescension to Italians and Americans—"your ambassador, excellent man." He had a lecture
on four great books of the world—wanted to know
whether the Italians wanted it. The Italian professor was
connected with some institution which gave lectures to the
English and Americans on Italian literature. Well, since
it was only to *insegnare* and not to *imparare,* he realized
there was no chance—since it was *senso unico.* These
things, the classics, were the breath of life to him. Epigrams in verse—"if you like epigrams in verse." Lord
Dunsany[21] on Mrs. Simpson: "I should say I did!"—as
good as the Greek Anthology: Leonidas of (Tarentum)[22]
—inferiority of Vergil to Dante—he had reread the whole
of the *Divine Comedy* coming here in a plane, reread it
every year. His visit to the Pope, had shown him a book

[21] Lord Dunsany (1878–1957), Irish dramatist and poet.
[22] EW is alluding here to the third century B.C. Greek poet
Leonidas of Tarentum, who influenced the later Greek epigram.
He is not known to have written anything but epigrams. About
a hundred survive.

of poems of all nations that Maurice Baring[23] had put together for [T. E.] Lawrence. The Holy Father had been impressed, had said, "There's nobody like these old poets" —then, as if with surprise, "Do you read Horace in England?" —Ah, yes: Horace went with port wine—if one started an ode of Horace, one used to be able to go on with it—his classical training at Cambridge. Billy Hughes later said to me that we ought to have taken him up on this, should have stumped him by starting an epode.

"The head of my family at that time, Lord Brownlow, was sitting after dinner and the servant came in and said, 'There's a fire in the library, sir.' —He answered, 'I'm quite warm here.' The house was on fire." He told this apropos of nothing and thought it was very good.

His version of what had happened in Greece: ruffians and brigands. He graciously questioned Hughes about happenings in Yugoslavia—"since you are well posted about it." "Tito was not even his name. It was Broz."[24] Storrs wound up with an air of triumph.

[EW's note: "What follows is not an accurate account of further conversation but notes for a story I wanted to write which would be partly based on this occasion."[25]]

Hughes must make an attempt to say something about the classics himself, and Storrs will pay no attention, but continue to show off his familiarity with them by some totally irrelevant reply, as happened to me when, at his mention of Geryon in Dante,[26] I ventured to say that, in describing his ride on the monster, Dante had anticipated the sensations of going up in a plane.

[23] Maurice Baring (1874–1945), British novelist and poet. See EW's essay on Baring in *The Devils and Canon Barham* (1973), pp. 77–91.

[24] Tito's name was Josip Broz (1892–1980).

[25] EW develops this conversation in *EWB*, pp. 163–69.

[26] *Inferno*, Canto XVII.

Hughes, however, must end by falling back into an official attitude himself, as he did when we were talking about Sforza.[27]

Filicaia's sonnet about Italy, but Sir Ronald seemed not to know it. The Hughes character finally quotes Latin and translates, telling himself that he will at least attract Sir Ronald's attention: "I can dispense with your version, admirable though it is." Lousy epigram about eating, which he compares to the Greek anthology.

Somebody like Morra has commented on the hoarding by the English of the culture of other races, whereas the classics are a part of the background of Italian education. A "certain analogy" between England and Rome. Also, how the English always speak of "going out" to places. Hughes has wondered whether, in different circumstances, he might not even have expressed himself more strongly and further.

Sir Ronald was a storybook Englishman, who was partly or wholly Irish; [Hughes] said to me afterwards that he could earn money any day in a music hall.

(Notes for a projected story about a Negro.) He'd like to tell those good people what he thought of them. (Roi Ottley on the people who wanted to sell him their daughter.) The Forum depresses him because it seems like the southern states—a touch of Chattanooga.

The *Time* correspondent who always went in by parachute, but this wasn't any better than a *Time* man arriving on his legs. (Quoted from Hamburger or somebody.)

[27] Count Carlo Sforza (1873–1952) was president of the newly formed Consulta which served as liaison between the Italian people and the government until a parliament could be elected.

Family orchestra: pale heavy-lidded stupefied baby, seven children. They had things like little saxophones, and one of the boys doubled with cymbals. The man who played the accordion was the mainstay of the thing. They were playing the *International.*

Walk to Ara Coeli and through the Forum: Looking up at the sun going down from the corner of the Victor Emmanuel monument—the clouds, above the domes and the umbrella pines, had that faint yellow clay color and a delicacy beyond that, even, which clouds could have had, against a pale blue background, on a painted ceiling, with the quick swifts swooping and flickering among them. When I first saw this sunset, its soft luminosity was brought out by the flat chalky white of the Victor Emmanuel monument. At the top of the Ara Coeli steps, looking down toward the old brown circus, I heard the bells ringing quiet and spaced, not insistent as in other cities. The Forum looked better in the evening than it had in the late morning when I had seen it with the Barretts: brown and gray, with the greenery that subdued Italian tint that so seems to lack vividness and freshness. —Now it did not look quite so rubbishy. The little kids that want to show you the way at the slightest sign of hesitation—they don't seem to want money, though. The fragments of walls, and columns, as you look down at them from the street, loosely lined up or piled, as if they were on their way back to the quarry again. The empty eye-holes in the brick and grass of the shapeless agglomeration of the palaces of the Caesars on the Capitoline Hill, with, on top, a growth of cypresses and other trees (of which I don't know the names) that seem to have grown with no tending, like the weeds—the old sallow arches and fractured walls like swarthy but faded old men with hairs growing out of their ears and noses. Miserable little kids with gray clothes and dusty legs playing in bunches while sometimes their mothers sit about on the ruins—several were astride a length of column, playing train, I suppose. The old rounded stones of the Via Sacra, where Horace, as Barrett reminded me, met the bore—with great lacunae among them. —In order to get out of the Forum at the end toward the Victor Emmanuel monument, you have to climb up a dusty path and clamber over the low wall by the aid of a small section of column which has been propped so that it leans on a block—a detail of the general messiness which the whole place cannot seem to help having.

The British are said quietly but carefully to be getting *the hemp business* into their hands.

Hamburger on an afternoon spent with UP and Hearst correspondents, in a big top apartment with a balcony across the street belonging to an interned German baron. The Hearst girl was living there with a woman Red Cross worker. It had been boring—they had talked about how somebody slipped when he was landing from the boat and how old somebody else nearly fell out the window when he was drunk.

German broadcasting from villa outside Milan: Broadcaster used to turn up drunk, one night was unable to broadcast—when they left they smashed everything up; see also story about hunting woman broadcaster in *Stars and Stripes,* June 5.

Hamburger on Italian girl thrown out of window by American soldiers on the Via Veneto: "They'd finished with her—broke the poor girl's back."

Admiral [unidentified]'s aide turned up limping and

bandaged, but not as the result of action. He'd been tripped up by some American soldiers, under the impression that he was a British officer, as he was coming out of a villa outside Rome.

American colonel in the hotel next door to the Hôtel de la Ville was unpopular with his men. When he was ill and had taken to his bed, they hired some musicians, including an accordion, to play all day outside in the street.

Mrs. Daehn,[28] Via Aurelio Saffi. First day I went to see her—climbing the backbreaking hill with its interminable flights of steps—little villa with garden in back—poor soil in which things did not grow, some American seeds—beets and carrots—which they had planted. View out over newly built-up part of Rome: arc of monotonous yellow apartment houses, Protestant cemetery with its cypresses, big Benedictine monastery. House across the street with all one side sliced off as the result of bombing, some windows without glass. In her room, some of the panes had been replaced with opaque glass, others had been simply boarded up.

Shabbiness of her room: faded prints on furniture, screen that shut off narrow and sordid bed—Genoese tapestry on wall. Her corner, where she sat—no ikons, I noticed—pictures of the Tsar and members of her family —photograph of some mountain landscape—volume of Dickens on the table beside her chair. Bottle of red wine. She read *Time* and the *Stars and Stripes*.

She was six feet tall—had once weighed 45 [kilos], on account of the lack of food, but now weighed 50, which was better—old black clothes, worn black shoes—stooped and almost as thin as a skeleton, had been starving, "dire

[28] Mrs. Sonia Daehn, from a Russian family of once immense wealth, had lived in Rome since the Bolshevik Revolution. *EWB*, pp. 138–47.

hunger," though much better off lately—neuritis of the spine, bad heart and kidneys, had to spend most of the day in bed. Her yellow skin as if she had jaundice—great gray eyes, blocked out in her face by the straight eyebrows and the pockets of discolored skin below them, liked dimmed or blinded windows (Lensky's eyes after he was shot in the duel), one of them horribly bloodshot, swimming in blood, as if a vessel had burst—the wrinkles of collapsed and sallow skin in a face which would not otherwise have been wrinkled. Her dignity and ease—her "Yes, yes, yes, yes, yes" (sometimes repeated) which I felt to have some connection with the court—now not in the least unamiable but based on the assumption that it was always impossible to tell a person in her position anything. If you did tell such a person something that she did not know before, she had to make a point of being markedly impatient. She was making her own cigarettes, had tobacco loose in a box.

[EW's note: "The Russians are likely to say *da,* as Mrs. Daehn did, five times; the Germans *ja* three times; the French *oui* twice; the English *yes* only once."]

Gentleness and fine timbre of her way of speaking in her rather deep hoarish Russian voice. Russian quickness of perception and reaction. "What have you got here, my dear man?" at sight of my musette bag with food that I had brought them from the American PX.

Attitude toward Europe congenial to an American, because based on being outside it. She asked whether we were disgusted with Europe. The tourists had spoiled the Italians, encouraged them to be idle. In Florence, you couldn't pull down an old building that was rotten, rotten, rotten, without letters from spinsters protesting. They liked them to be picturesque. The European countries, that seem little to Russians, were so cramped and so furiously nationalistic. —She thought the Italian Fascists quite a different thing from the Nazis because they wanted to encourage the individual. She had at first been in favor of the Germans. In Russia, the people had given themselves up in droves to the Germans—before they found out how brutal they were.

Her voice sank as my visit went on—I had not myself been saying much—as if she were partly talking now to herself. Perhaps, she said, the ones who had been killed in the first days of the Revolution had been more fortunate than those who had lived. (When we went to Rome in '64, Olga Fersen told Elena that Mrs. Daehn had taken drugs, poor old lady.)

They seemed mostly to have taken "paying guests," and had had a great many Americans.

The walls of the Troubetzkoys' room were covered solid, in a characteristic Russian fashion, with very poor watercolors and good engravings of Moscow and the Neva (the latter the long panoramas that matched the St. Petersburg vistas), one of Orenburg. The shorter of the old ladies was assertive and pungent in the Russian tradition of talking out of turn. The pale blond daughter (Olga Fersen), of indeterminate age, as if the young people were fading out, too, with the general fading out of the family. The blond and very tall grandson who couldn't imagine a Soviet girl being ill.

We listened to Attlee's speech on the radio, interrupted by strains of dance music and spasms of Italian—they commented on his cultivated voice. Labour was not socialist. Yet they all seemed to take something of the kind for granted: one of the old ladies said that she believed the public utilities ought to be nationalized. And if all that money had not been put into explosives, it could have been used for schools and hospitals and parks. Somebody had said, under the old regime, that Russia ought to be like the United States.

Mrs. Daehn's occasional Americanisms. Her son had written her every day, but the letters had taken a month or more, the packages even longer. She knew that she couldn't live in America on $500 a year; and here she could go about in rags, which she wouldn't be able to do in New York. About the only thing she had to look forward to was seeing her family again. [EW's note: "Her brother was the Sheremetev in whose company I was later on to have some rather comic adventures in Charlottesville."] She asked me, her face lighting up with a smile as it very rarely did, whether my family were good correspondents.

Dinner: little glasses of sherry before: gray bread without butter, spaghetti with pinkish rather flavorless sauce, salad with chopped-up lettuce and beets, little preserved cherries.

Russi (Antonio, with whom I took Italian lessons): *"In Italia, cinismo, mo' sfiducia"*—among the people difficulty in believing in ideas. —They would not die for an idea—but in contrast, there were *"delle persone individuali che hanno ricattati coloro giro questa manchezza."* Difficult to find in histories of other countries such examples of individual idealism as in Italy—Garibaldi. (Also, for France after Sedan.) After having been defeated by the French with chasspot rifles—(Napoleon III sent the Pope French troops)—Mazzini, Bruno—rich in great contrasts —prostitutes and heroes. The Italians produce ideas for Europe—but the new Garibaldis must think as Europeans, not as Italians.

Primitive local buses: I saw one which was pulled by a motorcycle and was fenced (dull green) as if it had been built to transport cattle. They go at a terrible clip.

The Vatican Museum. Columnar strips of painted wall (dating from when?): hippogriffs, sphinxes with wings and curling rears like sea horses, spindle-legged and needle-beaked birds, hawk-beaked and double-headed eagles, scrollery and tendrils, goddesses with twining branches, delicate vine leaves, slender trumpets, general impression of spidery tendrils, winged cupids, graces or allegorical figures poised like tightrope walkers or equilibrists, squatting winged sphinxes—feathery flowers, cupids, holding red spidery lobsters. On dryish cream-colored background, dryish greens and blues, yellows no longer luminous and dried bloodstain red. Tongues, serpents, twining tails (twirling). There was also a somewhat different perhaps later kind of thing that involved satyr masks, lions' faces, female beings with impenetrable complacencies.

Walter Newburgh: Two kids at station: one stuck a hatpin into the American and the other grabbed his bags.

Italians removed paving stones at Naples, so as to slow up trucks and steal flour. Newburgh was in charge of the flour warehouse. The Italians would slit the sacks, and the kids would scrape the flour from the floors of trucks.

The British officer in charge of the station who had worked everything out with toy trains and said it would be impossible to get food through. An American corporal got into an engine and had the trains shunted around in no time so as to get the food cars through.

Italian with bogus passport who brought a bishop with him.

Walter was worried about the French designs on Italy —implied that they were invading it.

We had rather a pleasant amusing conversation sitting around a table in the Hôtel de la Ville bar—while, beside us, the British correspondents sat slumped in their chairs and silent. Hamburger spoke of some firm of lawyers in

New York—Levi, Levi and O'Brien—"You know, that big firm—one of them went to jail." Isadore Kaufmann said, "That was the Irishman." (I hadn't seen him since college, where he wrote for the *Lit*. He had been working for the Brooklyn *Eagle* and was in Rome as a correspondent.)

Newburgh: AC,[29] Americans 40 to 60 or one third. Our army promotion system on a rationing basis played into British hands: with them, rank went with the job. There had been fellowship at mess between Americans and British when they first came to Rome, all mixed up together, but they later dissociated themselves from one another. English [illegible] behind nominal American head—civil servants for British, who treat us like colonials—playing Santa Claus with our food and oil and manpower—as Sumner Welles[30] said, we're the tail to the British kite—the English treat the Italians like Indians—sending in lots of economic missions to get Italy commercially and financially under control—apple-polishing for superiors. Walter had tried to be incompetent, but he couldn't keep it up. Mixed British and Americans at morning parade in Africa, complete confusion always when they dispersed.

Newburgh had attended a banquet given by Myron Taylor for visiting senators, at which they had paid to the tune of $60 a plate (my apologizing for mess to people like Morra).

Via dei Cappuccini: old black sandals sprawling in shreds across cobbles near urinal—melancholy.

Nights in Rome: cocks crowing at dawn—seems curious in a city—and screech owl: it made me remember the

[29] Allied Commission.

[30] Sumner Welles (1892–1961), U.S. Under Secretary of State, 1937–43.

Latin word *strix*—perhaps in the Borghese Gardens?
—American soldiers howling songs. Philip Hamburger
said that there was one drunken soldier who would lurk
at night in a doorway and dash out, baying like a hound at
everybody that passed. Crash of people pulling down tin
fronts of shops—loud reports of exhausts, explosions of
trucks—all more marked in the general quiet. Party for
enlisted men down the street—man pounding piano who
would try rather ineptly from time to time to go into
something new, but give it up after a few bars and go
back to the few tunes he knew.

Terrific cats. —Whistle of occasional trains which one
couldn't believe were really going anywhere—they were
just standing in the station and whistling a little—exas-
peratingly, pathetically—to show they were still alive—or
like dogs breaking out into yelps at the sound of a passerby.
Street singers at morning.

The feeling of turbid atmosphere one got as June wore
on into summer—under the clear pale blue innocent dome
of the sky. Black market (my adventure selling my sleeping bag) outside the Fagiano restaurant—old slightly
misty emanation of corruption and apathy—"the people
from the North would go away holding their noses"—
iridescent scum on the surface—"a body is found in the
Colosseum about every morning." *Roma, 1943* of
Monelli.[31]

To walk out, after a hot afternoon, into a tepid evening
—the gray streets, the slow people spreading all over the
pavements—in the dark pavementless cobbled side streets,
sometimes howling at the top of their lungs—all in a kind
of stagnant medium of atmosphere.

[31] Paola Monelli (b. 1894), author of *Roma, 1943* (1963).
EWB, pp. 74–77.

Going to the hospital of the Blue Nuns [where Santa-yana was living]: The Via Claudia with its cobbled walk —its scratched yellow clay wall on one side and its dense texture of purplish-pink brick Roman ruins on the other —rubbed, eroded, with sand-castle holes and disheveled dry shrubbery hanging down from the top—then a tunnel of low acacias overhanging the street—an old wall that screened off what?—then a street of eighteenth-century gamboge buildings—then the Via di Santo Stefano Rotondo: wall of fine eroded brick—dry grass along irregular top—bricked-up arch of radiating bricks—deep scars gouged out—iron lamp with an electric bulb on a black iron arm—man and girl quietly kissing. Cobbled road with old gutters making undulations on either side. —The hospital cypresses—orange building with green shutters and tinnish dome that looked as if it had been an observatory.

Borghese Gardens: Behind the old chipped reddish weedy Roman wall and the stone gates with the modern eagles, an atmosphere, in the spring, of gaiety, leafage, light, bright color—a mixture of grandeur and informality —so much larger and more casual than Paris or London (D'Annunzio, Respighi's *Fontane di Roma*).

Later, in the afternoons, up to June 16, when I left, I would go every day for apricot ice and little pink or chocolate *pasti* in paper frills and pretty but, from the American point of view, rather unsatisfactory fruit-juice drinks, to the Casino del Lago, inside the shady and peaceful enclosure, surrounded by a little iron fence, behind which were posted at intervals small antique classical statues, dim in the shadow; and along the graveled walk of green oaks (*cerri*), so cool and reposeful in the summer heat, after the dusty main drive of the park, their green-ness now a little gray—a large gray stone lion grasping in its paw a sheaf of stone arrows and resting on what seemed to be an improvised brick pedestal, which did not fit it and which on one side it overlapped (in the wall outside, loaded down with vines, sculptured griffins and an embedded sarcophagus side); to the small restaurant with its big umbrellas, wicker chairs, pink wide-branching rhododendrons in clay jars, its portico with classical columns, as if it were a little temple, its radio warbling continual grand opera or concert renditions of Mozart, which would surprise me by turning out to have come from the Metropolitan or the Boston Symphony Orchestra—rather sympathetic easygoing waiters, who soon appeared and then let you alone.

The British Indian soldiers' club at the entrance to the park—I never knew what it was till I got lost one day and came around behind it, where their outdoor restaurant was concealed. The Indian I saw walking in the park, with green turban, black beard all around his cheeks, and black glasses, carrying a cane.

June 16 conversation at the Silones'[32] *with the Barretts and Hughes:* Protracted crisis about forming the government: the Liberals didn't want Parri,[33] because he would come out clearly as a Republican, and were waiting (abetted by the Christian Democrats?) for the presidency, as Mrs. Silone said, to drop into their laps like a ripe fruit after all the other possibilities had been elminated one by one. The people were getting childish (Mrs. Silone), making an exhibition of themselves before the world. It annoyed Silone so much that they never got to the meetings on time—he would come as arranged at five and they wouldn't turn up till six (*sulle cinque precise*). He was

[32] *EWB*, pp. 170–74.
[33] Professor Ferruccio Parri, Premier of Italy in 1945.

lugubrious and in bad humor. Came in obviously very tired toward the end of our conversation and said that if we continued to talk English, "*ça me reposera.*" He lay inert on the couch, smiling politely from time to time.

Hughes's line: The British were going soon, both from Italy and from Greece, because the soldiers wanted to go home, and they needed troops for Germany. It was, however, a good thing, at the present time, for them to hold down the North of Italy, because otherwise there would be riots at political meetings, and a lot of people killed. Barrett pointed out that they mostly went gunning for Fascists at night. "But if they held meetings they would be able to massacre them wholesale." I set out to smoke him out: made him admit that the English had an interest in what they were doing in Italy and Greece, and admit that, like other Englishmen, he hated to confess to doing things for interest—but immediately tried to slip out of it by falling back on the compromise position that the British were busybodies. There had been a fight in the Piazza Barberini—the Americans had looked on and enjoyed it, egging the combatants on, while the English had been worried about it and thought somebody ought to go down and stop it. I reminded him that the English had never hesitated to foment violence when it was to their purpose. Yes, but they'd be worried if there were more Syrians than Arabs, would think the sides ought to be evened up. —Also, the Americans could be impartial in Europe because they had no serious interests at stake. —The Americans were really just as hard-boiled when it came right down to it and talked their own kind of hypocritical nonsense. Why should the English get out of India to let the Americans step right in? We asked him why it was so difficult for him to contemplate the possible position of England as a member of a European federation. Mrs. Silone pointed out, in her gentle voice that at moments became almost inaudible, the possible role of England as the leader of Europe toward a socialist world by means of a Labour government. He then said that conversations like this were conducted on two levels: an idealistic level—I interrupted him, saying that that was the stock thing to say, and I thought he lacked any idea of the international socialist movement as a historical reality. He said that he was going to vote for a Labour government but he didn't think that it had a chance—if it got in, it wouldn't accomplish much. The English were afraid of losing their high standard of living. Silone somewhere [at] this point introduced a little interlude on Swiss imperialism: they sent their capital abroad to Swiss-Italian or Swiss-Brazilian (?) companies which compelled the people of other countries to work for them; Lenin, in his pamphlet on *Imperialism*, on the export of capital abroad. —Hughes confessed, under pressure, that he could not contemplate with equanimity what he called the decline of England—by which, however, we made him admit, he meant the breaking up of the British Empire (the question of the standard of living could be made to follow from this). —We Americans, he reminded us, were now criticizing the British from a very comfortable position. —The more we talked, the more clearly I saw, behind all the various British smoke screens, the purpose to oppose Russia, the old balance-of-power point of view; but now they could only play the old game rather gropingly, didn't know where to have Russia (as in Greece)—afraid of countries going left for this reason—how much pressure are they bringing to bear on the formation of this government in Italy? Mrs. Silone had told me that the AC (Allied Commission) had let it be known that it was not true that it was backing de Gasperi.[34] It was probably true, as Hughes said, that the

[34] Alcide de Gasperi (1881–1954), Premier of Italy, 1945–53.

British had expected the Americans to have a line and had been let down at finding they didn't (telephone exchanges: Freedom, Independence, etc.)—but of course, in any case, the British would have opposed a too liberal line. —I now deplored the failure of the Americans to live up to their role—our streamlined official propaganda, Dorothy Thompson,[35] and the flag of the United States of Europe. —Going downstairs, at last, I said that I was really gloomy about things, and we laughed. Hughes said, "We've had it!"—this, used humorously, was a favorite phrase of his, and I think was significant of his state of mind. He told us that he would once have talked as we did, but his experience of the war (six years) had discouraged him. He had once thought that the other nations —the Italians and the French and all these people had different ideals, contributions of their own to make, but they were all just as tough and just as intent on the main chance as the British. —I told him that this showed an advance because it meant that he no longer took national differences so seriously, and that he ought to be ripe for the point of view of international socialism.

I can't help wishing there weren't so much human excrement in the corners of the grass-grown great backstairs of Santa Maria Maggiore.

[35] Dorothy Thompson (1894–1961), American columnist and political commentator, at one time married to Sinclair Lewis.

LONDON, 1945

[EW's note: "I went back to London to try to persuade Mamaine Paget to marry me; but she was still devoted to Arthur Koestler, who at that time was in Israel."

[Mamaine Paget was described by EW in *Europe Without Baedeker* as "a London girl whom I very much liked. She was an extremely bright and able girl with the same sort of all round competence that the young Englishmen from the universities have." They knocked about wartime London together and one gathers that Mamaine enjoyed Wilson's constant liveliness and inability to be bored in a new environment. He had the proofs of some of his *Hecate County* stories with him and she read them. When he proposed to her she proved cautious, and less impulsive than he was: "I don't think I can marry you or indeed do anything to make our relationship fit any conventional pattern, if it doesn't do so anyway. I don't think you know me very well either." Her decision was final and the romance was thereby short-circuited. She was much more interested in Arthur Koestler, whom she eventually married. EW's passion for her was strong and he carried it

back with him to the United States. A number of his letters to her—the last dated 1954—are included in *Letters
on Literature and Politics.*]

June 17. Flying to London. Corsica: Looking down
through soft melting snowy clouds on the grim and granite
island—peacock green in the shallows against a dark blue
that was almost indigo—butterfly colors, stainings of batik
—then off over the great blue-black of the sea.

The South of France looked drier than it had in the
spring—you could see the summer drought into which
everything had fallen, like this period that had followed
the war. —Then the long red sunset in the sky.

Flying over Paris at night: the lights looked wonderful
underneath—the amazingly short stretch of the Channel:
first the lighthouse winking on one side, then on the other
—then scattered lights in a darkness which one conceived
as the green of England.

London: Mamaine's story about the Stalinist friend who
came back from prison and thought that everything was
so awful in England that he wanted to go back to prison
—another friend who had come back and stayed at home
only two weeks: wife had had a boyfriend and had taken
to drink—he was a terrific gambler and had been gambling
all the time in prison—they would even bet on how many
men were going to be converted by the priest. He had
immediately gone to gambling again.

The man who had been feminized by playing women
in prison theatricals and who could not seem to get over it.

The Green Park Hotel, in Half Moon Street, which
seemed to be a condemned brothel—with its lift that ac-
commodated only two and that with the greatest difficulty;

the floor creaked and seemed to sink ominously when you stepped into it. I was given a little room with yellow walls rubbed by greasy heads above the bed—little daybed with horrible brown cover that seemed to be impregnated with dirt—wooden washstand with no towel—brown carpet with rhomboidal pattern, stained and full of dust—piles of dirt in plain sight in corners—small shit-colored coal grate with dismal gas logs in corner. The dining room, with slovenly wretched waitresses—stains of soup, eggs, and jam on the table that seemed never to have been wiped off.

Half Moon, Curzon Street, etc., *whore district*—curious little nexus of streets, with small Christian Science church in the middle that looked almost as gray and old as any other London church.

Odette: Nice-looking, not *abîmée* like the other women along the street ("Come here, sweetie!" "Hullo!"). She had a firm strong body, good breasts. She said she was thirty-five but hardly looked it, though her buttocks were perhaps roughening and sagging a little. Bright smile with strong white teeth, very little makeup. She came from Montmartre, had been in London since '39. Brown suit and beret. She worked during the day for the French Red Cross, wrapping up parcels, and was knitting the director a sweater, which would have cost several pounds to buy but this way only a few shillings. She talked about her expenses, the overhead on her room, etc. She wanted eventually to go back to Paris and start a lingerie shop. The English, she said, were cold, they unbuttoned the *pantalon,* and then goodbye! The Americans were *bruyants,* but they were *loin de chez eux* and no doubt behaved all right at home. The Canadians were *ordinaires.* "*Il n'y a que les Français, les Américains, et les Belges pour faire l'amour."* The Americans were gay to go out with, they liked to have a good time. Some of the Poles were nice. She had said she had another engagement when she discovered that the officer who had spoken to her was a Negro. Her professional neatness. The purple girdle that left her black bush exposed; but she would also strip, leaving nothing but shoes and stockings rolled down to her ankles. Her green room—purely for professional purposes —with a framed photograph of an "oxidized" friend and some *Vie Parisienne* pictures. She produced a rubber condom and worked energetically and authoritatively. She got restless when I simply wanted to lie and talk, even though I paid her for an hour and a half. She finally got out her knitting. What had De Gaulle taken into his *cipole?—"vous ne comprenez pas l'argot?"* (They must have got this from Italian *cipolla.*) Otherwise, the wonderful French generalizations expressed in language almost classical. —When I met her a few nights later, she said, *"Bon soir. Vous avez l'air d'aller rentrer à la maison très sagement. Vous avez très chaud."* Disparity between her politeness and sobriety, on the one hand, and the things she did professionally, on the other. Her story about *ami* who had married and then come back to her. He had told her that his wife was cold, but then of course he didn't ask her to do the things *qu'il exigeait d'une petite femme des rues.*

The compact little blond English girl who, after I had been with Odette, showed me my way back to Half Moon Street and was very nice about it—though I had to decline her invitation, telling her I had just been to see a friend. "You've had it? Charming," she said.

Electioneering with Harold Laski: Enfield and Watford, (later Sutton): Enfield—little bay windows and brick doorways—gray sandy-looking sides of houses (called rough cast or sprinkled ash)—meeting out of doors in noon sun—yellow bricks, dim or neutral red tiles: pale faces, quiet people—blue and gray, occasionally khaki clothes—all in Sunday clothes, the men wearing coats.

Conversation with Laski.

Churchill: "I am in favor of traditional Britain, with a few measures of reconstruction."

1 percent of the people owned 55 percent of the total wealth.

Mass unemployment incompatible with democratic institutions—Churchill must know this—Spain, etc.

1 percent of the army officers from working-class parents.

In 1919, 91 percent of the diplomatic corps had been to Eton.

In 1939, 67 percent (when war broke out).

Davies (the candidate): We can provide houses here in Enfield quicker than the Tories will do it—no stunts, etc.

—We must never again have the degradation of conditions that had occurred between the two wars.

Housing, nationalization of the Bank of England, education.

Enormous Major Freeman at Watford, who slightly depressed Laski before the meeting by telling him that they had been taking the line that poor little Harold Laski didn't have any harm in him.

Laski's speech.

We all knew that the Battle of Peterloo was won on the playing field of Eton and that the Battle of Sidney Street was won on the playing field of Harrow.

Churchill talks now about his good friend Marshal Stalin—if he had talked about his good friend Lenin, there wouldn't have been a Second World War.

London at night. It is still almost as dark as it was before the war was over. On Piccadilly, in the summer air, tepid and stagnant, there was something sort of awful about the aimless tidal movement of the soldiers and tarts as they had clotted in groups on the street—the aims of the war accomplished, the tension of the war relaxed, these human amoebas were left to drift about in the back eddy of England. What had the war worked up to? Nothing, vacuity—these unintegrated human organisms with no training in directing themselves, with no strong impulses toward self-direction.

Tottenham Court Road in late-gathering darkness—gruesome-wry trees with tufts of leaves at the end of the branches like the necks and feet of plucked fowl—fronts of bombed-out houses like masks—peculiar desolation and horror of this effect in the midst of an inhabited city.

Roger Senhouse, when we were leaving the Travellers' Club, standing and waiting to get a taxi. He said it was "a kind of hell—standing and waiting, while one saw all the people one loathed most get into cabs." This is very typical of the present competitive spitefulness of the English.

Woman I took to Oxford Street in my cab: When I said that Italy was in very bad shape, she replied, "But they are very lighthearted about it, aren't they?" When I answered that they were far from lighthearted, she said that she understood that they were very unwilling to do anything for themselves.

Walking with Mamaine, we passed a sort of open shop with shelves full of *dead crows*—a bad smell. These perhaps provide those slivers of "duck" which one finds in the restaurants and which I noticed no one ordered but me.

Mamaine complained that the headlines in the papers were dull. Graham Greene said they felt a nostalgia for the hum of a robot bomb.

Woman at Sutton Labor meeting: typical face of Europe at the present time—such faces I had seen in Milan—chin and nose thrust forward, eyes intent and yet staring, face gaunt and rather wolfish—they had passed into a phase below anything we had known in civilized modern life.

ITALY AGAIN

Return to Italy, night of June 30–July 1.

Notice on American army club: "Reserved for GI's and their Lady Guests." So they are calling the prostitutes Lady Guests. The word *signorina* had also been ruined by being applied to these girls.

Walter Newburgh's apartment at the top of a house in the Via Pinciana with a magnificent view of Rome: much the same as the one from my old window in the Hôtel de la Ville, but including, also, the Villa Medici, its twin-towered bisque building, its mysterious round solid grove, its cabbage gardens, its poultry yard, behind walls, as well as the Appian Hills with the small eminence of Horace's Soracte.[1] Bright orange light of sunset. But the apartment, which is enormous, with many rooms, seems unlived in and uninviting. French and English books and Russian classics—big imitations of paintings and inlaid-wood furni-

---

[1] Mountain in Etruria about 24 miles from Rome. The mountain was considered sacred to Apollo. EW is alluding to Horace, *Carmen* 1.9.

ture. I lost my cap and *New Yorkers,* and we wandered
some time from room to room before we were able to find
them.

July 4. [Lenor] Fini and Lepri: In the old palazzo in
the Piazza Gesù, you never could remember which entrance to take and always had to call the *portiere.* Interminable shallow marble steps, made for unimaginable
grandeur—on the bottom floor, in the shadow, a naked
white man with a sword and a gigantic semi-squatting
figure, which took on, in the semi-darkness, a sort of surrealist irrelevance and incongruity—great funeral vases,
vaultings and flowered entablatures, the monstrous phallic
figure, the bearded man with a book who gave the impression of sitting on the can.

The view over Rome from their windows: infinite lines
and planes of roofs and upper stories: dry pale buff and
gray-blue which were matched by the pale blues and pinks
of the sky, in which the sun was setting. Later, a firework
display in honor of the Fourth of July: yellow and green
clusters of stars, which eventually became rather monotonous—the English, as I suggested, were keeping it down.

Barrett had rather a trying time showing the sights to
Americans who had just arrived from Naples. Awful little
man with dark glasses who had just discovered Rimbaud:
—"Have you read Rimbaud?" —Barrett: "Yes." —"Well,
if you haven't, you ought to." He had a plentiful supply
of whiskey, which he was princely about giving away, and
an accent which seemed to be a southern accent that had
somehow assimilated itself to French.

The GI's, as Barrett said, would come up to a girl on
the street, crane around and look at her face—then grab
her. She would let herself be grabbed; but, according to

my observation, would then stop for a long argument, standing back against the wall, in order to settle the terms.

Trip to Littoria [now Latina] and Fondi[2] *with an UNRRA*[3] *sanitary engineer, July 6*: Cisterna[4] (see also trip to Ninfa): (bombed station like a gnawed oatmeal cracker—hills like thin steel blades against pale sky, knife-like outlines)—exposed staircase like broken conch shell which shows the inside spiral—spattered and specked walls, balconies hanging in shreds—one gutted interior was equipped with a ladder to get to some rooms still usable—in the main square was a headless white statue with one arm upraised, standing on what looked like a rockery but was really the fragments of the base sticking out in four directions and sometimes resembling the heads of beasts. (Cemetery: *In Christo Quiescentes*—walled— "Sad to see that shattered." This is from trip to Ninfa.)

The little *capanni* at Fondi where the bombed-out *contadini* lived: little straw huts like hollowed-out haystacks such as had mainly been used for animals before— beds inside where it was dark and airless—one woman was making dough—open to *zanzare*—one woman with sickly brown dog, one of whose ears seemed to be stunted —irrigation pump turned by wooden bar. You walked around the well, fine vegetable garden and fruit trees. She insisted on giving me more plums than I could carry, beautiful bluish bloom on deep shiny red-purple base that showed when you rubbed off the bloom. Patched together from other things, feet in rags tied on with string—they had sprayed her hut against the mosquitoes.

---

[2] Littoria (Latina), 35 miles southeast of Rome, pop. 68,781. Fondi, 29 miles southwest of Latina, pop. 24,417.

[3] United Nations Relief and Rehabilitation Administration.

[4] Cisterna, 8 miles northwest of Latina, pop. 20,718.

July 7. Dinner with Mrs. Daehn and her household: borscht, stuffed tomatoes, plums, little loaf of gray bread.

Tall daughter with pale blue eyes and pale blond hair (Olga Fersen), who spoke in English with curious drawling cadences that seemed a mixture of Italian and Russian.

Mrs. Daehn: How were they in England? "They all hate each other!"

When I told her she ought to come to the United States, she said there'd "have to be dirty work at the crossroads first." She meant that her American boarders would have to pull wires for her.

With the Princess Troubetzkoy or the Countess Fersen (I'm not sure which) you got down finally to the bedrock of her Tsarist mentality—when she kept insisting, in defense of Fascism, that the people had been satisfied—they had sent an anti-Fascist sanitary engineer (I had learned that there was only one in Italy) out to the malaria region, on condition that he should not speak against Fascism— this proved how liberal they really were.

Mrs. Daehn was amusing about "displaced persons"— said that *they* were displaced persons.

The French and the Italians were conventional—they wouldn't ask you to dinner to eat what they eat (et).

Her knowledge of the McCrystal cocktail party, which she called a "reception."

There had been gangs on the streets that used to *catch well-dressed people and undress them*—a man was supposed to bring 20,000 lire, a woman 15,000 lire—this had happened to a professor they knew of.

The Italian driver of the PRO[5] *jeep* who took me over to the Via Aurelio Saffi; hurled the car through the streets,

[5] Public Relations Officer.

cursing the pedestrians and purposely threatening people on bicycles. Also, the oldish man who drove us out to Littoria, taking the holes and rocks in the road head-on, and on one occasion passing a big line of trucks at full speed while a line of motorcycles was coming from the other direction. This drove little Italian UNRRA captain crazy.

Hamburger: Lieutenant colonel who arrived in a staff car in Venice and asked a soldier to show him how to go: "Sir, you've had it: from here on the city is built entirely on water."

Hamburger had been talking to Campbell, the man with the gigantic farm who had been in Russia. He had just come from the Pacific and had been in Okinawa Wednesday. Campbell had told him about American jelly bombs, the most formidable weapon yet invented, which could cut a way right through a jungle, so that the army could march through and burn people to a cinder in thirty seconds. Hamburger grinned at this, and I probably did too. This is *the new sadism,* irresponsibility about human life. (See conversation in London with John Strachey and Humphrey Slater.[6] Strachey said with grim humor that Germany, since the bombings, was "rather changed." Warsaw had been wiped out.)

Hamburger on woman beggar with "dead baby"— thought that it must be doped.

Major Simcock:[7] I went to ask him about Russians: everybody who had left the Soviet Union since 1929 having to be sent back, by the terms of the Yalta agreement—

---

[6] John Strachey (1901–63), author of *The Coming Struggle for Power,* which popularized Marx and Lenin; see *The Thirties,* p. 142. Humphrey Slater, journalist; *EWB,* p. 34.

[7] *EWB,* pp. 159–61.

the bogus lists they presented of Russians who were supposed to have disappeared, etc. He said that he was not
authorized to talk about the Yalta matter—but "could
write volumes" if he were not a simple major. He told me
only that Russians of whatever age and sex were claimed
by the Soviet Union as prisoners of war. Then he went
on, apropos of nothing, to talk about himself. In the East,
he was called the "Wild Irishman"—I unquestionably
knew how fast a reputation traveled. He was absolutely
honest, and when he said he'd do a thing, he did it. Had
held 5,000 blacks at bay alone. Had been fined twice for
beating men in the Sudan—£25 and £50—he had asked
the judge how much it would have been if he had killed
the man, and the judge had said £5. He didn't like to beat
people up but sometimes it had to be done. He went on
to say that if an Arab ever came into his office without a
hat, which was a mark of disrespect, he didn't say anything, he kicked him, and the next time, the Arab would
come in with his hat on. It was no use to try to punish
them by not giving them supplies, because they'd have
their food and their vices anyhow—it would just mean
that somebody else would go without. I couldn't figure out
his political point of view: he said he hadn't voted for
anybody for many (14?) years, because there had never
been a candidate who was the kind of man he'd like to
see run things—but he thought that everything would
collapse if Churchill should die or be defeated. Had been
in Soviet Union in 1920 and 1936—as Metro-Vickers
engineer, but had not been involved in the affair of 1926
—he always kept his politics in his pocket. I had thought
we were fighting for freedom, hadn't I? He had never
seen so many dirty tricks in his life, on the part of everybody! Had been in all the countries, knew all the languages—could learn any language in three months. —Irish
type but very much Briticized—ruddy complexion, pale

blue but glaring eyes—had completely English accent, but his oratory was Irish, and he stopped after every statement to watch your astonishment, approval, or awe. Only good German a dead German.

Everybody in the army missed the ads in *The New Yorker* (omitted from the foreign edition). I had never realized before how much we got our ideas from these—I found that I missed them myself.

Caffè Greco: dingy and narrow, little black horsehair seats that ran along the wall, little round or oval gray-veined marble tables, bad landscapes and portraits, and rather annoying little medallions on the wall of the famous men who had come there. One of the ridiculous little hallway-like compartments that should have been thrown into one had a horrible *jour blafard* from dirty gray panes of glass in a skylight. Waiter who spoke languages and had a humorous-familiar tinge, as if he were playing a character role of the 1840s. —I didn't like it—too much of the past, made me want to get away. —Rope curtains cut it off from the street, sordid.

Vowels in Italian.

What the Allies really ought to do, now that the war is finished, is to try to prevent anybody whatever from being executed or shot for any reason.

Newburgh on British and Americans at Tizi-Ouzou: sixty-five miles southeast of Algiers—so-called school for military government—really a pool. Instead of reveille or roll call, they had to have morning parade—were lined up in huge courtyard of a fashionable girls' school "like Poughkeepsie"—the British commandant would appear on

a balcony, look at his wristwatch, and announce, "Gentle-
men, the time is now 8:45. Parade dismissed." The British
and the Americans were mixed up together, and the
Americans would immediately break ranks, whereas the
English would execute a right turn (which we call a right
face), salute, bring the hand down smartly, and march
forward. The Americans would then walk right into them.
The English would snap feet (everything they did was
calculated to make a sound so as to keep them in unison),
whereas Americans had rubber heels—the English had
hobnailed shoes. Both sides made earnest efforts to get on
with the other, but the tone was set by the British, who
had their tea in the afternoon. The cleavage began from
the moment that they got on the ship from Algiers to
Naples—and they had "been cleaving ever since." The
AC was "a shotgun wedding."

Trip to Milan, July 12.
Details of airport and vicinity (see earlier): Hollow
half-tower, wrecked sagging collapsed metal scaffolding of
airport.

On our way over the mountains, a man in our plane
said to me that he had been in the mountain campaign
and he didn't see how the doughboys had fought through
them.

Coming into Milan, the mottlings of snow on the mountains looked like patternings merely on the blue of the
sky, for the blue of the mountains was scarcely deeper—
sky of a blue *"sempre un poco stanco"* (*Cantachiaro*).

The Albergo Diana is now a pleasure spot: much talk
of parties at the Italian-American Press Club—excellent
dinner in outdoor dining room full of leaves—chestnuts

and oaks—little fancily speckled globes, colored Japanese mats suspended in the trees—wicker furniture, blue flowered or checked tablecloths, good-looking girls.

Concert (see program): the delicate music, delicately played, in the great old castle, with its gold-crested blue dragons swallowing agonized men and its squash, tomatoes, and cabbages planted in the moat. —Cultivated and well-dressed *borghese*—who sat next to me—he was afraid the English and the Americans would go—had been alarmed to hear that the Americans were going—there would be a terrible civil war—the Communists would bring the Russians in.

"Casa distrutta dai liberatori anglosassoni" (S. Carolus). *"Casa incendiata,"* etc. —*"Anglosassoni assassini."*

Blond girl riding a bicycle who put her hands to her hair, riding without hands. —A broader type of beautiful girl.

American in café, under the patched glass of the big *galleria:* tall, serious, war-tempered, dark greenish uniform. He had been laying and detecting mines—the kind that had two charges, the second one of which exploded them and scattered ball bearings; then, later, bits of wire that gave a terrible slash. We had mines like these that were worse than the German ones. In one place the Germans had left about three times as many dummies as real ones. You cannot use detectors where there were a lot of shell fragments around. In the case of booby traps, you just have to suspect everything. Two officers had gone into a house; the American had sat down on a bed, and whole house had blown up, leaving him holding part of bed—the British officer was suffocated in the debris before they could get him out. They would drag the mines out with long ropes and explode them with TNT. One man threw himself across an exploding mine—another threw himself down and was injured and got a Purple Heart. The man who was telling me this had gone back, after one of these incidents, and started talking to his men and fainted. On another occasion, he told me, he had been blown to a considerable distance. How had he felt? "Shaky." —But you have to hand it to the Germans: all these mines and things were wonderful work—before they had those Bakelite jobs. He had a specimen of the kind of clockwork bomb that had been used to blow up the Naples post office three weeks after the Germans had left—it was a wonderful thing, all in aluminum—he had set it and it had gone off within two minutes of the time—there were only seven or eight of these around.

July 14. Visit to Lieutenant Colonel Hershenson:[8] Big agreeable Jew. "Here's the picture": fifty-six prisoners— *partigiani,* accused of crimes ranging from robbery to rape —they had made a jailbreak Tuesday—the partisan guards had presumably let them escape—now had to change guards for the more reliable carabinieri. The partisans had been disbanded. "When a man comes to me and says he's a partisan, I tell him that there are no more partisans." Now a demonstration was being threatened by an organization of Italians come back from prison in Germany, who were proposing to gather in the square outside and march to the prison. The British head of AC security and an American major came in to see Hershenson. "They were buzzin' around them like blue-arsed flies —they were loungin' around, didn't get up when we came

[8] *EWB,* pp. 226–28.

in—I told them to stand up—if the poorest Italian comes
into this room, you'll get up out of your chair to greet 'im
—I told 'em that if they went to the Vincitore (?), we had
a reception committee ready for 'em and we'd extend the
hospitality of the Allied Commission and take care of 'em
with cells in the prison. It was just like when Togliatti[9]
tried to make a speech, we talked to 'im and he went right
away!" Percy left—Hershenson and the major examined
the invitation to the demonstration that night and the
literature connected with it. I explained that the symbol
that appeared on all this was the Phrygian cap of the
French Revolution. They were rather surprised and dismayed by this: "Does that mean the French Revolution?"
Hershenson, after the major had left, told me that he
thought it would be better for everybody concerned for
the Allies to get out of Italy—a baby had to learn to walk.
About the armistice terms: some said that they had been
kept secret because so disadvantageous to America—
England had secured Naples, etc.—others, because they
were so bad for the Italians that the Italians themselves
didn't want them published.

Boy on street like the children I saw the first time I was
here: drawn face, frowning brows, glazed eyes—tall but
in short pants.

Das Kapital in almost all *libreria* windows—strangely
displayed between Rimbaud and Catullus. One bookstore:
"Libri socialisti; non si vendono qui." Also Apollinaire and
translations of Rilke's letters and Barbey d'Aurevilly's *Del
Dandismo e di George Brummell.*

[9] Palmiro Togliatti, Communist Party leader, Minister of
Justice under Parri in 1945.

July 14. Bastille Day celebration: the man in the park who told me in thick dialect that he had never been a Fascist and showed me his Communist Party card, and the place on his leg where he had been shot by Germans. He was back in the factory now—what his father had suffered from the Fascists—how they had dealt with the Fascists in the factory.

I sat on the grass watching the open space before the decorated arch: Italy, United States, England, Soviet Union. Two small blimps inscribed FRATERNITÀ. It was pleasant to hear the band playing the *International,* now that it was no longer the anthem of the Soviet Union. Suddenly people, with lots of children, began to swarm across the grass from behind me. Immense crowds from then on—loudspeaker: *"Attenzione, attenzione! Sulle vent: due ore precise,"* etc. *"Questa e la notte della liberazione. Gli nomini libri sono allegre!"* Yet there was something rather admonitory and even menacing about this as it was pronounced by the metallic voice. A few couples were dancing here, where the crowd made a circle about them, but, in spite of a prizefight ring, a small circus, a pop stand, and little ice wagons, there was no very delirious gaiety. —A PRO man who took me around in a jeep. He thought it was all a gesture to cement good relations with France in compensation for the "stab in the back."

It does not seem absurd, in Milan, to see a statue of Leonardo and a street named after Dante.

Little dark wiry lawyer at the press party: had been active and very clever in the Resistance. Said that Italy was a small country, but big enough to devote oneself to. He came from the North, just below the Austrian border.

Communist headquarters: tall girl with one eye lighter than the other; Dr. Busetti was wall-eyed. They were waiting for the results of Potsdam and the British elections.[10] Busetti pointed out that the night of July 14 there had been a million people in the streets: the woman immediately added that it was a demonstration for the United Nations.

Talk with UP man: The Communists were warming up with demonstrations—it is so long since the Italians have had any—calling out undertakers, etc. (explanation of proposed jail demonstration)—July 5th strike of 300,000 had been orderly, they appeared in the streets with banners demanding more bread—a committee had gone to Rome that morning with demands for wage concessions, and they had granted $20 to $30 more a week. The circulations of *L'Avanti* and *L'Unità* had increased. Italian industry had hardly been touched by the war. The British were perhaps sabotaging it for competitive reasons—the motor industry. The *Corriere Informazione* (Crespi's) and the Venice paper still had their old backing, though the attempt was being made to have them honest liberal sheets. At Turin, Valetta[11] was still running his factory from behind the door of a real estate office, the stock was all owned by the same people—"That was my first shock." He thought the "threat" that had been mentioned in the *New Statesman* was there, though not explicit. The governments lasted only because they made no decisions. The Communists would hide behind the Socialists, would fol-

[10] The last conference of the war was being held at Potsdam, Germany, with President Truman attending. Churchill was defeated in Britain at this time.

[11] Director of Fiat; *EWB*, p. 233.

low them out, if a crisis arose; but Nenni[12] would sell the Communists down the river. What had protracted the crisis fifty days or more had been the question of the Interior—the control of the police.

Journalist who was starting to explain demonstration, then, after interruption, beginning to tell me he hoped to go to America.

One of the prettiest girls I ever saw sitting with a man at a table on the sidewalk, eyebrows; and she had succeeded in getting red high-heeled shoes. This shows what they can do with cosmetics and clothes. —*Girl with hair in process of becoming undyed:* half golden, half brunette.

Poletti,[13] *July 16:* He had just had lunch with a Swiss from an Italian-speaking canton who had sheltered refugees, etc. His telephone conversation with a lady whom he called *tu* and *cara* and with whom he was evidently on terms of affectionate intimacy. I smiled, and he explained, after he had hung up, that she was a heroine of the Resistance, a story in herself, forty-five. He talked about the Eyetyes, though Italian himself. Only 60 percent of the partisans had been disarmed—they didn't know what they had got from the Germans and the Austrians. The policy was to give the Italians enough coal and materials to keep the Communists from getting too much of a hold on them—without (I gathered) allowing their industries to become formidable competitors with the English. The workers, if the excitement was allowed to die down, would think: "Well, perhaps we can't swing it."

[12] Pietro Nenni, Socialist Party leader, was Vice-Premier in 1945.
[13] Charles Poletti (b. 1903), the Italian-American politician.

Parri's lieutenant: Fascist youth organization; Abyssin-ian War. He saw that Fascism was a complete bluff; no clothes and no equipment, soldiers bleeding to death with dysentery for lack of a little ice. He went underground, and was sent to Germany, ostensibly for health. Austria was more fanatical than Bavaria, but there were plenty of anti-Nazis. The German officer who was sure that the Germans had a secret weapon, a powder of which a little pinch destroyed utterly. The women were stupid—espe-cially when amorous: he had got a lot of information from them.

Last Supper: The windows opening behind the figure of Christ onto a dimmed but still shining vista—the subtle shades of green and blue, and the tender and lovely modeling of the hand, still exquisite where so much was effaced in that shell which had just been roofed over.

Europe: the countries like animals' dens, foul with their excrement, clogged with shed fur, bones—the badger gets into the woodchuck's hole—great squealing and squawk-ing and clawing.

I have become so *anti-British* over here that I have be-gun to feel sympathetic with Stalin because he is making things difficult for the English. It is the atmosphere of Europe—like the lowest circles of Dante's *Inferno:* dis-trust and hatred. I'll be glad to get back to the States and shake it off.

Non-bourgeois in Milan all afraid that the Americans will go away and leave them to the mercy of the English.

Rome. Mrs. Daehn: They were lamenting the English elections. —Her long black back, like an old crow—hump in shoulders, black-stockinged ankles and feet that hardly seemed to be shod but to end in some harder substance, her too-long-worn heelless slippers, as if they had been bird's feet.

Klaus Mann[14] at the *Stars and Stripes* mess. He was pleasanter, less pretentious than when I had seen him in New York, as if he had struck his level as a reporter for the *Stars and Stripes,* but still incurably German. He was raving about some Italian who was exhibiting anti-Ally pictures of caricatured GI's and Italian girls picking up their skirts to them: "It oughtn't to be allowed!" [Actually he was pathetic. He ultimately killed himself.]

Dreams about Margaret,[15] in Italy, after I came back from London, for the first time now in years. "Don't tell me," I said in one of them, "that this is another of those dreams where I'm going to wake up and find you dead!"

General Theron,[16] the administrative head of the South African forces in Europe, whom I met at one of the Ritrovo dinners: He would keep saying, rather pathetically, "I'm not an Englishman!" but he had a sort of low-bred English way of talking that indicated an English element that seems impossible for these British colonials to get away from. I was told that he was "socially ambitious," and wanted to be South African Ambassador to London. He is blond, and the little South African girl radio broadcaster thinks him very good-looking. He surprised me by a line of attack that I had not encountered

[14] Klaus Mann (1906–49), son of Thomas Mann, editor of literary review *Decision,* 1941–42.

[15] Margaret Canby, EW's second wife. For earlier references to his dreams after her death, see *The Thirties,* pp. 365–69.

[16] *EWB,* pp. 161–62.

before: he told me that the United States was really a British dominion, and that the British dominions all had to stand together to defend the principles of "fair play" in the world and see to it that people like the Germans didn't go around bullying people. Well, he insisted when I demurred, the United States and South Africa had one thing at least in common—the United States had had a revolution against England and the English had never forgotten it—the Boers had fought the English, too, and then they had made peace, and the English had stuck by the terms of the peace, and the South Africans had been very much impressed by this (I couldn't really understand what the line of argument was). Yes: the United States had a lot in common with the dominions—everything but a King, and (giving me a broad wink) it would be a good thing for us to have one—we gave our President more power than a King. The King could appoint a Prime Minister only on the advice of the South Africans.

GREECE

I was told that there was a lady who wanted to meet me who was *a direct descendant of Dante's Count Ugolino*. It turned out that the reason for this was that she wanted to write for *The New Yorker*.

Greece:[1] Splendid little American lunches in pasteboard boxes that we ate in plane: hard-boiled egg with salt and pepper, one beef-spread sandwich, one cheese sandwich, one peanut butter and marmalade sandwich, one cookie, one small container of cut-up peach and pear compote, one small bag of assorted fruit drops—with a pasteboard cup for water.

Dull stretch of Italy—parched fields—between Rome and Bari. The sea, slightly corrugated, the flecks of white that seem to be permanent—why?

Then complete change with Greece: the country paler, barer, soberer than Italy, not so much cultivation, hence grander and more mysterious, fewer visible ribbons of road —not the deep earthy clay tints of Italy, but a kind of bug

[1] *EWB*, pp. 236–323.

or bisque—the mountains dim and serene—the fawn-colored earth in its haze, which shades into blue of the mountains. Absolutely smooth dim blue sea, glistening with a fine grain of silver in patches. —Islands with marblings of beaches looping with the pale brown shape of the land—the patterns and tints of Greek vases. Finally, just before we reached Athens, we saw the bulbous or oblong shapes as distinctly overlaid in relief, on the bright even blue of the water, as if they had been cuff links on cuffs. —Coming into Eleusis airfield—pale gray of stone, pale green of foliage, pale yellow of clay—colors not well distinguished—but general grateful impression of simplification and gentle austerity.

The GI in the truck going into Athens said that Athens was a fine place, more like an American city. Atkinson afterwards said it was cleaner than Italy.

You realized on the streets that this was the place where the people had nothing—but they were more self-respecting than in Italy: few beggars or prostitutes, little servility. No makeup or gay dresses or chic shoes for the women—men somehow more decently dressed than in Milan. The city seemed depleted of inhabitants—as if everything that was going on was underpatronized and understaffed. People serious, cared nothing about making a show. Women not nearly so attractive as in Italy—round faces, round eyes.

Dim lavenderish mountains rising above bright blue water (on the way from Eleusis).

When I went up on the Acropolis and looked out around Athens, I realized more than ever that, if one had been born in Greece and never seen any other part of the world, one would not have a very distinct or vivid idea of color: acacias, olive trees, little fig trees, and cactus all blue-gray—hills and earth indeterminate tints—(effects of light and shade so much stronger)—yellows that shade in and out of pink and brown—you would have to have vague words that covered these indeterminate shades—yellow that turns red toward evening—one reason for the clarity of Greek, which has none of the Italian substantiality. —Greece, from the first moment that you see the Ionian islands from the air, makes you realize all that was vulgar in Rome, all that was trashy in the Renaissance.

The Modern City: houses dry yellow, streets pale gray, everything less ornate than Italy—simpler, more severe, more uniform—clean and well swept—a fine bit of bombing here and there, buildings nicked by machine-gun fire.

No Catholic church—only modest, unobtrusive churches, *white* houses.

Kiosque with books on flagellation. While I was looking at them, a British officer bought one.

Pavlides[2] *house at?*: 15 percent Communists in Svolas[3] government—governments [?] of Cairo and mountains—delegation to Cairo—the Greek government put them in prison (the English-made government)—navy mutinied, would not fight unless government changed—Pavlides was in training camp, refused to obey orders for thirty-three days—the officers refused to go with the sailors—had lost twenty days—the admiral came to them, then the British

[2] *EWB*, pp. 246–56. EW met the Pavlides family through a Pavlides daughter married to Alexander Barmine, the Soviet chargé d'affaires in Athens in 1937, who later fled the Stalin regime. Young Pavlides had been a partisan.

[3] Alexander Svolas, an Athenian professor, was a socialist and partisan, originally with the EAM (National Liberation Front), from which he later resigned. *EWB*, pp. 280–88.

came and said, "We want the camp," and put them in
lorries and Prisoners of War 307, twenty-six days—the
sailors found it was a Communist meeting—the British
lined them up and escorted the ones who wanted to leave
with bayonets—from 891 only seven went out—(this was
before the Greeks knew it was Communist-led)—they
wanted to take the crown out of the flag, enraged the British—before that, the British had called them rebels, but
they would not salute ship after the crown removed. —60
percent deserted the mutiny and joined the fleet (Pavlides
among them). The Greek officers made categories: A.
sailors who from the first had disagreed with the movement; B. people who had sympathized but done nothing
and were on leave or in hospital; C. people who had
shouted and done something; D. the leaders. A., B., and
C. are free; D. are supposed to be in London.

All men with beards were consigned to the C. category,
because the partisans had grown beards. One man who
was writing something about getting the right amount of
vitamin content in food at home was taken, because it was
considered insubordinate to show a patriotic interest in
Greece.

Scotchman who came and said they were costing
£25,000 because they refused to fight and did not convoy
merchant ships and the Germans sank them. They
laughed and said they were glad to hear that because they
understood that without Greeks they could not fight
Germans.

It was said that the British provoked the movement in
order to find out who was Communist, who not.

Modern house with pale straw-colored walls, white ceilings, green latticed blinds, pale cupboards of natural-
colored wood, green-and-white linoleum imitating tiles.
Cactus collection, heavy clusters of grapes draping arbor

that sheltered back door, goldfish pond very turbid green with slime, trees of yellow roses, dahlias, and petunias. Flat roof and crow's nest like a ship—all white. View of Hymettus, Piraeus.

The cactus, the house, the aromatic smell were all rather like California—glass plant.

The richer residential suburb was Ψμχικσ. The last battle against ELAS[4] had been fought through here and the houses were nicked by machine-gun fire and with paneless and blindless windows. British signs in spots and British soldiers who seemed to be having rather a dreary time. House of Prince Paul[5] with white imitation bit of Greek frieze—naked figures and horses—relatively big but not big by American standards. House where the Germans had been, still surrounded with barbed wire and with "blocuses" for machine guns. Big girls' school, now British hospital. Houses a little more pretentious and tricky and not in such good taste as in the other place.

Room where I slept. Precautions against mosquitoes: net and burning thing like punk. Loud strangulated cry, as of a dog choking on a bone or of someone being resuscitated from drowning, that I had difficulty assimilating in my dreams; finally I woke up toward morning, went to the window but couldn't see this bandersnatch. I wondered whether it was some kind of monkey. Later the thirteen-year-old boy said to me: "He shouts like a man. He jumps with his two legs. He is green." I imagined something very queer till I recognized it as a frog—"$\beta \alpha \tau \rho \alpha \chi o s$," the boy said; and it pleased me that the Greeks should have superfrogs appropriate for dramatization by Aristoph-

[4] ELAS was the National Popular Liberation Army, allied with EAM but more to the left.

[5] Prince Paul, later Paul I of Greece (1901–64). He succeeded to the throne in 1947 during the civil war and reigned to the time of his death.

anes—perhaps the οὐ-όττ was this sound. I was even further charmed when one of the ladies came out of the house and said that the frog went κοάξ κοάξ.[6]

Curious impression they gave of having simply waited till the Germans went. It was all over now—it had inconvenienced but not profoundly disturbed them—calmness after the passing of a barbarism. Independent and democratic—no real feudal nobility.

Not demonstrative like Italians—general quiet and sensible tone—good taste. Children rather serious—listened to all the political discussions. The boy said that the English and Americans didn't seem to know their own language, because they hesitated so much for words; remarked also that the Greeks had celebrated enthusiastically the results of the English elections, whereas the English had been very quiet. They were able to eat for the first time after four years. The nephew who said that he always tended to forget that he could go home in safety at night, he had got so used to dodging the Germans. Fear of the doorbell at night. One day you would have a friend, the next day you would not have him, the little daughter-in-law said, smiling. The Germans killed fifty Greeks for every German killed—they stopped a train that was going to the seaside and shot every man, woman, child, and baby on it—or they would shut off a block and take all the men. If lights were left on at night, they would machine-gun the windows and kill the people inside the house.

It was cheerful to see from the Pavlides house the twinkling lights of the suburbs of Athens: the first lighted-up city I had seen since I had come to Europe.

Somebody said that their present position was that they

[6] *EWB*, pp. 256–57.

believed all men were brothers, Greeks, Italians, Americans, Germans, etc.—with the exception of Churchill—and Leeper[7] and Scobie. They wanted to be let alone in their country—no Germans, Italians, British, or Americans.

Mrs. Pavlides [the mother of Alexander Barmine's first wife]: blue eyes, thinning and whitening flaxen hair. She came from the island of Samos, where everybody had blue eyes. She must once have been very pretty—with a sweet liveliness and desire to please. She worked in a Montessori school. They all accused her of being EKKA.[8]

Her son, an importer of rice, etc., from Baghdad—a solid businessman who made rather a show of being left about Greece but did not approve of the Communists. His wife tried to sabotage his story of the mutiny by poking her head under his arm, trying to shove him off the couch, etc. He said that she took everything from the Party, didn't know what to say about anything till she had received the Party direction. I said that I wondered they managed to be so happily married with such a serious issue between them—he replied that this was their only difference. In the East, he had not found the English especially honest, they would do anything to beat their competitors. They had tried to have him and the other members of his firm put in prison as Nazi spies. Among the English-speaking peoples, he had found the New Zealanders the best behaved. The Americans tried to grab every woman they saw and were sore if they could not get her. The English in Athens had given a dance and invited a lot of married women without their husbands—one husband who had come they had kept out.

---

[7] British Ambassador in Greece during the postwar period. *EWB*, p. 285.

[8] The National Party of Social Reconstruction, which was more democratic than EAM or ELAS but weaker militarily.

Nephew who had taken degrees in physics and mathematics but had waited eight years for a job had been giving private lessons. Seventy percent of Greek people illiterate, 3,200 teachers out of work. He thought a Left government would alter all this. He said that the American journalists had told the truth about Greece; the Briton, with few exceptions, lies. (Roi Ottley had told me that he had found, throughout his trip, that the British journalists were all propagandists for their government's policy.) At the time of the big riot, when the British had been mowing down the crowd from the top of the Grande Bretagne Hotel, American correspondents had gone down into the square, and the British had stopped firing. The Greeks had had so much to do with the English that they had rather got to like them, but they had had to change their attitude since December. If you succeeded in getting the English to come to your home, they never asked you back. He told the Greeks they only liked the Americans because they hadn't got to know them yet. Didn't believe in the disinterestedness of UNRRA—roots that would bear commercial fruit. Greece had done as much as anybody to stand up to the Germans. He made fun of the old liberals like Plastiras.[9]

The Greeks were allowed to receive only £30 a month from abroad, which wasn't enough to live on—the British were afraid of the money's being used for Communist propaganda. Mari's school friend Lulu [Mari was Barmine's first wife] had studied medicine, but had not finished because she had lost money on account of the war. She had married a lawyer and gone to live in Salonika. I like my husband and he likes me, but that's all.

[9] General Nicholas Plastiras became Prime Minister during a chaotic period in the government of Greece and lasted only a few months.

Had had to sell carpets and a lot of other things in order to get enough to eat. I felt that she was rather able but discontented.

Cousins who came in, the second evening. Two sisters —the husband of one had a post in the government. Well dressed, white suit, half-white shoes, panama hat—very polite, spoke English well. Other sister banal and bourgeois—appalled by British elections—was Attlee as intelligent as Churchill? Horrified when I said that in America they didn't sympathize with British policy. The Communists would have shot everybody if they had won. Greek Communism mere fanaticism of ignorant people— she had asked her maid what she would do after the Revolution. She would have to be a maid, as she did not know any other kind of work—the girl hadn't thought of that: she had thought she would be a lady—that was what Greek Communism was like! They were cousins of Paul Claudel's wife and of the Greek girl who became Miss Europe and married a rich American.

Forest fire—poor Greece. The Germans had stripped the mountains of the primitive forests they loved.

Out of the 7,000,000 population of Greece, 1,000,000 were killed during the war, 600,000 by starvation.

When I first got to Athens and saw the damage, I assumed that it had been done by bombing; but it seems that all these buildings were bombed and shot up in the course of the December civil war. The police headquarters had been completely blown up and most of the other ruined buildings, I was told, were places where the police had been. My room in the hotel had bullet holes in the door and in the plaster of the hall wall—one of the bullets went through the door and made a hole right above my bed. On the roof outside the windows are lying barbed-wire setups. The Grande Bretagne was one of the only strongholds of the government.

Θεατρὸ Λυρικόν: 'Αν Δοολέψεις ΟαΦας. There was a riot a month ago by government people at a performance of *Julius Caesar*—they shot Βεάκης and Παννίδης and somebody else [actors at the Lyrikon]—Βεάκης had only just recovered and come back, so was applauded. He had been with the partisans in the mountains and had lost his daughter, who had fallen into a ravine while riding. One of the most eminent actresses, a rival of Παξινούς, had been taken to the mountains and shot by the partisans for her relations with the Quisling Prime Minister (unless the other side had done it themselves). (?) When I met him in his dressing room, made a little speech and said that he was glad to speak to an American: they had fought and won their freedom and then they had lost it, and the Americans were the only people who knew what freedom was. This was an embarrassing moment for me—I said that all I could do was to write about Greece. They had cabled to the United States about the riot in the attempt to let the American people know what was going on. The subtlety of his expression and the sensitiveness of his face were thrown into relief after seeing him play the old man.

When the girl who was giving me lessons showed me how EAM had been on one side of the street (name?) and the British with their tanks on the other, I said that it had been terrible. "No," she replied almost casually. "Our men showed how brave they were."

(Barrett's report that he had from somebody about the Russians—knocking people off bicycles in the street because they had never seen bicycles before, shitting on the floor in the toilets. Apparently, the reluctance of the Russian authorities to let the Allies into the sections of Berlin allotted to the Russians was due to their wanting to get them shipshape so as not to let the English and Americans know how primitive the Russian soldiers were. Also, reports of raping in Germany by Russians, Americans, and English.)

Sentries and "inundated with 'em" (I forget with what —this a British phrase).

Anecdote about Russians capturing English at Bulgarian border.

Bloody awful
Nine hundred years old at least
400,000 inhabitants
Made him feel like some sort of Yorkshire comedian whereas he thought a man ought to keep his accent (Major Eaton)
Mountains become dull mounds, the pale and colorless sun
Scabies, lice, malaria
Homeric official
Jumping mouse

Bread wreaths
A poor show
Makes them feel better—worse
Archbishop
Women in black wailing and chanting
Left-wing speech—about to boo him—schoolmaster—mayor
Bugle set off donkey braying—ringing bell

Kidnapping of Gen. Keipper
Thirty-three men killed when Germans destroyed town
—Crete

Churches spared
Bones on floor
Girls with gold-braided black blouses and reddish snoods
with gold flowers (?), silver necklaces and strings of gold
coins
Laurel twisted on poles, Greek flag

Three bombs through roof of museum, blocks taken
from royal tomb
Type who talked French, abused Platon (the curator of
the museum)

British displacing Americans in UNRRA.[10] Clumsy
organization
Little white house where leading citizens were shot by
Germans
Man who had built fence out of air bombs—bleeding
Ammunition ship blown up
Accident in jeep—man's nose squashed sideways
Fields strewn with shreds of ammunition
Children playing with cordite
Looking for mines, simply hitting the ground
Explosions while talking
Sounds of man being beaten up
Civil war expected
Hole in bridge—skidding
Towns destroyed

[10] Brief notes set down during EW's visit to Crete. *EWB*, pp.
357–88.

Mines and bombs where you swim
Olive groves cut down
One part of oil for 50 of oranges

4 a.m.—round up people, shoot men, give others an hour to get off with animals, methodically blow up houses one by one, churches had been their headquarters.

Germans had gadgets and luxury articles—orderly—thought there were more British than there were.

Respect for Cretans, nation that boasted it had never been subdued—Achaeans, Romans, Saracens, Venetians, Turks, Germans, British.

Cretans thought he was a stinker.

Soldiers treated like cattle while officers lived in luxury. Churchill stoned in Egypt, his pipe was full, Griggs was hated.

Eaton thought it would give them a chance to show what they could do instead of complaining and taking no responsibility.

(Incident at correspondents' party.)

Contrast between going to Crete British and coming away American (this refers to the planes). "Do you mind puttin' this on, sir?" Man who checked on who I was and where I was going, Greek officer who shot his breakfast. American pilot, "How did you like that landing?" (he had bumped). —Going back: did not ask for my orders, windows open, everybody lying around, plane plastered with pin-up girls.

Engineers at airport who complained they got no publicity—what were they there for, work had no point, hard to have any initiative for it. They liked Lt. Kriegslanser.

They wanted to know whether they couldn't get ice cream in Athens just like at home—doughnuts covered with sugar. Beer.

Acropolis looked ghostly.

Holding up the traffic changing the guard Sunday mornings.

Story about Churchill and Damoskynos: "a scheming ambitious medieval prelate."

Arsenic and Old Lace

Delphi: The grim and simple mountains just out of Thebes that looked like thin flint slabs against/along the sky—iron destiny, hardly human.

"Carry on (at once)—you carry on in there" (to Eva S.). —Most of the time is spent swimming.

(The British mess.) Incident at dinner: we have no manners at this end of the table—water polo—ducking the officers.

Hills across the flat and dull water like a more massive and sullen Whistler.

Man going on leave to England.

[American] engineer said they [the British] always behaved as if they'd never seen him before, but he burst right in.

Lack of confidence of local doctors.

Man who drove me to ruins: Conservative government didn't have very good record, did they? His whistling *Star-Spangled Banner.* Silence at first, as if with British officer. Officer said it was all right—man who drove me that it was pretty deadly—also complained about Greek girls—afraid to be seen talking to British soldier.

Batman standing like butler—asked me how I'd like my eggs as I came into mess for breakfast.

Lanyards.

Greek Orthodox priest would never mix like padre.

Two ladies who had been in jail for sheltering British soldiers: New Zealanders were nicest, Australians "rougher," English "very selfish." Eighty women and children in one room—big pail in middle for everybody—weren't allowed to relieve themselves if it wasn't there—not allowed to read. One of them had spent six months, other eleven.

EAM had been all ready to blow up the Grande Bretagne Hotel.

Man who picked me up on my way back from Glyphada—British YMCA—glad he had been to Milan to get better idea of Italians than in Rome—liked Greeks better than Italians, but they told him he would change his mind—thought the British probably ought to get out—had only been here a week.

The Miami [a nightclub]: M —. Smarais: kissed man, then banged him with tambourine, shuddering start of pleasure when partner kneels and kisses her above the crotch. People liked to talk about her—a legend: slept with all nations, Germans had had her up for English lovers. *"Elle ment avec une facilité inouïe."* Story of journalist who had just been to London: *"Trois compliments méditerranées—seulement trois—avec un effet foudroyant."* (They had bowled some woman over.) Game: Churchill wished he were Mussolini because Mussolini had shot his son-in-law. —I wish you were the town of Hiroshima and I *la bombe atomique pour tomber dessus.* I wish I were a *cigarette pour brûler entre vos lèvres.* Called up at 8 and said the enemy had withdrawn.

American who wanted to know whether the war between Athens *and* Sparta were still going on.

New Zealand girl: vegetarian, but thought it had been a very good thing that Greek actress's throat had been cut. Japs ought to be taught their folly, Hirohito deposed.

Large painting of room in museum (Vatican?) at the Siph's, with [?] in the middle. —Couple who talked French at home with one another.

RETURN TO ITALY

August 22

Greece: Meager, arid, abstract—contrasted with rankness and earthiness of Italy. The terra-cotta lichen-covered hills—the islands stood out on deep violet water like pieces of a picture puzzle, in rounded shapes of bottles, blobs, a roast turkey.

Italy: A relief, after all, to see trees and plowed fields below and to find, on the road to Caserta,[1] so much vegetation—straw (?)—ricks, a high eucalyptus drive, smell of manure and sulphur, and swamp, fruits and vegetables grown systematically.

The grand and gigantic buildings, with statues three times life size—and a fleshly world; the women, dark- or yellow-haired, on their red or white clogs; the Corso Umberto and the Via Roma a vast meat market; many little boys, one of whom offered me "a nice woman." Back in the thick night atmosphere, the unlighted streets of Italy.

[1] Caserta, headquarters for the Allied Forces in Italy, 1943, and scene of the German surrender in Italy, 1945.

Uplift campaigns: "Drive carefully. Death is so permanent" (thought up by smart advertising man); "Flies Foul Food, Kill that Fly, Flies Contaminate Food, Flies Feed on Feces and Food, Flies Spread Dysentery, Diarrhea, One Fly Killed Means a Million Less"—long eucalyptus-lined drive between Caserta and Naples.

How the Americans hated Naples!: man with hard *r*'s and permanent grouch, whose commanding officer had just told him that they might be here a year.

Little kids in streets—apparently stayed there all night —sleeping on curbs along buildings and mudguards of cars.

Italians in GI clothes—they and the submerged GI's becoming almost indistinguishable.

Pregnant ·women—with wretched little babies—sores on the children's faces, pink mottlings of disease.

Cheap and fancy white and black hearses like pastry, loaded with flowers, a common sight in the streets—so many must die, they make a fete of it. White ones with crowns on top like Christmas tree ornaments. One big black one drawn by eight black horses with crowns which were lamps at each corner and quantities of spiraled columns and elaborate jet carving, like a Renaissance bed.

Lemonade stand set up by Red Cross in Via Roma.

Big pink buildings with green blinds—ridiculous gigantic plastery-looking statues.

Bay of Naples now hard to distinguish from colored picture postcards, etc.

Silver things on collars of horses: bells, rosettes, half-moons, madonnas, saints, and birds.

Street shut off on account of mines and part of beach shut off.

The inhabitants of Naples seem sometimes to have only the same relation to people as octopi, small mollusca, and crabs brought in by the marine tides.

Scarcity of dogs and cats in Italy and Greece.
(These are miscellaneous notes, some from my first stay in England.)
Book: Our conversation at dinner in London with Humphrey Slater and John Strachey: Strachey talking about Germans coming back to Germany: —"They will find it rather changed—superficially, perhaps." Laughing about the wiping out of Warsaw. Humphrey Slater said, if anybody had told us before the war that we'd be laughing ghoulishly, etc.
(This was my first meeting with Mamaine. I took her home in a cab.)

Other colored correspondents [than Roi Ottley]—one of them had gone to Harvard. Anti-white papers like the *Afro-American* (Baltimore) made a lot of money. Roi Ottley tried to tell one of them about white officers who had tried to do things for their Negro troops. He replied, "I'm only interested when the Negro gets kicked in the pants." Every white face is an enemy—lies they print in those papers—"it's a war."

(I originally intended a volume of stories, but only one was written—"Through the Abruzzi with Mattie and Harriet."[2] The notes below were intended for these stories, and they do not necessarily represent real happenings.)

[2] See *EWB*, pp. 97–137.

Five Views of the Ruins of Rome—The New Piranesi
—Ruins of Rome—Six Views of Rome. Jacket: A Piranesi
and a devastated village

Abruzzi

Communist and Mrs. Daehn

Santayana and Dewald (Has been in Milan?—seen
pulverized Mantegnas?)—with Santayana slips into school
and college attitude of very bright well-liked pupil.

American and British—(on Sforza and Nenni)

Fini and Lepri

Black Market (buying a Negro)

Caetanis (Hotel situation followed by ride to Ninfa)

Dorothy Thompson or Clare Luce? (Dorothy Thompson and the flag of the United States of Europe)

Dorothy Thompson and husband[3] despise *Time* man
(in Paris lives in special quarters) but think they are in
New York themselves.

Lee White—white correspondent, formerly a socialist,
tells Negro correspondent that he's lucky to have a cause
that lasts: "You're to be congratulated."

Negro story: Ottley and Italian family who offer him
daughter, religious pictures in house—wonders whether
he ought to consider the incident gratifying because they
did not draw the color line or insulting because they had
counted on his jumping at the chance of sleeping with a
white woman. —Smartness of Roman girls—fornicating
in the Forum (memory of Horace)—buying a nigger—
he finds him naked—girls in the caves and ruins—soldier
who got killed by mistake by a stone when he wouldn't
come out—blacks from Basutoland—Italians scared of
them—they depress him about the Negro in general.

Hughes and Sir Ronald Storrs (Clare Luce)

[3] Maxim Kopf, well-known artist and sculptor who married
Dorothy Thompson in 1943.

Career newspaperwoman and husband competing, with rooms on different floors, and insulting each other over the telephone like Hemingway and Martha Gellhorn.[4] —*The Rome Assignment*—food at Cecchi's: eggs with vegetable salad (*uova a l'italiano*), ravioli, mushrooms, langouste, two kinds of cake—chocolate and a paler kind with a maraschino cherry—cocktails in hotel and two bottles or more of white wine—fuss about getting car to go there. In public, check pinching—argument in private about divorce and their child. He realizes she is under some new influence—or what?—simply got it out of herself.

Evelyn Waugh in Rome?

British and American official running-down (even on the part of intelligent young men like Hughes and Barrett) of people on the wrong side of their governments: Nenni when arrested, Sforza.

Notes on Anglo-American Relations

England: Henry Yorke [Henry Green][5] talking about Vermont, Florida, as if Vermont were a town in Florida that had the same root as vermiform. —On White's, of which [Victor] Weybright[6] (whose name he pretended to think was Waynefleet) had recently become a member. He was obviously shocked and alarmed. Weybright said there were only eight American members—a Jewish member had been one of his sponsors. Yorke exclaimed: "He gets a dirty Jew to get him in—another Jew—which you're not!"

---

[4] American writer and journalist who married Hemingway. See *The Thirties*, p. 557n.

[5] Henry Vincent Yorke (1905–73), British businessman and novelist who wrote comedies of manners under the pseudonym of Henry Green.

[6] Victor Weybright, American publisher.

Evelyn Waugh began by pretending to think that I was a "simple man" from Boise, Idaho, and, alternatively, that I was a Rhodes Scholar, preoccupied with Henry James. Raved about Sergeant [Stuart] Preston,[7] who had made such an impression—he had been staying around Windsor and they thought he was going to marry the Princess Elizabeth. Later, in his rooms at the Hyde Park Hotel (where I was also staying), I talked about the antagonism to Americans, and he acknowledged it with a wicked gleeful grin in his bright little hard eyes, but went on to say that it was really based on jealousy. He talked about the opportunity for Americans of buying up fine things cheap. At White's (to which he had asked me for a drink), he said that England had better ruins than Italy. When I said that they would have to put up an annex for the overflow from Westminster Abbey, he said that he didn't think there were going to be any more distinguished men. (I said some derogatory things about *Brideshead Revisited,* and this really rocked him. When I quoted some absurd sentence, he said, "That doesn't sound like me, does it?" He handed me the book and said, "Find it.") I asked him when he talked of Europe as something different from England, whether he thought of England as not being Europe.

C. M. Bowra[8] on Eliot's American education—he had read a lot but didn't really understand anything—a very stupid man, slow. Of course, he could pick out the only

[7] Sergeant Stuart Preston, a handsome young man with a marked personality (later an art reporter on *The New York Times*), was taken up by London society and moved in high literary and artistic circles as a kind of ideal American soldier, possessing all the social graces.

[8] Sir C. Maurice Bowra (1898–1971), classicist, critic, and Warden of Wadham College, Oxford, 1938–70.

good line in Massinger! Bowra had never read Walt Whit-
man, who (he said) was a great writer in South America.
I said that Whitman was *our* greatest writer. "Better than
Whyte-Melville?"

Sylvester Gates:[9] countered my story about officials at
airport with two about his last trip to America. When I
complained about British ignorance of the United States,
he remarked that most American books were so badly
written that it was hard for the English to find out about
us. Experience of little girl at school: "They took Oliver
and I to the movies." Anecdote about Roosevelt's not having charmed Oliver on his visit to the White House and
wanting him to come back and be charmed, and about
Oliver's saying to Roosevelt, "I can hop, can you?" Complaint that the GI's weren't bad, but that the officers were
awful. Purse snatching, assault, following women out of
the underground—it later turned out, however, that, according to Gates, his sister-in-law Joy had just been sleeping with every American in Cornwall. She said about the
photographs that all the soldiers had that she thought they
were general issue, too: wife with two children on a porch,
the girl always fair, the boy always dark. The soldiers who
used to take their girls into the garden of some kindly-
disposed gentleman. He had told them not to hesitate to
use it, and then found he couldn't go out without walking
on a couple. When he complained, the GI's, in revenge,
filled his mailbox full of used condoms. On another occasion, an old Chinese scholar had been shot down by some
American soldiers who had come onto his grounds and
whom he had been coming forward to receive cordially.
—Fear of Luce publications and broadcasting ships.

[9] A longtime British friend of EW who studied at Harvard
Law School. See correspondence in *Letters on Literature and
Politics.*

They always bring up the Negro problem when anything about the English caste system is said. —When I talked about the different languages spoken in England by the different social classes, Gates said that he couldn't understand the American Negroes.

Vanity Fair and *Bleak House, Way of All Flesh*

"The natives are hostile," "different from one," "we've had it," "most of the time is spent swimming," and [A. N.] Whitehead's autobiographical sketch, "carry on," "cheerio," "yes" (they had a special way of saying this).

Mamaine saying that the Americans had done the British a service, because they had made themselves so disliked in Europe that people were glad to have the British. She seemed to know nothing about American history except Burke's speech. She said that the difference between Europeans and Americans was that Americans had no sense of history. Didn't it make all the difference with Americans that they had been in Europe?

Her two stories about Henry Yorke and John Strachey. *Dinner with Strachey, Mamaine, and Slater.*

Kemp Smith said that the British saw the Americas in their atlases as about the same size as the British Isles.

Italy: Philip Hamburger said that when any Allied military body was first formed, the British and American officers would have the same rank, but that the British would immediately be promoted.

At the hotel here [Rome], there had been trouble about the mess. The American correspondents had protested about the badness of the food. The position of the British had been that they didn't want to eat any better than the people at home. The Americans accused the British of selling the food on the black market. It turned out that the lack of sugar was due to the fact it was all being used up for the little cakes the English had at tea.

Walter Newburgh said that the AC was four fifths British in administration and four-fifths American in supplies. The British were now sending the older men home, so that the Americans only now had parity with them. If you were an eager beaver (the opposite was a goldbrick or coaster), the British said, "Fine!"—and you became an office boy to some British colonel—and never got home because the American army said you were still needed. The U.S. army wouldn't give promotions with the job the way the British did. According to our system, which was intended for a small peacetime army that only had to garrison Hawaii, etc., there could only be so many majors, etc. The British had Italy completely under control, had had their long experience of colonial administration. The gas was American, but it was always doled out by an English sergeant or a soldier at the gas station. Our man in the AC (what is his name?) was a figurehead.

Fodor said that the British were only all right up in Austria, where it was rainy as it was in England. The British colonel or whatever he was had treated them with the utmost cordiality at Salzburg, asked them to dinner, and sent them around in his car.

The sergeant at the British P.O. said to me the second time that I gave him a letter for Mamaine, looking at the envelope, "Fair enough"; the third time he said, "It's as good as gone, sir."

The English virtues are almost now merely a natural wonder, like the Carlsbad cave or the Grand Canyon, unless for social purposes.

The English Revolution took place in America, and since then there have been two parallel social developments that more and more put each other out.

Churchill (half a romantic Anglophile American) disgusting and intolerable now war is over.

Perfide Albion, *la morgue anglaise,* international reputation as hypocrite.

Hamburger at Trieste:[10] The British talked about the Jugs and Jugland—border incidents, the Jugs are coming through the lines—thought they were at the Khyber Pass. He said they spoke of the Jugs in such a way as to suggest hairy savages crawling around on all fours—creatures who had once been good police dogs but had now turned into dangerous wolves. *I Lavatori,* the Lavatory—president of council speechless with indignation at having been put in jail—"I don't know whether it's his wife, all I can say is that she's a woman." He was a fisherman, and they kept referring to him as "the fisherman"—provoking him to such retorts as "After all, Christ was a carpenter!"—British officer undertook to brief them on the Jugoslavs, after having held up for days their efforts to see them: "They carry their politics with them." Hamburger asked whether the British didn't do that, too. —At the British mess, an altercation occurred when they told him that the Americans would have to help them fight the Russians, and he was asked to leave the next day.

American officer who said: "A bicycle drove up and out swarmed four top-ranking warmongers, all complete with pips and squeaks."

[10] *EWB,* pp. 214–16.

When they asked whether these men had been arrested with warrants, the British officer talked of "military expediency."

My relation to the English and my relation to my father: accent, handwriting.

Partitions, plaster, sticks and bricks—

Expecting now the Japanese—

The circling swifts, the swimming roofs of Rome

Stains the clouds with tints of clay—
But crumbled ruins and smashed crates
Tourists' hotel at Milan—smell of bars
Himmler's death—crushed poison vial against his gums

English devices: They set out quietly to put over something so outrageous that you can't imagine any decent person would have the gall to attempt it, then, if you seem to be taking alarm, they try to make you feel that, if you objected, you would be behaving badly.

The Oxford brush-off: getting rid of importunate and troublesome questions by laughing gently about some aspect of the country or class or person which is totally irrelevant to the question in hand, and creating the impression that one has discredited it or him, that it is not to be taken seriously.

The moral line: indignation at the brigandage of EAM, they never fought the Germans; Sir Ronald Storrs's indignation over Tito's pseudonym.

Letting people down and then picking them up again. Tchelishchev[11] says, "They scratch and scratch, then (act-

[11] Pavel Tchelishchev (1898–1957), distinguished Russian-born artist. See *EWB*, p. 23. (EW explains his transliteration of Russian names in the preface to *EWB*.)

ing it out) they kindly put on a bandage." Dos Passos on their social banana peels.

Always allege some other reason in order that it may be impossible to put your finger on where the dirty work was done.

They have a special word, "civil," for what is elsewhere merely ordinary politeness.

Henry Adams on walking into a strange house, etc.: The Perfection of Human Society: p. 202 (*Education*).

(I left a party in London with Evelyn Waugh and some lady related to the Churchills, and we took a taxi together. He said in his well-tuned way—a lovely voice redeems his ugliness: "The Americans are politer than anyone else." I said, "Only than the British.")

Picking-up every morning of enthusiasm for art, etc., which surprises me—much more so than when I was young.

THE CAPE AND NEW YORK, 1945

Summer weather on the Cape, '45: First, during July, two strange spells of weather which were like the first days of autumn when the weather is distinctly cool, but the world still looks like summer. (Drought all the time: the grass was getting yellow.) Then a long period of horrible heat—suffocating, stultifying—days of overclouded humidity—crawling through a thick moist medium, almost like mud, or the semi-transparent glutinous substance of which jellyfish are composed. You would drowse, soaked in the humidity and your own perspiration, which seemed thus to merge in a general liquefaction.

[Elena Mumm Thornton, who became the fourth Mrs. Edmund Wilson, was born August 27, 1906, in Rheims, France, and was christened Hélène-Marthe von Mumm. Her father was German and her mother Russian (the former Olga Struve), daughter of a high-ranking Russian diplomat who had been ambassador for the Tsarist government in Japan, the Netherlands, and the United States. Her parents were in France at the time of her birth because her father was running what was a family business

—Mumm's champagne. After the First World War, Mumm's was confiscated by the French government as a "spoil of war." Her father continued production of wine in Germany and was based in a town outside Frankfurt called Johannisberg. Elena Mumm was the eldest of four children—one sister and two brothers. She never went to school, was tutored at home except for art studies in Munich when she was seventeen and later in Paris in her early twenties. She at first painted a great deal—actually did house decoration, frescoes, portraits—but gave up this work when still young. The Mumms lived for part of the year in Switzerland, mainly in hotels during her childhood and into her teens partly because one of her brothers had tuberculosis; they stayed in Davos, for a while (as in *Magic Mountain*—literally, because Thomas Mann was on the scene).

[Later the Mumms consolidated themselves in Johannisberg, where they lived in a big white house on a hill overlooking the Rhine. Elena was trilingual. She learned French, German, and English simultaneously, and some Russian. She had been christened in a Protestant church, but her mother was Russian Orthodox. Both her parents had died before she married EW, and one brother was a suicide. She had been living in the United States for a number of years, married James Thornton with whom she had a son, Henry. EW had met her casually at the Chavchavadzes' in Wellfleet (she had known Nina since she was young through her mother—émigré White Russians seemed to have—or most certainly had then—a network of hospitality and friendship). She was a paying, long-staying guest of the Chavchavadzes on the Cape and on one occasion she went with them to a party given by EW and Mary McCarthy at Wellfleet. Elena had been working for *Town and Country* as a proofreader but the editor soon recognized that she was qualified for work of a much less mechanical nature and made her his secretary. Early in 1946 *Town and Country* published the Wilbur Flick story, later included in *Memoirs of Hecate County*. Elena was by then an assistant editor at the magazine. She and Edmund went out to lunch together; they got on; and they fell in love.]

April 6. E. Passion for her: blaze-up in taxi, as on both our sides it had been smoldering a long time without our paying attention to it: she would say, this is getting bad! —this is strong! My night of agony, couldn't sleep, turned on light about three, finally was able to read Edward Lear's letters a little, went to sleep about dawn and had long fantastic dream, visit to seaside resort: there was the hotel with room at the end of corridor that I always entered with apprehension, I would find then, wheeling through it, some kind of half-human machine, then there was the town, then there was the *plage*. The people had deformed or animal or grotesque wooden faces. I was always a little bit afraid of them but walked among them, half conscious that I was inventing them myself, vivid, detailed narrative, fantastic though everything was, you could stop and study it as if it were real. Situation with E. was present in my mind and I felt that the consummation in a sense as far away even now as it had been for so many months. I found myself back in the hotel again and had to repeat the whole sequence. None of the creatures really did me any harm, though they were unfriendly and I was alone among them. Finally I had an emission in a nightmarish connection irrelevant to E. Woke up, my tension partly relieved but still tight-strung and soon becoming again passionate in my desire for her. —Before that, I had, on the strength of my drinks and our passage in the taxi, been self-confident and exhilarated. Told Francy at concert I liked her so much and touched her hand with my fingers; checked up Paul Rosenfeld[1] afterwards—we even went to a cafeteria and had a couple of little cakes after leaving the bar where we had been drinking.

Next afternoon, when we had so little time, we were both so keyed up and nervous, trying to get uptown in a taxi through traffic jammed up by soldiers' parade. Buses routed through side streets and buses in which the soldiers had come stretching up First Ave. E. almost went crazy when we were stuck in block where Racquet Club was, squirming with her feet and long legs, then controlling herself: "Never mind, did you ever see such a Simple Simon"—of old driver who kept saying, "Look at all those buses!" and making other wise unperturbed remarks. He sounded as if he were German and she looked at his name on the card and said, "I thought so!" —"This is your dream," she said to me. "You must make up your mind! Well, what do you want to do about it?" —I loved her body, which I had first seen in a bathing suit—I found that my impression was correct of its natural fineness and style in spite of her longness and tallness—taller than my usual physical type—there was nothing about it that displeased me—her breasts were low, firm and white, perfect in their kind, very pink outstanding nipples, no hair, no halo around them, slim pretty tapering legs, feet with high insteps and toes that curled down and out. Never too thin, her hips, stomach, and abdomen were lovely. —Reactions quite different from those of any other woman I had known. She would look at me fixedly, her eyes becoming gray and as if somehow out of focus or differently focused, a little wolfishly, as if she too had a strain of the German police dog. She would crouch with her head down on the bed or lie sideways against me, half crouched over my

[1] Paul Rosenfeld (1890–1946), music and art critic and a founder of *Seven Arts* magazine. See *The Thirties*, p. 244n.

hand and gnawing my knuckles. She would wind herself around me like an eel, telling me how much she enjoyed it. Her grasp of the language relaxed and she would say things that sounded a little queer in English. She would embarrass me by saying, I'm so pleased, when I should have been saying such things to her. She said I'm flattered—you flatter my breasts, when I was caressing them, confusing, I think, the English meaning of *flatter* with some French meaning. She thanked me when she left—though I'd really served her rather badly—after my dream having come only once—pressure of time, too—we had only about an hour. Would always run her tongue into my mouth when I kissed her before I had a chance to do it to her—and would do it so much and so fast that I hardly had a chance to get my own in. Would clasp her legs together very hard when I had my hand or my penis in her—seemed to have tremendous control of the muscles inside her vagina. Her frank and uninhibited animal appetite contrasted with her formal and gracious aristocratic manners.

(December, 1945) When Mother came up to see Dr. Kirby preparatory to having the cataract removed from her eye, they put drops in her eyes and produced the impression that the liveliness and brightness of her eyes had been [restored]. Rosalind[2] and I both noticed that she looked pretty, as she must have done when she was young.

E. Coming back from bathroom with white bath towel wrapped around her middle. Perfectly beautiful, long straight legs, standing with her feet apart, her round low firm breasts, with their deep pink nipples, hardly less

---

[2] Rosalind Wilson (b. 1923), daughter of EW and Mary Blair.

white: no coquetry about being naked, but happy and frank in her tall beauty. The picture she made in this pose against the bedroom door, which she had just closed behind her, was very characteristic.

So, in a different way, was the way she looked when we were making love, our eyes open gazing at one another. When she wore blue, her eyes seemed electric blue; at other times, they seemed gray; now they seemed an animal green, and she looked at me with fierce glee. After the climax, she writhed around to bite, so wolfishly—her mouth wide open—that I drew my arm away. Then she said, "Get away!" —All this had nothing to do with her ordinary sweet manners and her deprecatory laugh. She was, as she said, "well disciplined."

Also, contrast of British accent and rather social way of talking, which sounded as if they had been learned from some extremely well-bred English governess, with the things she said in erotic passion: It's such a pleasure, such a pleasure! —Oh, please do that! (from behind). I'd walk sixty miles for this! (my finger). Does this bore you? (the same thing). Oh, I never, never—. I love to have you touch me! I'll be dreaming of your hands (German *r*). —I think about you and come by myself, and that isn't right, is it?

L.M. Autumn 1945. Like a love affair with a nymph: too lovely while going on—unreal after it was over, looking back on her, she seemed at once too perfect and too little fleshly to be a woman. For example, she had no smell. Tiny opening and pelvic arch—impossible, no doubt, to have children. Beautiful waist and behind. Her little half-priggish, schoolmistressish way of telling about love affairs and "relationships" in a semi-psychoanalytic jargon. Magenta nails to match her hat and dress. Little hats with down-curled feathers of the seventies that she

wore with so much chic. —Unnaturally warm October—
she said that it seemed "infernal." —G. had been for
years like a somnambulist; managed to be in the room
when she was talking to her friends on the phone and
seem never to be aware of it. Her delivering her little
lecture upset him, because he had never been able to speak
in public. He began going to an analyst, and one of the
first effects it had on him was to make him come home
and ask her what she was doing seeing V. so much. Later
she told me that the analyst had told him that he had
been dead twenty years. She said that it had been her
insecurity which had made her marry him—he had always been like that—you felt more secure with a dead
man because you knew he would never go away.

1946–1949

CHARLOTTESVILLE, 1946

[EW was visiting Virginia relations. His father's mother came from this part of the country.]

Charlottesville, May. Went to see the university by moonlight, with Venable,[1] late at night after party when we had had quite a lot to drink; lived up to dream from childhood. Poe's room; Jefferson club—Poe—Woodrow W.—portrait of the young Jefferson, red-haired, long-nosed, and slightly sardonic, which V. had told me at first was a portrait of the young Washington, interesting because so different from any of the later portraits. V. had the key to Poe's room. He took me through the pavilion, now the offices of, I think, the Grad. School, in which the Minors had lived: Corinthian columns, friezes, wonderful back yard, bedrooms with great high windows. Statue of aviator, quite effective at night. Beauty of proportions of "Range" poetry created by Jeff and ideal of noble education in the humanities and in civic virtue.

[1] Francis P. Venable (1856–1934) had been president of the University of North Carolina from 1900 to 1914.

But they instinctively tried to keep you from getting in touch with the past, which they knew all too well they were not up to. They wanted you to drink with them and to get drunk like them so that you and they wouldn't have to think about anything but their superficial conviviality. It was also part of the kind of war that they waged against the Northerner: exploited him (the liquor they got me to buy at the rationed stores) and tried to get him down at the same time that they wanted to charm him and give him the traditional Virginian hospitality. I finally got to feel that they really wanted to prevent [the] Russian [Sheremetev, brother of Mrs. Daehn; see above, p. 97] and me from seeing Monticello.

My embroilment with the greedy landlady (she couldn't afford to take in single lodgers), in a taxi the first thing in the morning *"un incident du premier ordre"*—escape also from the relations. We visited Monticello. Bubblelike beauty of the house: splendid and charming without being imposing. As Dos says, he had no private life after the death of his wife—it was surprising to see how he worked in an outside room, adjoining his small bedroom, that opened right on the side lawn, with glass walls like a conservatory. Did not want to hear about industrial machinery yet continually contriving gadgets. *M.* said, Yes, he was *un grand seigneur;* but did not like his insistence on revolutionary symbols, as he supposed the cannonballs that were used as weights for the clock to be. Also thought that putting the beds in alcoves was an attempt to eliminate the baldachins which were associated with aristocratic pomp. Was Jeff's systematic suppression of staircases really inspired by some such impulse?

Jeff had created Charlottesville—a first-rate creative artist, given some kind of magic to everything that he touched—wonderful with how sure a touch he would situate the places on their little hills so as to involve the landscape in the work of art.

Castle Hill: spooky, big flaring-topped walls of box, through which the car could hardly pass. Old Miss Rives upstairs having her head rubbed by elderly colored maid. The worn books, English and French with a little Russian, of the Troubetzkoys in the eighties, the nineties, and the early 1900s—the worn portraits and busts of Amélie Rives.[2] The ghost that waked the guests in their beds and shocked them and told them to go home.

The big Jeffersonian house where one of the Minor cousins lived—she had married a northern boiler maker. The farm paintings that *M.* recognized, the Compagnie des Indes china, the fireplace brought from France; the lovely uneven lawn, the immense modern tulip garden that opened on one of the wonderful views. —The Southerners resenting and exploiting the Northerners, the Northerners scorning the Southerners, yet living on their boughten Virginian glamor.

The cynical New Yorkers one ran into—the lady who explained that the man who won the cross-country race was virtually a pro: there'd been more betting on whether he'd have the nerve to take part than on whether he'd win. (Pretty sight to see them running against the soft spring green: the red coats and the black or brown horses.) Impossibility of making Mrs. ? realize that we would not come to lunch.

Marjo's acquired southern accent that did not sound really Virginian—actually an Irishman who came from Maine.

Dreadful lightweight professors: Davis and Gooch, two

[2] Virginia-born novelist and poet (1863–1945), who in 1896 married the Russian Prince Troubetzkoy.

Rhodes scholars and Anglophiles. G. thought that there wasn't in the U.S. a single legal or political arrangement that hadn't been handled better in England—did not take at all kindly to my telling him that the English social revolution had taken place in America—What do you mean by a social revolution?—quoted Chesterton—mixture goofiness and arrogance. The chief feature of Davis's library seemed to be a handsome set of Stevenson. Professors in general seemed preoccupied with qualifying for the Fairfield (?) Country Club (with its fine low wide view and its lovely snowy and luster-lighted Jeffersonian octagonal room). Ambition to have light and easy manners of old-time Virginian gentleman rather interfered with seriousness of discussion or genuine interest in their subject.

Lady at party: feminine Virginian type; her hat and her way of wearing her hair had something of the pre-1910 period—would have known her as a Virginian anywhere. Did this type contribute, through Miss Langhorne, to the ideal of the Gibson Girl; or is it merely that the old fashion has, for some reason, lingered down here?

My surprise over the tablet to Minor and at being told by a friend and a Charlottesville contemporary of his that he was probably the most brilliant man of his generation in Charlottesville, could have been senator from Virginia if he had liked.

The graveyard with the Wilson and Minor graves, with B. Gildersleeve not far away—as well as the cemetery for the Confederate soldiers—many bodies that had never been identified. One cenotaph with a list of names had had to do for them all.

Queen Charlotte Hotel on the railroad track, shaken by the rare pulling trains. Lush and coarse summer foliage a rank green outside the windows. Old low wooden beds —quite clean. Enjoyed lying there in the quiet afternoons.

Negro section—"Niggertown"—right in the middle of the business street. You noticed that they were going about their business quite out of cooperation with the whites—belonged to a different system. They did not make room for them on the street any more than the whites made room for them. The Disappointment Club —would let the whites down, on the pretext of illness, just before a big dinner, etc.

The Minors: old Mrs. Minor hated the New Deal, thought it had encouraged the Negroes to be lazy by putting them on relief; was still indignant over Theodore Roosevelt's having invited B. T. Washington to the White House, and no doubt her animus against Eleanor Roosevelt had partly been stimulated by her patronage of Marian Anderson. When M. asked her whether the silver was her family silver, she said No: that she didn't like to talk about it in front of Edmund but their silver had been stolen in the war. Her father, also a professor, had lived in another of the pavilions right across the campus from the Minors—(the original distinguished Venable had been on Lee's staff, the only one, according to Allen Tate, who had been able to talk back to Lee)—they had said that Raleigh Minor[3] had had to marry Nancy Venable, because he would have been too lazy to look for a girl any further away (she told me this herself). I did not like her much at first, but had continually more respect for her the longer I stayed. She at least kept up the attitude and lived up to the responsibilities of the old order—the younger generation of Venable and Ann were already something quite different—they knew they were no longer important and tended to be slack and indifferent. But Mrs. M. kept them up to the mark and kept the family together. (She

---

[3] Raleigh Minor (1869–1923) had been professor of law at the University of Virginia.

had lately had cancer of the breast, and had had the breast
amputated.) She would drink one or two old-fashioneds
with the rest, but would restrain the children from drinking too much. Though she was not remarkably intelligent,
magnanimous, or even well informed, I found that she
was the person that I tended to talk to as their parties
wore on. The children were good-looking and cute—
Venable's oldest daughter was remarkably developed at, I
think, fourteen, and already full of blond sex appeal, as
Nancy Tate had been. When I first met her, it was in
town, where I was walking along the main street with
Susan [Wilson],[4] who, after she had left us, deplored the
fact that she should be roaming the streets alone. The way
she said to her little sister on the bicycle: I'm gonna let
you fall!

[4] A cousin of EW's who lived in Charlottesville. See *The
Thirties*, pp. 694–95.

CAPE COD

E. at Wellfleet, July—second time when she was dry: thrusting it down into her with deliberate strong strokes that finally set the spring flowing. She would groan—said it hurt at first but later on was wonderful.

Marvelous afternoon in room above my study: tuna sandwiches and white wine. I made her laugh a lot the time before with Russian stories from V. Nabokov: she would say: more stories! (When I had read her the German sex book, she had said at last: Enough theory!) Interrupted too soon by Nina. By that time I was reading her poetry and we didn't hear N. call. The next time she simply got herself a drink and sat down reading in the middle room. When we found her, she announced with nonchalance that the duenna had gotten herself a drink.

—She said she had no shame with me: Central Park— "We're in the shadow."

—When she first came up to Wellfleet, the first meeting wasn't so successful as later ones—as sometimes happens when you have thought too much about it in advance. Usually best when you have been seeing one another, are already used to one another.

—Her blue eyes looking at me from Nina's car one morning when I was feeling low: gave me moral support.

E. in Berkshires. Three times the first day and again the next morning. The Corot-like misty landscapes with trees along the little river. —Rich and dense and furry country and with its big trees and round leisurely-rolling hills: dense atmosphere full of moisture: cleared up the last day to reveal the rich wine vivid colors. She thought it would be gloomy to live there. We could watch the people—blond shoulder-length-haired girls—strolling on the main street of Gr. Barrington from the windows of the hotel room and on which I had half pulled down the shades: the big screen of old dark green trees, the dense verdure of the girls' school across the street. —Gigantic and expensive New England summer hotel: $15 a day apiece, meals American plan: usual badly cooked food— full of old ladies and small-boned *mesquin* Massachusetts men—row of rocking chairs on the extensive white porch.

E. —Sank it between her slim lovely legs. —Beautiful long slim legs, with scar below right knee, where she had had a surgical operation after a ski accident—couldn't wear high-heeled shoes on that account. Father had been for some years champion high-jumping skier of Germany. —White skin and blue veins more or less all over her. When she got sunburned at Wellfleet, her white bosom with the pink just above it looked like a delicious ice-cream brick with strawberry against vanilla. —She always jumped with both feet after making love. —Her crystal ice earrings and her blue ones—her pearls that she wore when she was nude—her little watch that didn't go any more—her red flat-soled pointed balletlike shoes that she wore most of the time at Wellfleet. —She thought it was degrading to make love in the dark—used to look me right in the eyes with a sort of fierce expression. —Small flat stomach, narrow hips, torso that easily showed the ribs— very high well-molded insteps—well-molded curved and rather long toes—she always had them lacquered because, as she said, she had to wash dishes so much—her little toenails were incredibly tiny. Only her neck and perhaps her behind showed a little that she was nearly forty.

—Her feet, even thin high ankles, like the feet of some deer or something: strong and firm big toe, other toes surprisingly diminishing, till you came to the incredibly tiny toenails of the last two. Folded together they looked so fine and white. Sensual pleasures of holding the insteps and kissing the toes at their base. I used to lie beside her and do this after we had just made love.

—Lying naked, with nothing on but her pearl necklace —a beautiful blond effect.

—Driving her down to Yarmouth—attractiveness of this drive, which I'd never felt to the same extent before: the bright and chalky air.

—Little spot, with its slight non-bushy trimming, very discreet and distinguished. —When I looked at it from below, with the light on it, I saw that it was a charming light brown like the soft short growth of hair on her head.

—Her vinelike legs and arms with hands and feet like leaves.

Last of the season—affectionate passage with Reckie— eaten by mosquitoes, did not swim. —Dull water, sky soberly tinted and even and smooth like the water. —Leisure and relief of after the summer.

—On the way there, the marsh at the corner of Gull Pond Road and the main road was reddening like an autumn apple—(a few days later the bushes were blazing with bright rose-red and gamboges).

R[ichard] Rovere's[1] first experience as a Communist worker. At Bard College—they formed a Communist group, sent to N.Y. for somebody to instruct and steer them. A guy arrived that they all liked so much—he'd been a real worker and talked the dem-dose-dem language —told them that the first thing for them to do was to get to work on the colored help, give a big dance and invite them, and show them what fine people they were, cared nothing about the color line. They threw themselves into it with great enthusiasm, hired a band and a hall. But quantities of Negroes showed up that they didn't know were coming, and when R. began to dance with one of the colored girls, he found that she was crawling all over him, and, looking around, he could see that the other girls were doing the same. Then—ding · ding · ding—when (J. imitated the station wagon) the police had arrived and were packing them off. The organizer had been a stool pigeon of the state police or the FBI, and the uninvited girls were all whores and pimps with police records.

Gull Pond, Oct. 4, '46: Coming down the path, where the fallen tree had been cut away till there were only a couple of limbs left lying in the path. I heard some animal plunging about in the underbrush and, looking, saw his V-shaped face through the branches, with the white nose and white streak up between the black cheeks and eyes, so that he looked, with the rest of him hidden, like some wood spirit or dog-faun; then looked down on the pond that all the bright and warm summer colors were gone and that it was all a soft uniform lead, with a shade or streak of grayish pink smeared along the middle, and the

---

[1] Richard Rovere (1915–79), American journalist and critic, was the Washington correspondent of *The New Yorker* for many years.

old green of the banks only just perceptible when you stared, in the dark walls that ringed it round. Light mists that seemed to emanate from the shore were rapidly sliding out. Absolutely smooth and calm: a little fish would now and then punctuate this perfect peace with a small and brief spilling of ripples. —Dark green walls of wooded high banks, beyond the darker and dimmer reflected hills —water a smooth dead and livid lead (livid and leaden).

Intoxication after making love: I don't remember feeling this when I was young, but have had it both with G. and with Elena. When I was young I felt refreshed and elated. Now I have a sort of drunkenness or druggedness that must sometimes remain for a quarter of an hour. It is as a dulling exhilaration, a stupefaction by sweetness. —I sometimes have a letdown afterwards—but at other times I feel energetic and cheerful.

Gull Pond with Reckie, October '46—

> I am Dr. Dugashvili:
> Let me feel your pulse, *moi milyi*
> If you are a Trotskyish-ka
> You must have a little *chistka*[2]

[2] In this quatrain about Stalin, EW has added Russian endings for his rhyme scheme.

RENO, MINDEN, CARSON CITY

[EW and Elena Thornton took up residence in the autumn of 1946 in Reno in order to obtain their respective divorces. In his book *The Cold War and the Income Tax*, EW indicates that his earnings from *Memoirs of Hecate County*, which had become a best seller, helped him "pay for two divorces."]

Drive from Reno to Minden, afternoon of Oct. 25. A little rain and snow storm occurred on the way and made some very queer contrasts of indigo-blue sky and yellow or copper trees. Then you had, above the dull tawny shadowed mountains, the pale blue of the clearing sky. The white ranches with pale cottonwoods or aspens and Lombardy poplars around them on the flat plain ringed in by the mountains.

—When a lightening orange of the sun came out in the fluid clouds above one of the barren summits, it gave me vague ideas of Japan, and I thought about how the Americans seemed never—up to the war with Japan at least— really to have got a hold on the Pacific. They had come

out to the Californian coast, delighted to find that Promised Land—so much food, such wonderful weather: it
made them well pleased and genial. Then the monopolies
had eaten it all up; then the San Francisco fire; Hearst,
the immigration from Iowa, the movies. A goofiness, a
vicious intolerance, bemused God-seekers on the sunlit
tops of mountains. Moving toward the setting sun: in-
valids who had come to die, suicides in San Diego. (The
gold-mining days in Nevada passing into the days of the
divorce mill and the restaurants full of gambling tables
and slot machines: men with decadent brown fringes of
beard and pasty and oily faces.) They had never got a
grip on the Pacific, did not know how to adapt themselves
to it, build on it, make it serve them for the [illegible]
work of their race. Buoyancy, mysticism, lack of solidity,
feeling of not going anywhere, of the California writers:
McTeague [by Frank Norris] and Saroyan, the relent-
lessly hopeless and the ridiculously hopeful, equally pur-
poseless. —Our satisfaction, our projects, our ideals for
society, subsided into mere well-being, were lost over the
ocean spaces, diluted into the light and the fluid clouds.
We were left with God, liquor, love—that no longer
spurred the passions or sharpened the will. All were pas-
sive, the Pacific had conquered us. We sat with the sun
in our lap, drugged, benumbed, and finally sterilized—
like the dried cats found in the desert, the mummified
Indians two thousand years old, exhibited in the Carson
City Museum. —Was there something still there for us
that the Japanese, that the Eastern Chinese, had had, but
which we could not get our arms around?

—Flurry of snow—snow-penciled crevices of mountains.

Minden: The fine fishbones of poplars, when the wind
had blown the leaves away, against the pale blue even
sky. —The square-piled stacks of blond straw, in which
we saw a ground squirrel disappear. E., with her blue

socks, black ballet slippers, gray slacks, light blue blouse,
gray eyes, against the high flat wall of the straw stack, at
the foot of which we would sit, getting out of the coldish
stiffish wind into a warm steady afternoon sun, as if beside
the lifeboats on the protected side of a ship.

The little square at Minden with a white bandstand
and tall gold-ball-topped flagstaff in the middle, and, all
around, little one-story model white western houses—the
streets lined with weeping birches of the brightest purest
white, with long twigs of a kind of dull maroon hanging
like old-fashioned beaded curtains. A young red setter that
first barked at me, making galumphing retreats, then came
and made friends with me when I coaxed. Smiling bespectacled housewife looked out of the front door. The
next day, a yellow cat followed us that was just the color
of the drying leaves. The cat, the leaves, the dry pastures,
the straw stacks, the buff that the mountains showed
sometimes, alternating with the pale slaty shadows. —Like
Holland: round-topped yellow haystacks, steers and sheep,
straight planting of poplars like Hobbema,[1] little ranch
houses islanded on the plain, straight irrigation ditches,
with little locklike dams at intervals. Brown white-faced
cattle that followed us to the big gate, thinking we would
let them out, gazing at us with their stupid gelded faces.
Black-and-white magpies with long wings. —The sun, a
mere white light, withdraws behind the rocky ridge, leaving the cold Pacific dark that always seems sudden and
sad to an Easterner.

Reno Roaring Camp: Covered wagon and very primitive but imposing cigar-store Indian outside, big wooden
wagon wheel embedded in outside wall. —Long bar, with

---

[1] Meindert Hobbema (1638–1709), the last of the great
Dutch landscape painters.

collection of bottles almost as varied and complete as the collection of guns and other weapons—saddles for bar seats that bucked when you put a nickel in—large painting of Custer's Last Stand, smaller painting, rather spooky and not so bad, of stranded covered wagon, under gray sky, with tatters of cloud trailing west, with a coyote, a little wooden, standing behind it, and a long rifle and white human and ox bones lying on the slope below. —Strung up under the ceiling along the sides of the room, fine specimens, mostly black and red, of brougham, gig, buckboard, etc.—the guns framed under glass and against yellow satin; red with pink and green stained-glass panes, and rosettes of varicolored electric bulbs that revolved; the cheap pistols, authentic or specimens of the same make and style, with which the Presidents were assassinated; a large knife that inflicted a wound which no surgeon could successfully sew up and which was sure to give rise to gangrene: Colts, six-shooters, blunderbusses, muskets, firelocks, guns with which "The American revolutionists beat Hell out of the British," guns used by Jesse James, many guns with beautifully chased metal fittings.

—The old calliopes, music boxes, hand organs, jukeboxes, electric pianos, old-fashioned pianolas that, when you put in a nickel, a dime, a quarter, or fifty cents, broke out in loud hootings, gibberings, cymbal bangings, of old tunes from ancient waltzes to *Alexander's Ragtime Band,* that were somehow the most gruesome feature of the place, which, galvanized out of the past, but quite without romance, the corpses of old prospectings, debauches, shootings, and harlotries. —The peep show, where the darkness gradually brightened to reveal a naked woman, apparently in three dimensions, as in a stereopticon, reclining on a divan (there was a dark red pillow lying between the picture and the place where you looked, in order to increase the illusion)—about her lips there played a smile of invitation, across the triangle of hair that crowned her thighs hung a dark wisp of veiling—and when the vision was brilliantly clear, the veil began to be blown toward her feet till it laid bare the whole of this; then it subsided, and the picture dimmed, returning to darkness again. Another peep show displayed the/a hanging of a badman and was not without its grisly effectiveness: first, you saw a colored figure of Justice, noble and feminine, on the flat background; then there materialized, in three dimensions, in front of this, the hanged man, with gray-sallow face, popping eyes, and lips drawn back from grinning teeth, who swayed back and forth. —A few gambling tables, many slot machines, a place where you shot at something—the whole place filled with old tricks and knickknacks, stuck into every corner: a wooden American eagle, large carved cupids in pale varnished woodwork. —Another covered wagon with an imitation of the desert underneath, full of oxen ribs and skulls. —In the middle of the front room, a large imitation campfire, with an oven made of stones and long-handled iron implements to handle the meat: a gray square of imitation desert, around which were grouped in a circle comfortable chairs and couches; in front of them were sawed-off stumps, on which the drinks could be placed. —The whole thing a perfect example of the decadence of modern Reno. —Collected by a man who wore an old-fashioned western goatee.

Carson City: Celebration for Admission Day: Oct. 31. So quiet and desultory, halfhearted music, lack of organization, inexpert drum majorettes, who, after the parade, performed revolutions, while the plate-faced shawl-wrapped Indians looked on. A few Indian-chief head-dresses, a few silver-studded saddles, a few coffee-colored (palomino) horses. Chamber of Commerce and Hollywood—designed as an attraction for tourists. Crinolines and embroidered shawls. Lincoln and General Grant. Only lively number American Legion dervishes. Sharp-nosed pale-blond girl: one with gold curls on horseback not bad-looking. —Young man at station with black sideburns, black shoestring tie, and pistol in holster—looked as if he had been affected by Hollywood Westerns.

Hunter's Lodge: Italian spaghetti restaurant crammed with slot machines and gambling tables. A woman shot large semi-transparent green dice over a green baize marked off in numbered spears. Man with face fringe and depraved gray eyes who looked blankly without joining one's gaze: Eight's the point in the gambling joint: Here comes the dirty old tray. The shooter goes away (or astray); Here come the boys from Minoite; How it is! How sweet it is; The hard way! —The easy way!

Pyramid Lake: Tufa masses that made glyptodon backs; black sand that Elena said reminded her of black crêpe de chine sheets, sprinkled with the white grains of some tiny limpetlike mollusc. Indian arrowheads among flat bluish stones, bits of broken glass. A whitened skull and long beak, bent at the end. Water sometimes jade, as in Max Ernst's painting; but, when we got there Nov. 30, a blue like the Bay of Naples, which later faded to something softer, then made a harmony with the dimming sky and with the shadows that blued the buff mountains, as they rapidly closed in to engulf them. (The shadow of the pyramid itself began to show as a sharp black nick, stretching up the rock-wall behind it.) On the way home, the water had assumed a pinkish-bluish opalescence that harmonized with the purpling mountains. —The mountains on the way, like the back of great tawny saurians; one with two horses on a dropped pachydermatous neck, that

Walter Clark[2] had always called "The Rhinoceros." In one place, in summer, there was sometimes a mirage of a ranch.

Clark's stories about the lake: bay stallion, with black tail and mane—saw him twice with his remuda herd of mares: first time, he was young—when he saw them, he drove the mares up the mountain, would nip them in the hind flank to make them go, then began to come after Clark and a girl who was with him—retreating, W.C. would stand still at intervals and yell, temporarily giving the stallion pause; then they were rescued by a friend who drove up in the car behind them, and scared him away with the klaxon. Four years later, he saw him again: he had grown to be gigantic and magnificent; he came after them in their car and they were afraid he was going to attack them, rearing up and throwing himself at the front of the car, breaking the glass with his hooves, but again they scared him away. C. was indignant with some man with a plane that he had met at a dude ranch who had told him about driving a herd of wild horses over one of the steep mountainsides. He wouldn't be able to forgive him if he ever did anything to that stallion.

At one point, on the opposite shore, where you could see a mountain pass, there was supposed to be an Indian burial ground that had never been explored and was always guarded by Indian sentinels. One fellow said he had rowed across and found a great wide staircase, cut in the stone; but Walter, when he had gone there, had not been able to find anything of the kind. A party that had been there before him in 1922 had reported that they had never seen anybody, but that they had had the feeling of being

[2] Walter van Tilburg Clark (b. 1909), American novelist, author of *The Ox-Bow Incident* (1940).

watched, and that when they had waked up in the morning, they had found an enclosure marked around them with the prints of moccasined feet and a long arrow sticking up in the ground. They turned back. Walter had walked through a narrow gorge, at the end of which, looking up, he had seen two big skulls made of tufa set high up on either side. Now it was hard to believe he had seen them—it had rejoined the domain of legend. He, too, had had the sensation that somebody was watching him there —and you sometimes felt it at the pyramid.

Beyond the mountains on the left, where the needles were [situated] (sometimes they were dramatically lit), was where the bones of the saber-toothed tiger and the three-toed horse had been found. —His story about going to the bottom of some kind of abandoned mine (coal?)— crawled through the narrow tunnel, began to get rather uncomfortable at the feeling of the top pressing down. In a small chamber at the very end, he was amazed to find, modeled in the clay, a panorama of pornographic tableaux, like the framed groups in a natural history museum—a sort of rake's progress, he said, with all the details very carefully done: there was, for example, a cupid designed on a chamber pot under one of the beds. —When I suggested exploring by plane the mysterious **burying ground,** the idea was not enthusiastically received. This, I gathered, would be to cheat on the game of playing pioneers.

At Minden: late in stay, two days in succession, after three or four drinks (I went in for double manhattans): I would be delayed for a time, then gradually and comfortably come, but with a final terrific vibration, during which I could only hold it in her still and stiff, and while the tense charges would be shot into her in close succession, she, too, would vibrate, rigid, and sometimes fart in complete dedication that let all her bodily functions go.

VIRGINIA CITY AND TAHOE

Virginia City, Dec. 6. —Late in the afternoon—4:30 or 5: the little Church of St. Mary's in the Mountains, with its red brick, its plain red slope-necked roof ending in angular shoulders, its white steeple and small rose-window and other trimmings, against the wide sky and far-rolling mountains—the sky a great hanging gray cloud of moisture, with flaws of a delicate blue that showed through the whiter strips of cloud, where both cloud and sky seemed more fluid than they usually did in Nevada, with a subtlety in these distances—the blue series of hills that receded and diminished like echoes, each a distinct shade —that was so lacking in the human form and even in the fine little church that had to brace itself and stand straight, pricking the [sky] with its slim little needle that ended with a wiry cross; but the sun, so little spendthrift, in departing, had, to the left, rubbed in a dull pink touch which balanced the cold ruddy church. Immediately beyond, the curving hills were dark green-gray and sallow: sagebrush and the barren dirt that had no longer the interest of containing gold.

The neat white-icing trimmings of the church answered the down-scrawling snow-ridges on the mountains in the background immediately behind (the re-echoing vista was further to the left). To see all this, one looked out from the steep terrace of the main street, where there happened to be a stretch with no buildings.

The other and older and abandoned and broken-windowed little church looked, where one glimpsed it down a side street, yellow-brown and with the triple-shuttered dome eyebrowed windows in the tower, like some kind of alley cat cornered and scared by an enemy, pulling its legs together and hunching its lean back.

—The main street under the snowy dome of Mount Davis, refreshing, though so barren in contrast: that long ramshackle wavering and tottering grim succession of brick or yellow or gray-clapboard fronts, with their balconies undulating in ruin and thin tall spindling pillars, like everything else, seeming about to totter in collapse, with the plank walls that heaved and sunk on that hillside that was worm-eaten with the old empty diggings—all so ugly and so crude and now so decayed, all the more grisly, I think, for the touch of elongated elegance that made it at least human, recognizable as the shed habitation of human aspirations and amenities, under the monumental desert indifference of the heavens and the hills.

—The saloons, with antiques and their dates, their chandeliers and old lamps and pictures. The best museum was the Bucket of Blood, where the stuff from the "Bowers Mansion" was exhibited; the most sociable, the Crystal Bar, which was also a soda fountain, where the women and children gathered. —The doctor who had been in town a month and whose wife came to get him from the bar. —Most of them were more or less deserted: one didn't see how they made it pay. The big high school and every-

thing else perched precariously on the side of the hill—
junky look of old lumber—the yellow naked piles of dirt
beyond—the old posters plastered around, some of them
fairly recent, some summer circus, but faded and no different from the ones that were carefully being collected.
(Clark's story about the little man who was stabbed by
the desperado, when he dared to put his arm around him,
and cut to pieces on top of the bar.) Not romantic, only
sordid, disgusting, at its most exciting, macabre. —Piper's
Opera House up in the hill—its mortal [illegible] inside,
old posters and photographs, wobbling stairs that were
barred off, sloping stage, dance floor that had been rein-
forced.

—On the way there, E. had remarked that the country,
with its gray sagebrush, looked leprous. —On the way
home, everything seemed done in washed ink: formless,
grandiose, murky, like the poetry of Robinson Jeffers
(which is also rather insubstantial in the California, not
the Nevada, way): great hanging bank of gray or black
mist, as usual perfectly immobile.

—lean façades with long cramped windows

—little brick newspaper office where Mark Twain wrote
the Jumping Frog.

E. Dec. 6. Under the barely grizzled and frosted raspberry blanket, her hips, which had grown bigger at
Minden, looked beautifully molded and her slender legs
disappeared into the tail of a mermaid. —When I came
back from the bathroom, I saw the light hit on her tail
and the back of her instep—I seized it and she began to
laugh—with her Russian V-shaped mouth and her green
eyes and pointed nose like her mother (quite different
from her German personality)—she had hidden the whiskey bottle but put it on the pillow next to her.

—Several nights before, when I had seen her lying
asleep—her head was off the pillow and lying sideways on

the bed, with her mouth in a satisfied smile and her eyebrows, so blond and urbane, good-naturedly satisfied—
and with her slim darling white blue-raised arm bent, with
the forearm thrown up and her head resting on it below
the elbow—so white and tender and blue-veined.

—All this then was so fine and seemed strong but was
rather fragile—knee injured in skiing, with its indenting
scar, impaired muscles, couldn't wear high heels (or did
this have something to do with going around with short
men?).

—Another night, while she was asleep in bed, she had
brought her hand against her temple, with the flesh at her
elbow brought squashed and round and the strength of
her upper arm accented, and her face—unlike the other
night—in repose and much stronger, with its full lips and
wide-nostriled nose, and eyebrows alert and eyelids not
stolidly dropped, and short brown hair over the clear blond
forehead—her foreshortened arm looked stronger—with
the sheet tucked back under her chin—wonderful curve
of hip under the raspberry blanket, so much fuller (that
is, just full enough) than when we had come on here—
with her awkward gait, her praying-mantis head. —But
she has always that beauty that shines like a light—the
intelligence you can't get a grip on or wrestle with in an
exchange of wisecracks, love that is tempered by intelligence and knows how and where to place itself. —She is
beautiful: she can't quite do it justice, with her manners
and ways of speaking taught her by her governesses and
her constitution (which revolves on in a large point of
view in the present inflamed nationalist situation) of German and Russian and French and Swiss.

—Propitiatory, too anxious to please; but extremely
capable, quite cool-minded, checks up the American
woolly-mindedness.

Lake Tahoe, Dec. 7 and earlier visit—first visit. Quite cheerfully Californian to get up, from the gray sagebrush and the dead barren hills, with which we'd been ringed round at Minden, among the pines and the snow, with the fresh smell of winter woods and lake water (not a rank or very fragrant smell but pleasant after the plain). The whole place, with its screens of tall trees, through which the wide lake was seen, and its lodges of reddish pinewood almost Japanesey, had for me the quality of a period piece —associating itself with old drawings for articles in the *Century* magazine, and with Aunt Laura's long visit, at the time I was a child, to the California relatives. It was, even at the beginning of this century, still something that was fresh for the Americans, a possession they had just discovered, that everybody wanted to take a look at—and the people who lived there would be crying, Our sunlight, our flowers, our restaurants, our magnificent redwood trees, our gaiety and plenty. —But then, as soon as you crossed the state line to Nevada, you saw that modern Los Angeles had crawled up and thrust forward its loathsome head: fancy snack bars, cheap cabins, the characteristic bad taste at once whimsical, commercial, and slovenly.

2nd visit: We walked out [to] a point of land, with clean reddish large-grained sand, greenish and liver-colored marking, of sand and rock under the clear water, naked pine trunks lying on the shore and brittle little bushes dried gray; and, at the end, out in the water, a little bay hemmed in by great gray sugar-loaf boulders. Complete silence: a floating duck flew off with a faint cry of alarm; one of the big cones dropped (without wind) from a tree, and we heard it hit a limb or two before it fell to the ground. There was a constant variety in the landscape: when we first saw the lake, driving up, it presented a steel-mirror surface; then, when we were close to it on the point, the water, as it rippled, had a fluidity, a liquidity, that was not exactly silky, not exactly oily, but seemed to possess some softness, amenity, that made it different from the hard eastern lake water; then, where bright light fell on a section of the mountains across the lake, they looked, in contrast to the dark walls on either side in the shade of the dark hanging curtain of cloud, paradisial and almost unreal, a pale blue at once fresh and dim, which had its counterpart in a blue patch of water that looked as insubstantial as some volatile liquid like other (?). Beyond there, the subtleties and softness, the felicities, of the California "scenery"—the prospect of unlimited amplitude, the landscape with no real frame or shape, the panorama that always unrolled with no beginning or ending—but in which there was so much to be enjoyed, so much natural assurance and peace—the western country, with its possibilities, that everyone had wanted to taste and see—but now grown banal and annoying with everything that, all too soon, we had brought to it: Reno divorces, Hollywood, sordid liquor, and love in the fairyland Elysium of a uniform climate (formless and "uncomposed" as the expanding landscape was, it was fine both in serenity and in subtle change: blues and purples and gray and inky glooms succeeding and blending into one another); and, on the way home, a brief golden sunset: the sun a round pale gold dazzling round font as liquid as the lake, poised on the edge of the hills, then quickly dropping and lighting them with a fringe of molten gold—then our descent to the desert—on our first trip the big bad blue and pink sky like a grocer's colored Christmas calendar, on the second, a dimmer form of this, and then the gruesome dead rocky formations in the swiftly thickening dusk, like cactus clusters stripped even of their thorns or handfuls of huge dinosaur bones—air in the plain as we sank down toward the bottom warm and dead after the air up there—drab and neutral colors, uninteresting darkness of night, surrounded by sagebrush and mute stolid steers.

At the rather pleasant little bar at Tahoe (pine buildings with red neon signs) I put 50¢ in a slot machine and got back three 50¢ pieces, then a dime in a third, which I lost. But the bartender charged me $1.50 for E.'s one old-fashioned and my one Martell brandy.

Crowninshield:[1] Jeanne Ballot had told me that he had called her up and said that he was John L. Lewis and had just done his eyebrows up with blue ribbons.

[1] Frank Crowninshield, editor of *Vanity Fair.* See *The Twenties*, pp. 32–44.

WEST COAST

[*Memoirs of Hecate County* was published in March 1946. By May it was a best seller and provided EW with much-needed funds for the complications of his and Elena's divorces. By summer the book was under attack from various "anti-vice" organizations and was the subject of court action in a number of states. While on the West Coast, EW went with Elena Mumm—after their residence at Reno—to San Francisco, where he discussed the *Hecate County* case with lawyers. Later that month he and Elena were married.]

San Francisco, December 11–15. —Memories of 1915, when I went out to the Exposition with Mother and Father—the elevators were modernized at the St. Francis, but I recaptured the tall figure of father going out through the front folding doors, myself getting lost among the stairways and halls coming in through the door on the side, where there was a confusion of levels, and reading in bed —Chesterton's *Of All Things,* I think—on a bed of which it seemed to me that the mattress had always a little bit fallen short at the head, as our mattresses did now—I had

wanted then to be famous as a writer: now I was, though
the kind of fame that *Hecate County* was having at the
moment in San Francisco was not very satisfactory. Union
Square had been built up; I recognized the queer murals
in the dining room at the St. Francis on the right of the
lobby, though I did not this time go into it. —It was fun,
after the Minden Inn, to look out the *oeil de boeuf* in the
little bathroom and see the stone lion's-heads of the cor-
nice. Below us the trees in the square, a part of its rectangular formal design, were being hung with long strings
of silver tinsel and colored electric bulbs—fun to watch
the people walking at the peculiar angle from which one
saw them—bold step or stride of the girls. —I realized the
period character of this part of California even more in
San Francisco: well-stocked bookshops still arrested in the
Stevenson-Kipling period; authors at the turn of the century that were no longer in evidence in the East: Gertrude
Atherton, R. H. Davis;[1] lots of Americana, especially
about the West. Things, I felt more strongly than ever,
had never been the same since the earthquake (a passage
in M.T.'s *Roughing It* shows that even before the big one
you were not supposed to talk about this danger): the
agreement to ignore the earthquake had always been and
had always remained a fundamental factor in S.F. life.
(Mr. Andrews at Minden Inn had remarked on the fact
that the principal fault ran right under Montgomery St.
We had a hell of a fire here forty years ago—MacInnes'
law partner at lunch.) But Maurice Farber's brother, who
had come back to San Francisco to practice psychoanalysis
and seemed to be finding the San Franciscans so cheerful
and so healthy that there was really little field for his

[1] Gertrude Atherton (1857–1948), best known for her novel
Black Oxen (1923); Richard Harding Davis (1864–1916), a
journalist who covered most wars of the turn of the century,
wrote lively if superficial novels.

ministrations—he said that it would take years to educate them up to being analyzed. A man with a neurosis may commit a crime, and if he does, he may not be convicted. Mark Schorer said that the attitude in the newspaper report to a case of rape, for example, was, We don't believe this.

Gigantic party for us at the MacInneses'[2] (Pacific Street, or Avenue, one of those steep streets, where you wonder that a taxi is able to park). Mrs. MacI. (from Oklahoma) met us on stairs with a touch of something like Hollywood Park Avenue. Enormous perspectives and spaces, wide stairways and big open doorways, with lots of light-colored California woodwork, so different from anything in the East—yet so much of that period of the '8os, the '9os, the early 1900s. The women here had period clothes, too, as I found last spring they did in Virginia. Amplitude and plenitude of California life, openness and hospitality. Mrs. MacI. was good-natured and simple, after her first slight touch of local swank. Two little boys and one little girl—mostly the images of their father, and, like him, as Elena said, having the appearance of being highly successful—full of merriment, good looks, and health, injected themselves into the party. The current jump of the big super-giftshop, the psychiatrist who testified at trials, the lady who had lived in Europe (with an enormous round-brimmed pink period hat), the young man from the D.A.'s office who had prosecuted *Hecate County* at the second trial—not attractive, but told me, the second time I ran into him, that he did not consider *Hecate County* indecent—"I thought it was rather silly." (I endorsed copies of the book for the two judges.) Later I autographed a copy of the book for one of the colored

[2] James MacInnes, the San Francisco attorney involved in the defense of *Hecate County*.

maids and a dollar bill for another. Paul Elder, who kept the big bookshop; a young and evidently well-to-do Jewish boy, who wanted to write but was not nearly so much on his toes as the type of the same kind in the East.

—We had some people in to cocktails at the St. Francis. Jim Paramore[3] had grown fatter and was approximating the shape of his father, but he had a somewhat worried bewildered look, as if the way that the world had been going had continued to baffle and surprise him till gradually his urbane eyebrows had been driven apart on his forehead. He was quiet—though, when things were said to him, he responded in his old manner, with a laugh or a repartee. When I said, in the course of a general conversation, that I had had an awfully good time in San Francisco when I had been there thirty years ago, he said, with promptness and sharpness that sounded a little bitter, "Everybody had a good time thirty years ago!" —I laughed and he laughed in his old way—but that was a little the note of the occasion. —The activity and profit of the wartime had lapsed and left rather a vacuum—they had been counting on having the United Nations there, but this had failed them and now they didn't know what to count on. They felt they were going to be important when our connections with the Pacific were fully made, but in the meantime they were out on a limb. —I asked Jim about Santa Barbara—he almost never went there any more—there was almost nobody he knew there—on the beach, since the war, almost nobody spoke English any more. In the earliest phase, you could see at a glance who'd already arrived at any party by the carriages outside the door, and when you went home afterwards, you could just get in

[3] Friend of EW and of Margaret Canby. See *The Twenties* and *The Thirties*, *passim*.

and let the horse take you there. —Reggie Fernald[4] had finally died—it was a wonder that he'd managed to stay alive so long. Clarence Matty had gone crazy and died. Chris ?, who had had the private zoo, had died (or killed himself?)—he had tried to get out of being taxed by making his animals public property, willing them to the town. Jim had just sold the old pear ranch, which had cost him no end of money. Stan Gwynn had fallen off the roof when he was taking a sunbath there one day, and they couldn't be sure it hadn't been suicide—he had never worked much even when he came back to San Francisco. —The stucco Greek buildings, the color of the crust of Camembert cheese, with their fountains and fluted columns, that were still left—the old Fine Arts Building— from the Exposition of 1915—still rather beautiful and thrilled me a little as I remembered meeting Alice at the entrance to go with her to Walter Damrosch's concert, and spending the day there alone: the nude figures, a girl and a youth, on the columns; the relatively pretty and smart-looking prostitute who had spoken to me at night in the street, as I was coming home from the theater (in my hotel bedroom at night I had fantasies of a complacent chambermaid). We found, in the city gallery, an exhibition of paintings that looked exactly like the things I had seen in the F.A. Building thirty years ago: artists like Gari Melchers, rather flimsy and sketchy American Impressionism of that period—they may even have been the same pictures. It was a very poor collection we saw, but the local painting and taste in painting was evidently not very good —the gift arts and crafts at Gump's—modern jewelry, pottery, etc.—seemed, on the other hand, first-rate. Col-

---

[4] Reggie Fernald, Clarence Matty, Stan Gwynn, EW's friends of earlier years, figure in the preceding volumes of the journals.

lection of a local character who had evidently had a genius for getting the weakest sketches and miscarriages of even the most uniformly brilliant painters (Picasso).

—Visit to Alice Osborne and her friend Mrs. Kress, in whose small house in Oakland she lived. Mrs. Kress's remark to Elena, evidently based on the newspaper story about her being six feet tall, about the chair which she indicated for her to sit on being better for tall people— made Elena feel, she said, like a Brobdingnagian. Grieg on the piano, Andrea del Sarto on the wall. At once produced a photograph album, with pictures of all the eastern as well as the western relatives—all extremely touching to me, and I realized as we were going back in the taxi, and I was trying to tell Elena about it, that I couldn't really make her understand—something that only Americans understood. I don't think I had ever realized before how completely all that was over: all those people, those Americans of the turn of the century who had come down from the early Americans, were either nobody now, like poor Alice, or had turned into something else. I have often felt, and then felt most poignantly, that, since I have the ability to express myself in writing, which hasn't appeared to the same extent among the rest of my family, that I must tell about them so that they should be expressed and should not die out without their goodness, their enjoyments, and their pathos being put on record. They were the first people after the pioneers who—like Jim Paramore's family—had loved fresh and futile California. Alice was shrinking now in her little white wooden house on the long cheap and boring boulevard which had just been renamed after MacArthur. It was true that she was an old lady, as she had written Mother to warn me—I should not even have been able to summon, though I remembered it had been there, what had been pretty and touching in her pale blond youth, if it had not been brought back to me by the pictures in the album—as Elena said, the missed possibilities one felt in the sensitive and fine-modeled face. She had been to art school (with the girl who married Boardman Robinson), had painted miniatures, of which she had kept a few (not wonderful) which she showed me in two rows in a big frame—had been working most of her life as secretary for an Episcopal minister in Oakland. —There had been the people—like the eastern Kimballs and Wilsons—and how frail they now seemed, and how provincial, too, beside E.; but they had been the Americans, the frank, the free, the first, the adventurous, who had lived in the society that Jefferson had said was something new under the sun. Aunt Laura had gone to California with Grandmother to visit the western Kimballs. It seemed to me she had spent a year, though it may not have been so long. She brought back an album of pictures—she and Grandmother, I think, just emerging from driving through a redwood tree—and talked about it for years afterwards: Chinatown, the beautiful flowers that they had in spring, for example. She brought back the baked clay top of a trap-door spider's nest and told me stories about tarantulas. —Grandfather Kimball's brother who had come out to get his TB cured. Big strapping girl at the lunch who, in 1915, had almost removed my hand in shaking it—she had married and was dead now, it seemed.

Thoughts about myself and family: My feelings in so many other family connections—grandparents, father and mother, uncles and aunts—that, falling below them in my character in some respects, I must make up for it by concentrating [on] my literary ability, not merely to tell about them, but to bring their virtues into my writing, make my writing exemplify their virtues. Raymond Holden[5] once

---

[5] Husband of Louise Bogan.

expressed surprise at my saying I admired my family (Grandfather Kimball, father and uncles especially) and even felt a certain inferiority in relation to them, and a necessity of proving myself in relation to them; he said that his own seemed to him such a lot of cold and glazed fish that he wanted to be as unlike them as possible. But it is true that their example has sometimes seemed to me what kept one up when I was depressed or demoralized. —And yet at the same time there is the feeling that I've got to get it, embody it in permanent form, better than they were able to do. Their various strengths and defeats.

—Legend of the wonderful food: I kept telling Elena about it in Nevada, over the flavorless fare of the Minden Inn. Disappointment: the more candid people all said it had long ceased to be true—the others all recommended Joe's. The French and Italian restaurants such as had still been going at the time of my trip in the twenties had entirely disappeared (as had also the little French bookstore on Union Square in a basement, where I had, in 1915, bought *L'Ile des Pengouins*[6] and *Colette Baudoche*). We tried the Backyard, a routine machine-finished semi-bourgeois, semi-bohemian dump. Then there was a new and classy place where the Grabhorns took us, where they tried to make you drink at the bar while you waited for a table even when the tables didn't have to be waited for. I liked it; Elena thought the food not first-rate. The Grabhorns had never been there before, and I doubt whether they will ever go again. The meal we had at the St. Francis wasn't bad; in the big dining room of the other big hotel we couldn't get any service: dark and almost empty, a stage where a show was eventually coming on: Chico Marx the next week, advertized as if a special treat. We

[6] Anatole France's novel of 1908, translated as *Penguin Island*, contains an ironic description of the Dreyfus case.

walked out and tried the grill, where we found exactly the same menu at considerably lower prices—revolting but rather pretty mural in soft pinks, blues, and greens, of (of course) the early days in the West: prospectors, big railroad men, etc., soaring through the air to California; a beautiful hussy of legend—whole thing had a kind of pansy touch.

—MacI.'s way of talking—slight pompous misuse of words—something was to be esteemed (*Hecate County*) —see his letters to me. There was also the element of the whimsical and the humorous, as when he had invented the story that Hearst had set out to get me because I had written in *The New Republic* that if all the money he had spent on Marion Davies were brought together, it would light the city of Rochester for 150 years.

BACK EAST

Dream about Margaret [Canby], mid-January '47. I had married someone else (not Elena) whom I thought I liked very much, then I got a letter from her in California. There she had been all the time and I hadn't realized, hadn't looked her up—I could have been back with her and not have had to marry again. I would write to her right away, but I couldn't undo my marriage—yet I was excited by the prospect of seeing her, of talking to her again.

Feb. 16. Sunday afternoon—full of lust. I had a slight hangover from our having the Hacketts to dinner, with Rosalind and Topie, and Jack Hall after dinner, the night before: E. came and lay in bed with me. I hadn't intended to make love to her till after I had shaved and had a bath, but, while we were lying in each other's arms, I felt, what rarely happens when a woman is actually with me, that strong combination of love and lust that usually comes when I am longing for someone who is not there. It was the idea of postponement, I suppose—the not taking her at the moment I desired her; and when I abandoned the notion of postponement, my appetite and passion mounted. We did 69 first. She responded to it, flushed darkly—which is rare with her—put her legs up so that I could push it down into her. I was terrifically swollen and hot—"You were so big!" she said afterwards —and she got that green wolfish look in her eyes that is so unlike her ordinary blue-eyed and sweet expression. I went on and on, not coming, but with constant protracted enjoyment, an enjoyment all (saltily) physical. It was like the dreams I had been having lately, in which I would go on for a long time in the confidence of enjoying somebody or be making love to somebody for a very long time without coming and wake up without having an emission. (Lately, for some reason, I had dreamed in this way of several of my old girls, from Edna Millay to Anna.) I suppose that as I grow older, I am getting slower in coming; but this seems to be an advantage from Elena's point of view. She came before I did, as a matter of fact; and then, when I followed, a minute or two later, it was not with the climactic impulsion that, when we were perfectly synchronized, she has met with her emphatic giving herself in a final vaginal squeeze that has sometimes almost forced me out, but with a shudder that was almost involuntary and release of semen that had been kept back and that seemed to my mind dark and blocked, not rapturously rhythmic and free. It was our most strongly animal encounter. The occasion, I suppose, was heightened by the fact we had snatched a moment—after having adapted our habits to a routine of having other people in the house—when, at the time when on normal days we should have been working or eating, sometime a little after noon, Rosalind was out of the house and Nina [Chavchavadze] up in her room listening to the radio. —My erection remained and it seemed not a game or artificial but a part of our hot physical love, and, when she came back from the bathroom, I told her to make it quite stiff. She was dry now and I applied some cold cream, and this time it was, as she said, very "slippery." I went on and on again, though it was less satisfactory now —sometimes thought of imaginary women, as I had not done the first time. She came—I continued a little longer, then laid off in a perspiration. Lay suffused with that enduring drunkenness. Then went down to my study and drank a bottle of ginger ale and ate what was left of the party nuts. She curled up in the middle room on the love seat with her beautiful bare feet, read a little (F. Perkins[1] on Roosevelt), and went to sleep. I went back to bed and spent the rest of the afternoon till late dinner straightening out the manuscript of John Bishop's novel: wonderfully quiet, clear-minded, content.

—The night before, when we had been sitting in the living room, hashing over the guests, she had lain stretched out on the sofa—she had taken off her little red ballet shoes and had her so wonderfully pretty pink toes up on the end of the sofa, so that I could just partly see them from where I sat. They had excited me, but I thought I had had too much to drink to be able to make love to her properly, so went on drinking with Nina and later in my study alone, till E. came down and rescued me. Sunday, when I had made love for the first time, I kissed her feet with much pleasure, running my lips over her toes. She had just cut and painted her toenails a few days before. Her feet, even when at their cleanest—and they are really always clean, because she takes so many baths—have that faint cheeselike smell that is almost a taste and that I like.

Elena said that women, just before their periods, were seized with an anxiety to clean up the house, put things

---

[1] Frances Perkins, FDR's Secretary of Labor.

away, etc., some idea of making a nest, which had something to do with the animal apprehension that they were
going to have a baby.

The Amens,[2] *spring and summer 1947.* We met John
in Central Park, sitting with what I took to be one of his
plain good-natured drinking girls. He got up and greeted
me with a lot of laughing. Later, when we saw him, I
realized that Europe had had some sort of effect on him,
at once revelatory and sobering. After many drinks, at the
end of dinner, he spoke scornfully of coming back and
finding people occupied with "their little books," etc.,
when there were so much more important problems in the
world. But when I talked to him about Europe, it seemed
to be merely a question of "having fun"—flying down to
Cannes or Paris—so much pleasanter than in this country. French story, *c'est là qu'il plaie*—filthy limerick: before telling me the former, he asked whether I understood
French. Marion and I did a little Edgarly at his expense:
the broadening effects of travel, etc. Except when drinking at the drink hour, he seemed worried, nervous, sad-
dened. One felt when one was with them a strain, the
strain of their being together after a couple of years of
separation—they had just had a holiday in Jamaica (they
had seen Dick Knight in Florida)—they were not really
in harmony or intimate. Marion presented blank calloused-
over surfaces, talked banalities (someone didn't have a
flair somehow) as she had always tended to do—for this
reason she had always been apt at Edgarly, but, I thought,
in a more lifeless and unconscious way; had lost a good
deal of her good looks and charm; her face was pale and
dry, her thin beak and round blue eyes seemed depress-

[2] John and Marion Amen, EW's longtime friends. See *The
Twenties* and *The Thirties, passim.*

ingly chickenlike—but on one occasion she wore a well-
cut dress—a purplish-blue flowered pattern on white—
that brought out her excellent figure, with large hips.
—John always brought in a crowd of his assistants and
associates in Germany, as in his Brooklyn phase he had
brought in his politicians and Jewish lawyers. —I asked
him how things were in Germany and he said fine—meaning, as it turned out, that an officer in his position could
live very comfortably there—Oh, it's terrible for the
Germans. One of his pals, a Seattle woman, married and
with children, had never been to Germany or France before, and had evidently had the time of her life: It hadn't
really been written about and ought to be! she exclaimed.
When I tried to pin her down to *what* ought to be written
about, it seemed to be, again, the kind of fun they had
had at Cannes: Why, it's a world where the children have
no parents, the parents have no children, the husbands
have no wives, the wives have no children! You're likely
to meet members of the nobility that just happen to
come in.

—It was curious and rather reassuring and cheerful to
find them in their old apartment, which they had bought
back in the twenties—though, in the meantime, they had
sold it with great trouble and loss. Now they were leasing
it from the present tenants—weren't sure how long they
would be able to keep it. And yet it was something of a
shell—piano, the old books in the bookcase (of many
years back, girlhood and young womanhood), the Zorn
etching of Mrs. Cleveland—and a model of the Nurem-
berg courtroom, which seemed to me to strike a note both
sinister and a little false, and on the piano, a queer-
shaped dark object as to which at first I wasn't sure that
it wasn't a modern *objet d'art*, with its craning mushroom
head, but which turned out to be a small machine used
for clamping documents together. The things that make

the humanity of a home had disappeared during their period of estrangement and the occupancy of alien families, and they couldn't seem to get it back. Yet John was much more like his early self—he had lost his brash publicity façade and I wondered whether he had been having a touch of the neurotic anxiety of his student days when he had been getting through Harvard Law and Louise Fort[3] had let him down. It was pleasant to see him again. He was dissatisfied, evidently, with getting back and going back to his law practice again.

I saw Frances Dell[4] there with her second husband, the son of Tommy and Margaret Payne: coffee-colored, pretty, and cute. They were living somewhere in Harlem.

—Those old highballs of the twenties—John and I both enjoyed sitting around over them, though Marion wanted to get us off to dinner. He couldn't imagine anywhere better to eat than a crowded noisy pseudo-French restaurant where we had to wait for a table—consuming Scotch Mists at the bar—and where he prided himself that he had done something smart by slipping the headwaiter $5 for a table no better than any of the rest.

July '47. Mother at Red Bank, climbing the stairs with the assistance of Jenny: My old bones are creaking. Poor Jenny had lost most of her hair—wore a little net—growth on her temple. Mother so deaf I had to sit down and write her long letters, which she couldn't always read.

[3] Louise and Henrietta Fort, longtime friends of EW. See *The Thirties*, pp. 270–75.

[4] Daughter of Stanley and Marion Cleveland Dell Amen.

BERKSHIRE FESTIVAL, 1947

Berkshire Festival, Aug. '47. —Strange combination, on the part of the townspeople, of unrestrained rapacity in exploiting the Festival-goers, with resentment against them for invading their quiet and moribund community: going in and out of their houses and occupying their bedrooms and making them feel that they are enjoying themselves and deriving inspiration right on the local grounds but from some sources unavailable to the inhabitants. Contrast between the hard-faced and ungracious women who keep rooming houses and run restaurants and, for example, Beethoven's "Hymn to Joy" at the end of the Ninth Symphony.

—Surprise of people like Aaron Copland and Elliott Carter at seeing somebody turn up who is not of the musical world: What are you doing here?, I didn't know you are that much of a music lover, etc.

—Weather heavy and misty, lazy and stifling days, when a bath does not brace you up. —We lay around and slept all we wanted to, though, and it was a great thing to hear music in the country when you were perfectly wide-awake, with none of the strain or distraction that hems in the concerts in the city: a couple of hours of brilliant and intricate sound in the dismal cave of Carnegie Hall between two sharply-bitten-off taxi rides and after a dinner that had to be hurried in order to get there on time.

—*Edith Wharton's house,* the Mount, on the road between Stockbridge and Lenox: white façade with rather small windows on the next-to-top floor with rounded tops, and a little gray cupola with a weather vane—all an imitation of a French château, which, I understand, it also follows inside: stable-garage (with big garden behind it) and gatehouse to match: winding drives, rolling lawn with terraces (terrace?), views of the hills and the little lake by Tanglewood—rich grassy and tree-grown country, so luxuriously upholstered, richly lined—Mrs. Wharton was here put away and protected and arrayed with sables (of vegetation) like the frontispiece to her autobiography.

—Kissing E.'s feet, with their insteps so high on the inside and their dense network of fine blue veins—rubbing my lips back and forth along her toes was erotically stimulating to me, and I would put my hand around her foot under the instep and squeeze it with an erotic pulsation.

—She had been tired and getting a little haggard when we first came, but by the third night, when we went to *Idomeneo,* she looked younger than I had ever seen her and was putting on a kind of little young-girlish act such as I had never known her to do. When I said at dinner that the fricassee of today was the chicken à la king of tomorrow, she gave a little polite giggle, and she paid me polite compliments as if she did not know me well. She looked very pink and blue-eyed, and the wrinkles had vanished from around her eyes. I had made love to her that afternoon without her coming, so that she was stimu-

lated by this, and this may have had something to do with
it. Unlike other women, she never wanted me to go on till
she came—she thought this was not the thing.

—Thunderstorm with loud spasms of thunder that
sounded as if they were cracking large trees, heavy down-
pour of rain and heavy atmosphere that kept us languid
and stupefied, heavy on our beds. E. lay without moving
for a couple of hours, just as I found her when I came
back from Pittsfield with the thermos bottle—she did not
wake up when I opened the door.

—We took a walk to find the house where Elena had
stayed six years before and had been very comfortable and
had breakfast in bed. She had wanted to show me also a
spooky and ornate old house that she remembered. We
went up a dark driveway, blinded by its turnings, looking
for it. There was a man in a driveway that crossed it, who
had stopped in a car and was doing we couldn't tell what
—I thought at first he was watching to see what we were
up to, but evidently not. Within the woods to the right
were houses and a light or two. Then E. saw the dark
grovelike place among the trees where the house had been
pulled down—we crossed the road, with its formidable
streams of cars going both ways, and found the house
where E. had stayed: big and white with long curving
drive. A dog barked. The drive wound around behind the
house, and a man came out and stood on the porch and
said good evening. It turned out that the old lady had
sold the house and gone to live in Florida or somewhere.

—The next night we took another walk which brought
us into something more like the country. I looked up and
saw on the right an almost completely dark pinewood of
tall thin trunks, tufted at the top, that extended up a
slope. It was one of the darkest woods I have ever seen,
and this seemed strange because it was not dense and the
sun was not yet gone; but the slope was screening it from

the sunset, which was only just visible at the top as patches of white or pinkish light, against which the trunks and branches were silhouetted. The whole effect was queer and made you a little curious as to what lay beyond the top of the hill—more woodland or something else? —Along the ground was vague greenery of some kind of low foliage. (Woodland useful for Dream Novel?)

WELLFLEET, 1947

[Wellfleet] Sept. 2. —The pond was dark through the trees as I approached, and then I saw a doe with a well-grown fawn, light and tawny against the green, that made away into the woods, and they were followed, after a moment, by another fawn. As I came down, a black-and-white loon flew away from the smaller pond. The cranberries, yellow, were reddening like little apples and crunched under my feet as I walked. The fringe of water-weed had disappeared. There was a fine white flowering grass, and some little pink-purple phallic-shaped thing. Something that sounded larger than a bullfrog splashed twice in the muddy pond, some distance from the shore and with an interval between the disturbances. The big pond was astonishingly beautiful: the shadow of the high bank with its pines made a dark and blurred stain, on which was a great stretch of dry pale blue (I don't know how to describe this lovely quiet distinguished color) which had the shimmering texture of a dancer's costume that imitates the scaly skin of snakes; and on this blue was a patch of bright sparks of light that moved and went on and off like a cluster of rocket stars. I never saw sparkling

on water so large and live: it was marvelous on the sober blue nappe.

—I went there again, with Dawn [Powell], in late September, or early October, when Elena was in Europe. It was about to rain when we started and a fine drizzle began when we got there that was saturating us before we left. As we came down the road, going there, we saw the same doe and fawn. Dawn had never seen wild deer before and referred to them later as Christmas card deer —and she had never seen cranberries growing. The ponds were dark and dull—I felt it was the end of the season for them.

—A few days later, I found ladies' tresses, very well-developed, and saw a brown, I suppose female duck swimming on the other side of the pond. I sat down so as not to frighten her, and she made a beeline toward me, swimming straight across the pond. She stopped a little way from the shore and began swimming around in a leisurely manner, as if she did not want to venture too near me, but were pretending with dignity that her behavior was unaffected by my presence. When I quacked at her, she simply swam away to the other side of the pond. Nothing I did caused her to fly away.

September 3. *Charley Walker*[1] has acquired what I take to be an *official mannerism,* when a question is asked him, of slightly raising his eyebrows and putting his head on one side, as if he hadn't heard you distinctly but wanted to give you his gracious attention. I had noticed the same thing on the part of the pompous English bookseller in the Charing Cross Road from [whom] I bought the Peacock and of the streamlined press agent at Tangle-

---

[1] Charles Rumford Walker, longtime friend of EW, known for his expertise in labor relations. See *The Twenties* and *The Thirties, passim.*

wood. Elena says that it is intended to put the other person at a disadvantage: it shows that the person who practices it does not consider the person who puts the remark
quite worth his constant attention and sometimes makes
him repeat it. In Charley's case, it probably gives him a
moment to think what he ought to reply to questions for
which he is not prepared. The consequence of living in an
official world is that you develop set replies and responses
to protests, interruptions, and pleas that reach one from
people outside it, and you have to stave them off if you
are not in a position to deal with them. The method of
staving them off becomes a part of one's official technique.
I had enjoyed seeing Charley the time before when we
had gone to dinner at their house, and we had talked
about our school days and I had held forth on Thomas
Nashe and the Zuñis: but tonight I got rather impatient
at the hollow and complacent ideas with which he was
sounding off. Gene Katz was showing that television was
going to bankrupt radio and movies, and that it was going
to introduce a form of popular [entertainment] based on
the lowest common denominator of its public; Charley
was trying to give the situation a reassuring aspect by insisting that, after all, the written word was still free: anybody could still write a book and say whatever he pleased
and get the book published. —I thought also his invoking
de gustibus, etc., showed a newly developed proclivity
toward academic officialese.

The Jenckses this fall, since it has been getting cold,
have been getting into bed at night under an electric
blanket and going through Dowland's ballads. Gardner
singing them and Ruth accompanying him on the flute.

*Ruth Flint's account of Shawn's false retirement at The
New Yorker:* He had announced that he wanted time to

Elena Wilson, Wellfleet

write and would be in the office only two days a week
while Vanderbilt took over. Some of his enthusiastic ad-
mirers got up a project to give him a silver tray (though
S. never drinks) with everybody's signatures on it, for
which everybody contributed $5. S. then sent V. great
horseshoes of flowers of the kind, R.F. said, that one sees
in delicatessen windows, which were very embarrassing
to him and stood around his office faded. He was—as S.,
who probably wanted a raise, undoubtedly knew—inadequate for the job—so that S. (having no doubt got what
he wanted) never left at all, and the extent of his retirement consisted of staying away from the office one Friday.

KATY DOS PASSOS

[Katharine Smith Dos Passos had been instantly killed when riding with her husband, John, at Wareham, Massachusetts, en route to Connecticut on September 12, 1947. Dos Passos, who was driving, was blinded by the sun and crashed into a parked truck. The top of the car was sheared off. The novelist lost the sight of his right eye and suffered minor injuries. He was under the shock of the accident and loss when EW visited him a few hours later. He remained hospitalized and could not attend his wife's funeral, which took place on the Cape.]

Dos Passos[1] *in the hospital, Sept. 12, '47:* We found him in one of the dreary narrow Bostonian rooms of the Massachusetts General Hospital. He sat forward in his bed and shook hands with us with a warmth rather unusual with him, saying it was wonderful of us to come. I had never before seen him show anything like emotion. At first, when we spoke of what had happened, his voice

---

[1] EW's letter to Dos Passos on his wife's death appears in *Letters on Literature and Politics*, pp. 447–49.

would seem about to choke or tremble. The right side of his face was red and swollen and he had a bandage over his eye. He told us that he had lost it, that the doctor had still to reconstruct it and that he would then have a "poached eye." He would be able to use the other all right, hoped to "take a glance" at the paper the next day. He said: "A whole wonderful thing is over for me now and I'll have to think of something else." Charley asked him how his ambulance trip had been, and he said that traveling at night in ambulances was not very pleasant: they lost their way in the dark, etc. He'd been so anxious to go under the ether, but when they had started to give it to him he had put up a terrific fight—they had apparently had to harness him up. "The physical discomfort," he said, "is rather a good thing—because it keeps my mind off the other thing." He said that there was nothing we could do for him except get the bags at Wareham, bring him the briefcase with his notes and books and the little bag with his clothes to the hospital, and take the rest to Provincetown. "The only thing is to rally around Edie."[2] Later he said that he had plenty of work to apply himself to right away.

Charley had told him at once to amuse him the story of Don Stewart's play, *How I Wonder,* which he had seen on its opening night in Boston. He had said, when I asked him, that his eye was rather painful, and I noticed that he twitched his legs as we talked, so I asked him whether talking made him uncomfortable. He answered that on the contrary he was glad to talk, and, as we went on, his strain seemed to relax, and the conversation fell quite into our usual vein: he asked about the Puerto Rico hurricane which had been heading in the direction of the Cape and talked interestingly about England. He had

[2] Edie Foley Shay, Katy's friend. See p. 30.

looked up a man who had written a book on the social life of the apes which he had read and been interested in, and "Katy and I" had got a sinister impression when they had spent an evening with him—it was just like Molotov! —he didn't want to talk about his monkeys: when the subject was brought up, he would drop it, saying that [there] were people working on it—he was well fixed, had a house, got enough to eat, held some kind of official post —that was what he wanted to talk about and all that seemed to interest him.

The funeral was going to be Monday. Thelma and Eben[3] had very kindly given a little plot from their lot in the cemetery—Edie was going to get "a little coffin." —I thought that he was still in the stage of thinking involuntarily about telling her how their friends were behaving and laughing about it with her. I had myself been imagining how she would have told me about the evening before at the Shays' of which I had just had an account from Chuckie Walker. He, having been, I gathered, the only one sober, had apparently been rather disgusted at seeing everybody drink too much and get to talking about other things—as if, he said, it were "some sort of party." When I talked to Edie on the phone, she had told me the same thing over and over again—what the doctor had said about Dos—and started an Irish lament which I was fortunately, talking on the phone, in a position to cut short. Soon after, Nina had called to talk to Rosalind, with, so far as I could see, nothing new to say. The next day, at the P'town house, Rosalind said, the drinking continued. Phyllis tried to get some practical arrangements made, but Edie only did her Irish act—would say, I'd should have offered you a cigarette but I'm a little vague today, and that she

[3] Eben Given, married to Phyllis Duganne, who wrote for *Collier's*. See *The Thirties, passim.*

wanted to go and comb Katy's golden hair. R. said that she hadn't even thrown out the faded flowers from the vases. Mrs. Foster, from across the way, had sat quiet but intensely curious. —There had been general disorganization in the household of the Walkers, the Chavchavadzes, and us, too. —Edie had said that now she would never get any more of those little notes from Katy!—a funny little secret correspondence, feature of their schoolgirl fantasy, that they had apparently been keeping up all their lives. —I should have liked to tell Katy about some of this.

—*Funeral, Monday 15:* suffered from lack of direction —neither Edie nor Bill[4] took charge, Walkers and Givens had apparently made most of the arrangements. Family and friends hung about in the bedroom and the room next to it and didn't emerge for the service. When clergyman asked Bill how long a service they wanted, explaining that it could go on for anything from five to fifteen minutes, Bill hesitantly suggested an intermediate length, then referred him to Edie. At grave, everybody, including the clergyman, left, except Nina, Eben, Rosalind, Topie, and me. Adelaide[5] enjoyed being busy and important: it brought out in her a certain chic, as it used to in her Communist days—black eyes, good figure in well-cut sober clothes, fashionable built-up soles of high-heeled shoes. House decorated with white flowers—little gray shallow coffin. Knobby had wired that she couldn't come because she couldn't get a nurse to come with her. Thelma —who, Nina said, was one of those people who "liked to fuss with corpses" and ought to have been an undertaker —wore what I suppose was her mother's mourning, with a big black "picture hat" on one side of her head. Eben

---

[4] Bill, possibly Bill Smith, Katy's brother. See *The Thirties, passim.*

[5] Adelaide Walker, Charles's wife. See *The Thirties*, pp. 161–63.

kept talking, at the cemetery, about how Dos's grave was
right beside Katy's as if he were already dead. Susan[6] told
Rosalind that one afternoon he had come to see her very
tight and insisted that she should come with him so that
he could show her something. He had driven her over to
Truro, taken her to a spot in his family plot, and pointing
at it dramatically, said, "You're going to be buried right
there! That's where you're going to be buried!" —But
people's personalities were very much subdued. It was as
if everybody was stunned. We hardly spoke or smiled to
one another. Nobody knew quite how to behave in that
house, with Dos, the center of the household, not there.
At the cemetery, the crowd melted away after the clergyman, going light on the "earth to earth," had barely made
a gesture with his fingers of dropping earth into the grave.

—After the days of horrible weather—the day before
had been at once hot and sticky and drenched with dismal
heavy rain—it brightened up in the afternoon, and the
view from the cemetery was lovely. The Given plot is
just on the edge of the hill, across from the church on the
neighboring hill, and just below it is a big grove of
unusually tall pine—beyond is Pamet River and the bay,
all silver in the four o'clock light—the waterway winding
in between the sands and the marshes. The little cemetery
looked light, clean, and dry—with its millstone and its
old-fashioned tombstones, up there, along with the bold
town-square characters, above what had once been the
seafaring community. I had tried more or less to dissociate
myself from them, as Dos had done at first, but we had
been living there, dining together, struggling with the native tradesmen and workmen, bringing . . . I thought how

[6] The dramatist Susan Glaspell (1876–1948), with her husband, George (Jig) Cram Cook, had been among the organizers
of the Provincetown Players.

they had lived on that water—and how much, in spite of all that was frivolous and "escapist," childish and futile in our lives, we had derived something from it and belonged to it—and Katy's death for the moment had given the whole thing dignity. I felt, as I had not done before, that we (Givens, Shays, Chavchavadzes, Walkers, Dos Passoses, Susan, Matsons, Vorses, ourselves) had all become a group, a community, more closely bound up together than we had realized or perhaps wanted to be. It was already a whole life that we had lived there—since Dos—who had always scoffed at Provincetown as a middle-class artist colony—had come up there to court Katy and had first moved in to "Smooley Hall."[7] All the parties, the days at the beach, the picnics, the flirtations, the drinking spells, the interims of work between trips, the moldy days of winter by stoves, the days of keeping going on a thin drip or trickle of income, stories and articles, bursts of prosperity, local property and cars, bibelots from Mexico or elsewhere, pictures and figures by local artists accumulated in P'town front rooms, walled in against the street—that was what our life had been when we had dedicated ourselves to the Cape, to the life of the silver harbor—and all the love and work that had gone with it, that we had come there to keep alive. The cemetery at Truro made me sad not only on account of Katy but because it reminded me of Mary—[brought] up our children together, long enough to feel grounded there and to have been molded to some solidarity. Musty foul smell of a dead rat associated with reading *War and Peace* in the evenings at the Walkers' house one spring, and later in my bathroom when we had lived in Polly Boyden's house and used to take walks up there—for me now, she was just as

[7] "Smooley Hall," a composite name for the Provincetown house shared by the Foleys and Smiths. See *The Thirties*, p. 482.

much gone, just as much destroyed, as Katy. And Polly's illness—about which Phyllis had just been talking to me, saying, characteristically, she's a very sick woman—seemed a part, too, of something ending.

Walk behind the house afternoon of Sept. 17: I had thought the day before that the hurricane was going to strike us when a wind began shudderingly to stir the leaves under the sky that threatened rain on the sultry afternoon; but today was clear and bright, the Cape September at last. The bushes and tall grass were full of partridges [pheasants] (a pair in the field next door just outside the little window of my study had even annoyed me that morning when I was working); goldenrod, deep blue asters—as I looked at the little asters, I felt what it meant to be still able to enjoy the earth, as I had after Margaret died—it seemed all worth so much when one thought of the dead, who were now aware of nothing. The silent back roads in warm and bright September. As I came back and looked out at the pinewoods and hills and little (square peak-roofed) white houses, it seemed to me that the country, under its spell of quiet and sun, was half empty in a sense, filled up with the Cape Cod past, with which we newcomers were in touch and on which we partly lived—Miss Freeman's house with its things brought from China, the Averys' house on Higgins Pond, the Wellfleet oystermen—the little cramped white houses with their angular gray roofs. I would play the phonograph while shaving, dressing—Jig Cook's Long Nook house, sitting on the porch there years ago when Norman was growing dahlias (it was not Jig Cook's but a nearby house): our jokes about Bill L'Engle[8] improvising on his

---

[8] William L'Engle, wealthy Provincetown neighbor of Dos Passos. See *The Thirties*, pp. 23–24 and *passim*.

organ, Dos said it was rather a small organ, we enjoyed our cocktails then—the little house across the road where I had visited Edna Millay that summer the first time I had ever come to the Cape—an old cart met me at the station (I think), in any case, I got off before I came to the house, got lost going cross-country, sweet-fun—I was in the house again this summer for the first time since then, the Cohens live in it now, and it is a middle-class little summer cottage, with modern kitchen and bathroom—it was queer to see that dining room where they had given me dinner, the doors down which Edna had come when Griffin Barry[9] had made her uncomfortable by laughing at her, the place where she had sat just below the stairs and read us some of her poetry—I even went upstairs and looked for the little room in which I had slept, suffering from my wartime eczema, the porch on which we had sat and huddled inside some kind of swing to get away from the un-"control"-ed mosquitoes which had made lovemaking on my part difficult and finally driven us in. The next day we had looked down on the beach from a cliff and she had pointed out to me Rob Minor and Nilla Cook,[10] a round little girl in a red bathing suit, whose figure she had admired. Jig Cook and Hutch Hapgood sitting on the porch that morning—Jig had quoted some Sanskrit. The battered Fifth Symphony records on the old hand-winding phonograph. Coming back from the beach, I kissed her behind a bush or something: her grin and summer girl-smile. Going to get the mail on the way back, I said, "By the time we're fifty years old, we'll be two of the most interesting people in the United States"—she said, "You

[9] Griffin Barry, Washington labor counsel. See *The Thirties*, pp. 455–56.
[10] Nilla Cook, daughter of George Cram Cook and Susan Glaspell.

behave as if you were fifty already." The old lady had
been extraordinary at dinner when I first arrived—we
were all having a little whiskey—she had said something
like "I was a slut myself; so no wonder my daughters are."
The three sisters sang songs they had composed together:
one of them had a line about *thweet, oh, tho thweet!*
There were Edna's versions of foreign folk songs, made
for Deems Taylor[11]—they were charming, I kept making
her sing them and couldn't get them out of my head.

—I thought, too, of the time at Peaked Hill, when on
some gay late afternoon, when we had had the Dos
Passoses and Spencers[12] over to dinner and had just been
into the ocean, I started to walk into the bathroom (that
wonder, that dream-convenience, that hardly ever worked),
where I didn't know the women were dressing, and had
a glimpse for a second of Katy half nude with her little
low breasts—the setting sun was shining through the windows and to the west, and the fugitive picture in memory
melts for me in the light and the atmosphere of liveliness
and the stimulating excitement of the drinks, talks, and
swims of those days. It seems almost as far away now as
Edna Millay in Truro. —Her (Katy's) figure was not
voluptuous but touching, and it added to, or made, the
beauty of the moment.

—That night, when I was sleeping between our clean
sheets just after Elena's return from New York, I was
waked up by a short sharp dry barking, just one bark
reiterated at intervals, which did not sound like one of
our dogs; but I went down to see if it was Bambi and
then heard that it came from the hill and took it to be a

[11] Deems Taylor (1885–1966), American composer who wrote
the music for Edna Millay's libretto *The King's Henchman*
(1927).

[12] Niles Spencer, artist and industrial architect. See *The
Thirties, passim.*

fox. I felt then, as I sometimes did when I listened to the whippoorwills in spring, that the place was really wild and alien, that I had no part in its life.

The next morning, September 18, a wire came that Mary Blair[13] had died—she had been "out to supper" the night before, Venita said when I called her up, and had died in her sleep.

[13] EW's first wife. See *The Twenties*, pp. 144–45.

TRIP TO ZUÑI

[The trip to the Zuñi in New Mexico was made by EW in December 1947 on behalf of *The New Yorker*. EW, as readers of his *Apologies to the Iroquois* know, had always been attracted to the American Indian—from his early years—and he wanted to see the Zuñi ritual dances which he describes with so much virtuosity as a high form of art.

[The text published here is the version expanded from brief notes immediately after the Zuñi visit; additions and revisions were made in the *New Yorker* version and there were further elaborations and changes when it was reprinted in *Red, Black, Blond and Olive (Zuñi/Haiti/ Soviet Russia/Israel)* in 1956.

[EW uses several Indian terms in his narrative:

[*Shálako,* or the coming of the gods, a yearlong cycle of ceremonies starting with the appointment of the impersonators and culminating in the elaborate fourteen-day public festival.

[*Sáyatasha,* an impersonator who oversees the conduct of the pueblo in matters both public and private. Also the rain god.

[*Hútutu,* a deputy of Sáyatasha.

226

[*Cúlawitsi*, the fire god.

[*Kóyemshi* originally were probably related to the clown society of the Plains Indians. Here are ten impersonators of the ancestral spirits whose ceremonies invoke rain and fertility.

[*Katchina*, earthly manifestation of the gods whose priestly duties include the appointment of the shálako and the other ancestral impersonators.

[*Newekwe*, activities less farcical than the Kóyemshi clowns, but also less important.]

December 12. —I was met at the Gallup station by a young man named John Adair, an anthropologist working at Zuñi.[1] He had to wait to pick up two Indians who were going back to the pueblo, and in the meantime advised me to buy some liquor, as it was forbidden at the reservation. Tough dirty bars and hard-boiled girls in the saloon and the telegraph office, though with something of the western handsomeness and robustness. Gallup, he tells me, remains one of the toughest western towns. It is a trading post and coal-mining town, and from the train it looks almost as ugly and grim as anything in the northern route. One of its principal industries is rolling Indians who come in to celebrate. They are invariably robbed and then arrested for drunkenness and thrown into jail. One of our Indians turned up, dark, bespectacled, lean, but the other Adair gave up, after waiting for him awhile in vain. We drove to Zuñi in a battered old station wagon over a very bad road.

He took me first to my quarters at "the club." The government center is a handful of little houses, with a small hospital (staff of nineteen) provided by the Collier re-

[1] See *Red, Black, Blond and Olive* (1956), pp. 3–68. Hereinafter given as *RBBO*.

gime. I had not expected such good accommodations: I have a clean, plain, shipshape little room, very well heated and with plenty of blankets (the nights are terrifically cold); good light to read in bed and table at which I can work; view of the big mesa from the front window—one dollar a day, with meals at the hospital: 7, 12, 5.

Adair took me down to his own house for dinner. He is living in the pueblo doing "fieldwork," and I was surprised to find him living in relative luxury. A two-room house built fairly recently, with running water, though no toilet. Rather good-looking red-haired wife, and two little red-headed children, one a very lively little boy almost seven or eight, the other a baby harnessed up in an armchair, so that it could not get into trouble. On the walls, pictures of Indian pottery alternating with colored [Paul] Klee reproductions—I thought that the Indian designs had all the better of it. The living room was heated by a small cookstove—the problem of keeping warm must be serious for them. The other room is kitchen, dining room, and bedroom. The little boy was later put to bed behind a screen in one corner, and there was a harness for the baby hanging from the ceiling that looked like a little swing. While Mrs. Adair was getting dinner, a colleague of Adair's came in to confer with him about the papers that they were writing for a big anthropologists' conference that is just about to take place at Albuquerque. They are both getting material for their doctor's theses—Adair among the Zuñis, the other boy among the Navahos (of whom there are six hundred living not far from the reservation). They are working on the same subject: what has been the effect of the war on the returned Indian veterans? Talking to them and listening to them, I got a rather unpleasant impression. It was impossible for them to pursue their researches without asking a kind of question that was sure to antagonize the Indians: when had they had their first sexual experience, how had the army affected their sex life, how had it affected their attitude toward the Indian community? etc. I was not surprised to hear that they had tried to throw Adair out last summer. An article on the Zuñi dances had appeared in the Gallup paper, and he had at once been accused of having written it (though this was not true). The point was that they had become annoyed with him, and had seized on this as a pretext to bring one of the only valid charges that an Indian in a reservation can bring against a resident white: that he is prying into their religion. (He had hidden his anthropological works that had pictures of the ceremonials.) The two young men discussed at some length the case of a young Zuñi who had taken rather badly to drink and was behaving in a disorderly way. Was it the conflict between the two worlds or was he simply an unstable character? —In the meantime, the little boy, madly excited by a new white guest, was showing me his Siamese cat, his moccasins, and his small pieces of Indian pottery. It must be queer for him to live in the pueblo: the grownups have fallen into the Indian habit of talking about the mythological beings impersonated in the ceremonials as if they were real creatures—tonight they were "bringing in the Longhorns"—fires had been built outside the pueblo, apparently to guide the masked impersonators who had been getting into their costumes at some remote place. (Driving in, we saw a big drum being carried somewhere in the darkness.) The child seemed to accept these characters in much the same way as children accept Santa Claus. The Indians live with these characters all year (I saw the ceremonial calendar, which shows that there is something or other going on all the time), and have emotional relations with them quite distinct from their relations to the actors. When the Mudheads, the sacred clowns, half-witted children of an incestuous union, take their definite departure in November and are seen going away to the hills, people feel very sad, though they may be on bad terms with the actors, whom they will have among them the same as before. —Adair says that the complication of the orders, cults, clans, dances, and ceremonials becomes completely baffling if you live among the Zuñis and try to get the hang of things. It is supposed to be the most complicated religion that still exists in the world—it is a web that binds them together and has preserved the little society intact. There are in Zuñi, besides the government school, a Dutch Reform school and a large Catholic school, but neither of these religions has made the smallest impression. The priest considers that he has made headway merely because, after almost ten years' residence, the people no longer spit on him as he passes.

Mrs. Adair turned out an excellent dinner of calf's liver, lyonnaise potatoes, peas, and lemon-meringue pie (about the last of which the little boy was much excited—he had not been allowed to have any that night and kept making commotions behind his screen and from time to time peeking out). After not having had any meat, she said that they were now being overwhelmed by presents from the Zuñis, who were slaughtering now for shálako—this was where the liver had come from. —I had had no lunch except a chocolate bar and an apple, and was ravenously hungry. After dinner, I felt as if I had been hit on the head and got Adair to drive me back early. Bob Bunker had been away on agency business and was supposed to come in later. (He was the Indian agent at Black Rock. I had known him from Cape Cod.) The night was black and bitter cold, and the stars were sharp and bright as I don't think they ever are in the East—they looked like silver-headed nails that had been driven in to show the constellations. —I always tend to sleep uncomfortably in the West, can't get used to the changes in temperatures:

always too hot under the blankets when you go to bed, then it drops and you have to pull them back.

December 13. I overslept the hospital breakfast. Bob Bunker came over to get me, and I took a long walk with him without eating anything—was much exhilarated by the stimulating brilliant weather and did not feel the lack of food. I have skipped a meal every day and am much the better for it. It is easy to do out here, because the food is mostly heavy: beef and mutton, potatoes, canned corn, bread (Zuñi bread, which is excellent—not like French or Portuguese bread, but very white and dense). We walked partway around the reservoir which provides irrigation for the Indians—got a good view of the big red mesa, Corn Mountain, where the Zuñis had gone to live for seven years to get away from the Spaniards—there are still masks and altars up there, which they continue to tend, though they pretend that they don't go near it. There is a great pile of stones at one end, and the gods used to appear from behind this, though they now, for some reason (perhaps because they can be seen from the agency post?), come from a different direction. Sagebrush and juniper—we saw a jackrabbit (last night a coyote crossed the road). Bob Bunker is a bright little fellow, with a good deal of charm, though very old-fashioned Bostonian in a way that I should have thought it impossible to perpetuate to this late date: dry, exact, conscientious, intellectually able, curtly and quietly self-important. It seems that the Indian Bureau did some energetic recruiting at the end of the war. He plays down a real enthusiasm for his work, and his version of it is that he let himself be roped in. Does not expect to stay in the service more than two or three years more. He came here from Albuquerque, where he was active in persuading three pueblos to accept the self-governing constitutions provided by the new Collier policy. He says that the

Indians turned out to vote on this, as they hadn't on any-thing before, and that the arrangement seemed to be work-ing well. He says he feels all right about Zuñi, too; the pueblo has never accepted the provisions of the Collier Reorganization Act,[2] but it is prosperous through its own efforts. They raise sheep and do a certain amount of agricultural work, but their great industry is silver work. He estimates that, during the war, when there were sev-eral army posts around here, they must have made a mil-lion dollars. Every house now has a radio and many have cars and phonographs. They are always knocking down the sides of the rather weak old wooden bridge over the Zuñi River, but nobody has ever gone over. Their thresh-ing machine is not a great success under communal owner-ship, as nobody has ever really mastered it and nobody takes responsibility for it, so that it is always out of repair. One man has broken away to the extent of running a garage, another of keeping a store. (The medicine orders of the Zuñi manage, as Adair afterwards told me, to keep going concomitantly with the hospital—which takes care, Bub Bunker estimates, of almost two thirds of the number it should. They think that the germs have to be dealt with, but that the other, more supernatural causes have to be dealt with, too: stinkbug sandwich as a remedy for the bad consequences of having been near something struck by lightning; washing in water used by someone else as a cure for spider bite.) Difficulty of getting the pueblo affairs administered by younger people who do not believe in witchcraft, which is so involved with their system of justice; charges brought through jealousy. —But when he goes over to see the Navahos, for whom he is also re-sponsible, it "makes him scratch his head." The Navahos

[2] The Collier Reorganization Act had shown important con-sideration of Indian needs.

are increasing at a great rate—"a way of keeping warm, I guess." They live miserably in their little huts, they have little social organization, and the R.A. has done almost nothing for them. John Collier[3] had for so many years blamed everything that had gone wrong on the failure of Congress to provide appropriations, and then when they had finally come through with a lot of money, the Indian Bureau had built at Windy Rock a giant headquarters for Navaho work, had equipped it magnificently for an immense staff of economists, sociologists, and anthropologists (who could not be recruited unless they could live comfortably), and then had managed to do nothing for the Navahos except persuade a few communities to consent to stock reduction so that their grazing grounds would not be blown away.

Lunch at the Bunkers': Priscilla Bunker is a half-English girl whom he first met at Truro. I think they rather look down on the Truro young people, and they do certainly represent something on a higher plane: more serious, *rangés*, etc. They have three children—he explains that they wanted to get this over as soon as possible—the last one had only just arrived, she had it in the little hospital. Her English mother had come on and was appalled by the country and the life they were leading. Had never been further from Boston and New York than Franconia, New Hampshire, and couldn't believe in the Zuñis at all —she thought that Bob and Priscilla were making up the things they told her. Priscilla has gotten rather bored and fed up with the life. They say that they can talk about nothing but Indians and children—have been out here now for years and long for a vacation in the East. They see nothing of the people at the post—fortunately, no

[3] John Collier (1884–1968), American ethnologist, U.S. Commissioner of Indian Affairs, 1933–45.

bridge-playing set—only people they see the Adairs, old friends from Albuquerque. But there is a delicate situation, because Adair has got in wrong with the Indians (Bunker deplores Adair's role as a catechizer of the young veterans). Bunker warned me not to give the impression that I have found out from Adair anything I know about Zuñi ritual—and I must pretend to be just a tourist. They are afraid that someone who knows about me from Adair or Santa Fe may come over for shálako and tell the Zuñis that I am a writer, and had even discussed before I arrived whether I oughtn't to come incognito. Bob Bunker has himself written a novel about Boston and is at work on another one, but has carefully concealed, at Zuñi, the fact that he has ever written anything. The atmosphere of a reservation is something entirely special of which I have had no experience before. The government agents are, in certain ways, completely at the mercy of the Indians, who, if they dislike them, can get them removed, so that the whites have to be very careful about giving grounds for charges against them. Liquor, for example, is not allowed; and, though the Adairs and the Bunkers have an occasional drink in a surreptitious way, Bunker thought it was a bad idea for me, under the circumstances, to run any danger of having liquor found in my room, so I have given him the bottle to keep. He has already run the risk of getting in wrong with the Zuñis by getting Adair out of his jam last summer; and he evidently feels that his mother-in-law did not create a very good impression recently by talking at the hospital about needing a drink— she couldn't, as an Englishwoman, believe in the restrictions either, and it was impossible to explain to her that the Zuñis could appeal against and make trouble for the whites. Her son by a second husband, English, an eleven-year-old boy, just arrived from England, where he has been in an English public school—Priscilla's half brother

—had been left with the Bunkers on a visit, and he, too
—though he enjoys his horse—has not shown the right
attitude toward the Indians, with whom he gets into continual quarrels. This has all amused me very much—as
has also the relationship between the scrupulous Bostonian Bunker, with his anxieties about what is and what is
not done, and the blunt Chicagoan Adair, who finds it
natural to walk into places and do and say what he pleases.
I have a feeling that, in their respective ways, neither gets
very close to the Indians. —The Bunkers have a Zuñi girl
who comes up and helps them out with the children and
the meals. She is attractive, as so many of them are: quick
and shy, dignified (she eats with them). Reminds me of
Teresita Baca,[4] whom it turns out that Bunker knows.
Teresita has married, has many children, her husband is
dead—you can still see that she must once have been
beautiful. Jesús, her father, is old and has dropped out of
politics. The Jemez pueblo, where they live, is almost two
hundred miles away—too far for me to go to see them.

Bunker drove me around Zuñi in the afternoon. Great
preparations going on for shálako: baking bread in their
beehive-shaped bread ovens, fresh sheepskins everywhere
from the sheep which are barbecued by the dozen. The
pueblo is quite different from any other I have seen, and,
it seems, there is none quite like it. It is no longer an
anthill of piled-up houses, as it was when Cushing[5] saw
it in the 1870s and as the Taos pueblo still is—but mostly
a village (except around the little old plaza, where the old
formation is still partly left) of independent houses not
very close together. At this festival every year six houses

---

[4] A Pueblo Indian whom EW met in New Mexico in 1931.
See *The Thirties*, pp. 103–7.

[5] Frank Cushing (1857–1900) compiled and translated Zuñi
legends and the creation myth. See *RBBO*, pp. 15–19.

have to be built or renovated to receive the arriving gods, and these are used when the festival is over. Usually the older generation of a family (instead of the newly married couple) moves into them—so that the village is always expanding and the architecture being improved. It is queer to see the newly built houses, with the little stickers that advertize the glass plastered in the corners of the panes, in which are to be received the grotesque bugaboo fetishes that they have been worshipping for thousands of years. The general aspect of the village is rather dirty and dreary. The houses, the ovens, and the earth are all more or less the same purplish chocolate color (the houses are mostly one-story affairs, with an occasional two-story mansion); two or three ill-looking trading posts; small corrals, which have sometimes caged eagles, kept for a supply of feathers; occasional pigs and turkeys (some domesticated wild breed, not like ours), also kept for their feathers; the most dreadful lot of half-wild mongrel dogs I have ever seen anywhere, many of them so much like coyotes that they look as if they must have coyote blood (dogs, it seems, are the only animals that the Indians are known to have had when the Spaniards arrived)—they do not treat them very well but eviscerate them and skin them alive as sacrifices in some of their ceremonies. (The Zuñis are better-natured and less quarrelsome than many of the other Indians, and it is an oriental gesture of their code never to give an ungracious reply; but, at the times that Cushing was here, they did have some pretty barbarous practices. People suspected of witchcraft were hung up by the wrists to make them confess; at the rites of adolescence, the men first put out torches by swallowing them, then made the boys extinguish the smoldering ends in their mouths; then there is another ceremony at which all the children in the pueblo are whipped, in apparently a purificatory way, since our habit of whipping for punishment is regarded with abhorrence by them. The hanging up by the wrists has been suppressed by our government, but nobody seems to know whether the adolescent ordeal is still practiced.)

I had dinner at the hospital at 5—ate all alone: a pleasant old Indian woman, the cook, put my dinner on the table. Then I went straight to bed and finished Cushing's *My Adventures in Zuñi* and read most of Ruth Bunzel's[6] *Introduction to Zuñi Ceremonial.* About 10:30 Adair dropped in and we talked till 12:30. Adair had sat under Ruth Bunzel at Columbia—a spinster with a cast in one eye. She had become probably the greatest authority on the Zuñis. She had come here and lived for years, telling them that she wanted to learn to make Zuñi pottery. She had learned this and had also learned the Zuñi language as no one else has done (has written a Zuñi grammar, which Bunker is now busy studying—characteristically, he has attacked it head-on, as I tried to do Russian —mastering the whole grammar first, which is of course unimaginably complicated, but hardly being able to speak a word). Then when she had left the pueblo, she prepared for the Smithsonian this masterly report, which explains the ceremonial apparently to the last detail. Since this happened, the Zuñis have grown extremely suspicious of anyone who comes to the pueblo except for some easily comprehensible purpose, and Adair said that the days when it was possible for Cushing to become a Priest of the Bow and one of the chief councillors, and for Miss Bunzel to attend esoteric ceremonies wearing the Zuñi costume, are inconceivable now. I think that there is a contrast here between the old American way of going into a situation and doing things and finding things out for

[6] Columbia University anthropologist who also wrote an encyclopedia of Zuñi sacred personages. See *RBBO,* pp. 21–22.

yourself, and the specialized, bureaucratized modern way of being sent by an organization which tells you what you are going to do and provides you with a set of ideas. Adair would keep saying that Cushing and Mrs. Stevenson (a contemporary of Cushing's, who also wrote a report on the Zuñis) "must have been very aggressive." The point is that, though he himself has been brash enough about invading the little closed community, he establishes no intimacy with the Zuñis, being responsible to no human relations which he himself has *nouées* with them, but only to the Anthropological Department of some half-baked university, which has assigned him, or allowed him to assign to himself, a ridiculous and improper task. He knows a lot, for all that—my interesting conversation with him.

December 14 (Sunday). In the morning Bob Bunker appeared with a large pasteboard box containing tons of anthropological books sent me by Adair and a little coffee heater and percolator, with some grapefruit, rye crispies, and a pot of marmalade, so that I could make my breakfasts here. —I waited to eat, however, till lunch, when I went over to the hospital. Afternoon writing up notes. Shower and short walk before going to Bunkers' for dinner. —Very clear sliced new moon with its simple bright star behind it in the fading pink of sunset that bordered the cold western night. This and the chilling night air after the bright stimulating air and the stone fence in the dark around the government post reminded me of Santa Barbara in the late fall and winter of 1929, when I lived in the Hoffmans' beach house,[7] and of Santa Fe, etc., in 1931. Places come back in my life after long intervals: I even felt that Naples and Rome, where I hadn't been

[7] EW's stay in Santa Barbara at the Hoffmans' beach house is detailed in *The Twenties*, pp. 459–90.

since 1908, had naturally recurred in 1945 and were places where I was at home. The most curious feeling of recurrence here, totally unexpected, is the feeling of representing an opposition and working underground—like our expedition to Harlan, Kentucky, my visit to the Boulder Dam strikers,[8] adventures in Moscow, precautions with the British censorship in the last war. Coyotelike dog that recognized me in the dark. —At the Bunkers', I found a Calabrian Italian who came from Newark, New Jersey, but had been living for years in Albuquerque, where he kept a small picture gallery and bookshop—married to a lean pale western girl, as tough (not in the bad sense) as a rawhide shoelace, whose father had kept a small grocery store at the Jemez pueblo. Her name was Mercedes and she looked rather Spanish. Later the Adairs came in. Guests are arriving for shálako, and the Bunkers and the Adairs are going to be filled up with people sleeping on couches. The Bunkers say that their children are far more interested in it than in Christmas. The little English boy made a little English joke about having seen a Buffalo Dance, which he carefully explained for us after he had sprung it. The Italian had for years been resisting the glorification of "the Indian" which he had had so much of at Albuquerque and Santa Fe, but had finally decided that he would come over to see shálako "without saying anything to anybody." Mabel Dodge[9] and the badness of her influence. Her son John Evans is in the Indian Bureau, and one night he had said to the Italian: "There are only two people who understand the Indian: my mother and one other" (obviously meaning himself). That phrase "the Indian" sickened Bunker. He said that, after

[8] Harlan, Kentucky. See *The Thirties*, pp. 160–91; also Boulder Dam strikers, *ibid.*, pp. 332–33.

[9] Mabel Dodge Luhan, friend of D. H. Lawrence. See *The Thirties*, p. 92.

two or three years working at Indian administration, he was unable to talk about the Indians at all with the romantics who never had to deal with them. The Navahos called themselves Dinne, which literally means "the people"—regarded by the Indian-fanciers as a heroic and a picturesque conception, as if it meant "the great people" or "the chosen people," but actually a number of tribes had words of the same kind, and they were practically equivalent to "we." An appeal had been made by radio for help for the Navahos, and now, to people's surprise, great truckloads of clothing and food were arriving. *Time* has published a picture of a Navaho mother and child, with a story about their wretched condition—evidently an attempt, they thought, to discourage supplies for Europe. There had just been a story in the Gallup paper, which everybody resented very much—also with a picture of a mother and child—declaring that the agitation for help to the Navahos was "all a hoax," that they were perfectly "fat and healthy." —Adair had been suspected of witchcraft. He rented his house from a certain Flora Zuñi, and a family who was having a feud with her wanted to rouse public opinion against him and deprive her of a profitable tenant. There was a child in the pueblo named for him— they all had to have American names for the census, as well as their regular Indian names and their esoteric names. There were men named Gingersnap and Chicken Grammerphone. —Last year at shálako there had been two mishaps: one of the shálako gods had fallen down in the footrace, everybody had vanished at once, the god he was impersonating was supposed to strike him dead, but, as the god seemed to disregard it, the priests took it into their hands and whipped him; another god had stumbled coming over the wooden bridge, and his mask had been hung on the door of the impersonator's house, and the family had gone into mourning. —They didn't have a barber in Zuñi, because enemies might get hold of the cut-off hair and use it to exploit or to sap the other's strength—all cut-off hair was buried.

Priscilla looked very cute in a red embroidered mandarin coat and little black pants. More Anglo-American difficulties: she was trying to train her little half brother to say *dahnce* instead of *dance,* so as not to create a bad impression in the West, and he caught her out with glee at the dinner table pronouncing it *dance.* —The Bunkers had a frightful time when her mother came out for the baby. Mrs. Toy, who has something wrong with her spine, so that she has to be operated on every six months, began having convulsions and losing her memory, one of her arms and one side of her face became paralyzed, and in her spasms she would become cross-eyed. The doctor had diagnosed it as encephalomyelitis. They found somebody to go East with her. —I went home about 10, leaving them deep in their Albuquerque gossip, and read more anthropology in bed.

Fantastic situation of concealing anthropological works. Comic idea of man who comes out here and reads up the enormous reports of Stevenson, Parsons, and Bunzel, which describe everything to the last detail and have photographs of all the masks, and then is not allowed to see the shálako, because the Indians are afraid he will write about them. —There always was an atmosphere of tension, the Spanish-American wife of the Italian says— she had been anxiously warned away from the skull dance by the earlier subagent; and lately it had been increased— perhaps by the pressure on the old religion of the outside world.

Exactly the same kind of thing evidently goes on in Santa Fe as in 1931. The people who follow Collier; the people who love the Indians but want them let alone. The people who make a specialty of the Spanish-Americans (Cushing is now a saint) and the people who make a cult of the Navahos and the people who make a cult of the pueblos. Bunker says that it is all the difference between individualism and collectivism, country and town. He is obviously on the Navaho side himself. John Adair contrasts the ease with which one circulates among the Navahos with the difficulty of knowing the Zuñis.

I walked down to the pueblo, starting at about 2:30. Big Mesa—known as Thunder Mountain—well salted with snow today. The pueblo is in an amphitheater, dramatically commanded by this mountain. The mesas, merely tablelands produced by erosion, are in some way reassuring and human—colors continually changing: pinks, purples, reds, dry yellows. Mesas in the distance sometimes dark. The red clay bridle path reminded me of riding from Boyd's Ranch[10] to Taos or Santa Fe (which?). Indian woman in blanket riding a horse, stopped to let him drink in the river; Indian boy showing off on his pony. At the pueblo I wandered around a little, looking for Adair's house. It is very strange and interesting to come down among the adobe houses and the crude egg-shaped ovens on the bare grassless earth the same purplish pink as the ovens and the houses, smelling the wood smoke, while the Indian dogs run out at you (one family of incredibly mongrel half-grown pups, all different). It reminded me at first of the old and poor parts of Italy, but it seems as much older than Italy as Europe does than New York. —Rum and conversation at the Adairs'. A square-jawed bear-trap-toothed visiting Hopi came to the

[10] The ranch where Margaret and EW vacationed in 1931. See *The Thirties*, p. 92.

door, looking for someone else. —Adair took Italian and me for a walk around the town. Development of the architecture: they had changed, it seemed, from round to square beams because these were easier to dust. Great preparations: baking, chopping wood, etc., going forward on all sides; trading post full of Indians buying things. The upper part of the mesa was reddened and made distinct for a moment by the setting sun, then suddenly left in shadow; on the other side, the clouds were a dull brickish red that corresponded with the earth and the mesas—the little shallow river shining palely in the falling twilight. Some of the people have frank friendly faces, others look grim and hard-bitten—the men look cut out of some very hard substance. Gaiety of the bright blankets against the monotonous background. Women with thick feet and legs, rolled up in their white puttees; young girls, also all wadded out and swathed with blankets above, but with spindling little legs underneath. —Old shell of mud and beams that is all there is left of the first Christian church. In the graveyard a wooden cross stands—there are no tombstones, no mounds for graves, and no grass or anything planted: they bury them anywhere, and the whole place is a mass of bones, everybody is buried in this little space. —The sky became perfectly beautiful with an effect such as I have not seen anywhere else: the new moon was now blurred, it was thickening and had lost its thin sliced form in a large soft cloud of a darkish gray; the sky behind was a clear pale gray, and below was a lemonish dying light —the whole thing reminded me of the coloring of certain black-and-yellow butterflies—perhaps because I had read that the Kóyemshi (who corresponded to the Kóshares here) have black butterflies' wings in their drums, which are supposed to make them irresistible to women.

Supper at the Bunkers'. It has dawned on me that they always have the front door locked (which opens on a lit-

tle porch) and only use the back door (which lets you in
through a hallway and the dining room–kitchen), so that
people cannot walk in and find them drinking—at Adair's
we were instructed to put our glasses out of sight when
anyone came to the door. There is also the problem of the
anthropological books. Bunker said that the maid Margaret
Zuñi had looked rather surprised when she had seen him
reading Stevenson, with its colored plates of masks.

Early to bed, after rereading Elena's letter, which
warmed me and cheered me up. I have enjoyed being here
by myself but, without Elena's reassuring presence, I have
been brooding over my faults and misdeeds, and having
some bad dreams.

December 16.[11] We went down for shálako about 4.
The Bunkers brought all three of their children, and
Priscilla had an awful time with them, as the little girl
wouldn't go to sleep and they didn't get back till 4 in the
morning, poor Priscilla not seeing much of the show. The
Adairs also had a pretty heavy time, as something like
twenty anthropological students from the University of
New Mexico descended on them, and little Peter was old
enough to be interested and had to be carried around on
John Adair's shoulders. I didn't care much for the students, but I was struck, as in Nevada last winter, by the
quietness of everybody compared to the East, where young
people of the same kind would have been laughing and
shrieking—they were almost as quiet as the Indians.

We got there just in time to see the first set of gods
come over the ford of the river, which had been built up
for the purpose. Incongruity of dead dog and old tin cans
strewn near where the procession passed, and large grunting pig in corral. The effect of these crude corrals, the
mud houses, and the muddy river not entirely devoid of

[11] See *RBBO*, pp. 23–43.

refuse was to make me think of what I imagine as the abject savagery of Africa. The effect of the gods is uncanny: Sáyatasha (rain god of the north), with his blank black-and-white noseless Pierrot face and his long pennon-like lateral horn (long life); the two Yámuhakto (attendants of Sáyatasha and Hútutu), with their cylindrical green heads; Hútutu (Sáyatasha's deputy), with his large fur-fringed ears; and the two Sálimopias, with enormous black raven feather ruffs (the others have things around their necks like black-and-white-striped life preservers)—each of the Sálimopias has a long pipe-nose and a plume of yellow feathers on his head—the one who comes first is the warrior of the zenith, and his face is a checkerboard of five colors with red sunbursts at the ears, representing a sort of spectrum of the sun at midday; behind him comes the warrior of the nadir, just the same, but with a black head and blue eyes and snout (ears different, too). We missed Cúlawitsi. The soft queer whistling call is going on all the time. They bless the village, holding little ceremonies in six places—in each a hole is dug and prayer sticks buried—people follow them from place to place. In each they perform maneuvers. Sáyatasha stalks up and down with a long stride, rattling his cluster of deer scapulas whenever he brings down his foot; his retinue maneuver with him, but the two Sálimopias simply mark time at one side, turning as they do so. There are at least three tempos involved—striding, tramping, quick marking time. The bird call keeps up, and when the final evolution brings Sáyatasha and Hútutu facing one another, with the attendant of each behind him, Hútutu utters his call: Hú-u-u-u – Hú-tutu – Hú-tutu. It sounds like the cry of an owl—all the cries are soft and expressionless, not human but completely birdlike. I thought the wooden noses were whistles, but one of the anthropologists said no, they made the sounds with their

throats—in talking to one of the actors and another Indian, the latter had said to the former: "Gee, you make
that sound good!"

In the meantime, the giant shálako were sitting in front
of a house in a field back of the trading post. As we
watched, they were brought down to the ford to a slow
tramping rhythm of jingling bells. It was dusk now and
difficult to see them. They had evidently calculated the
time so that it would be quite dark by the time they got
across the river. They were squatted in a row of six across
the road just beyond the corral. The last orange-yellow
light faded in the sky to the left. It began to get very cold
and our feet froze. People had been sitting on the big
ovens for warmth, and Mrs. Oleson got a loaf of Indian
bread still hot—it was delicious, we all ate it—made of
sourdough—they have semi-sexual shapes which the
whites are unable to ignore—then everybody (whites)
got cold and left, except Bob Bunker and me—we must
have waited an hour and a half, walking up and down to
keep warm. Black blanket-cloaked figures kept coming and
going, sometimes with flashlights—cigarettes were seen in
the darkness where the shálako were sitting, but no light
was ever flashed on these save when the headlights of a
car revealed for a moment the monstrous birds with their
fan-shaped crests of feathers. The bird call continued all
the time, as if it were across the river. At intervals the
shálako snapped their beaks, never at the same time, but
one after the other, like counting off in the army. At one
point they were doing this at the same time that bells in
the Christian church were ringing. At last, the jingling
rhythm of the bells on their ankles was heard, and six
delegations came to the shálako, one by one, from different
directions. One man, the shálako's attendant, was always
in costume. They had been attending ceremonials in the
houses, I think. Finally, a hymn—quite beautiful, evi-

dently of joy and welcome—was raised in the dark, and the procession came forward. It was impressive, the great thick twelve-foot figures, bent forward, with their crests, feather-beards, and long beaks, moved past one by one with their escort, and we followed them to their houses. (The expense of entertaining them was so heavy—would often bankrupt a family for the year—that this year two pairs had been doubled up, so that there were only four shálako houses.) I saw the reception at one of the houses: the bird sat down outside the door and snapped its beak in response to the welcoming chant—sprinkling of prayer meal, etc.—Bunker and I had got separated, and I got lost trying to find my way back to Adair's house. Perils of wandering around a pueblo at night, there is no street lighting whatever and the houses are not lined up in streets, but are situated every which way. Dogs bite you. Later that night I fell into a small pit; Bunker barked his shins and fell over various things. Finally I got to the main road and inquired at a very modern house with an electric light in the front door and many maps on the walls inside. An elderly obliging Indian told me that John Adair's house was just across the lane but that the place was all enclosed in haywire and I should have to go around. I groped along the fence, which I didn't remember, decided he hadn't known what he was talking about, and inquired of a couple of Indians coming along the main road. It was a Navaho and his wife—the man had had something to drink. He said, We are three strangers! and assumed, quite wrongly, that we were looking for the same person. Finally I found the garage and Chavez told me where to go—the man who first directed me was right. (Terribly hungry: soup, coffee, bread, meat, and beans. The rest of the night till after three consisted of going the rounds of the houses at intervals, returning to the Adairs': wakeful children, people asleep stretched out on the couches, the chairs, and the floor.) The Navahos come in great numbers, they are enormously impressed by the Zuñis, envy their accomplishments and sophistication—they have taken on, it seems, a good deal of pueblo culture, but these complicated rituals are beyond them. But when they come, they are afraid of the Zuñi witches, who are also more "sophisticated" and more dangerous than theirs.

—First trip with Girofalo, the Italian. On the way, he told me of his fourteen months as a psychiatric worker during the war in a hospital at Battle Creek: orgy of experimentations and sadism on the part of the psychiatrists, who had helpless GI's for victims: insulin, electric shock—did far more harm than good, rivaled the horrors of German doctors working on the men in concentration camps—had taken him months to get over it, his job had been to make out case histories. —We came back several times to the Sáyatasha house—looked in through the misted windows. The Kóyemshi (Zuñi equivalent to Kóshares) were sitting against the wall with another row of men sitting close in front of them—they would hand them reed stogies to smoke, which was part of the ritual. Their Mudhead idiot masks (purple-pink) were pushed up on their foreheads and revealed their faces, lean and aquiline, often elderly—solemn to the last degree and queer contrast to the clown faces. Sáyatasha, his mask removed, too, was sitting in the far corner and chanting interminable prayers—six beats always ending in a kind of short wail. The congregation sat on the other side of the room. They don't like outsiders to come into the room while this is going on and there is no reason why they should. It is the solemnest kind of religious service and compared very favorably, I thought, with any other that I had ever seen. —Some evidences of hostility—though usually quietly expressed. A man had told me to keep

back in the afternoon, when Sáyatasha had been entering
this house, and now, when John Adair arrived, a boy
(who he thought had been drinking) told him to go away,
and then, when we said we wanted to watch, had answered: "Don't watch!" The Bunkers had been here or
elsewhere and a man they knew had put out chairs for
them in the front row, but someone else had forbidden
them to sit down and had made them leave. Later, in one
of the shálako houses, one of the old men had come across
the floor and said to one of the whites: "Kindly remove
your hat." —We saw the young people coming and going
as we hung around the shálako house. Three boys who
had evidently been in the war amused themselves by talking Italian: *"Come sta, signore?"* etc. A boy and a girl
did a little necking sitting down on the rail of the porch.
He enveloped her round little figure in a bright red dress
in his big blanket-cloak—they didn't seem to kiss but to
rub cheeks. Then he carried her off in his cloak, laughing
softly—it was a very pretty sight. I am told that the boys
and the girls take advantage of the occasion to stay at
home while their parents are out.

   —*First shálako house* visited (about 12). This made
upon me a terrific impression. The shálako's attendant
was wonderful (the two dance together). Eyelids dropped,
cheekbones accentuated by black, line drawn on face, this
and spot also somehow suggest scars—intense and serious
look—sharp rapid rhythm with brown bare feet and sharp
yucca wand held out at an unvarying phallic angle, also
marking the rhythm. The giant bird, towering above him,
goes to a lighter rhythm, then will swoop back and forth
across the room with wonderful swiftness and nimbleness
—this must be very hard to do. Turquoise altar at the end
of the room and the whole place hung with bright shawls
and blankets. It was something of this energy and color
that Dyághilev and Nizhinsky brought into the old-

fashioned (Russian) ballet (*Sacre du Printemps,* etc.);
but here it is also their religion: the discipline, endurance,
and energy required for such a dance (which goes on all
night, though the shálako has two men, who alternate)
represent the backbone of the community and keep it up
to its standard. They are sustained and invigorated by attending it. Orchestra-choir always sitting in a huddle, facing one another, with rattles and one drum. —These are
probably the most vital and effective religious ceremonies
that I have ever attended.

Second house: Two shálako and two attendants, not
quite so good. The houses are built with windows that
open from one room to another, apparently for the sole
purpose of being used as boxes for the privileged. Mrs.
Stevenson on social differences in spite of the collectivist
economy—I saw some evidence of this.

Third house: The shálako here was doing a *pas seul.* He
was absolutely terrific and must have been a star to be
allowed to have the whole stage to himself in this way.
The enormous false body was made to vibrate as if it were
alive—whirl, glide, and swoop. The tempo changes from
time to time, and there are subsidences to relax the dancer,
but these are extremely brief and allow him merely to
mark time a minute as he poises at the end of the room,
smartly snapping his beak. The effect here became so
hypnotic that I finally found it rather upsetting and
wanted to get away. Mercedes Girofalo said that when
she sat down and watched it, she got a sort of thrill out of
having the great bird swoop down on her. The shálako is
formidable, godlike, yet, stylized though it is, it is an
imagined living creature, which they love. And it loves
them: it is performing this dance to show them that it is
pleased to be so generously received and banqueted, and
it is consecrating the house for them, bringing plenty and
family fertility.

Sáyatasha's house: The prayers were over here, and the dancing was going on. Sáyatasha, unmasked now, alternated dancing with his stately stride and rattle. The slim fire god, always a handsome boy, almost naked, with colored spots painted on his legs, had the same set lips and dropped eyelids as the attendants of the shálako. Two Mudheads were dancing with them here, now wearing their masks. The wiry half-naked human bodies (special physical types seem to be cast for the various gods) make them less unsympathetic than they appeared in the pictures I had seen, with their great warts and their tadpole faces. They go around from house to house, dancing and doing their act. When they are not dancing, they go among the audience, grabbing people and making jokes in the voice that they assume for their character: an oozing wheedling simpleminded voice. One of them seemed to be imitating Hútutu; one of them, I understand, tries to recite Sáyatasha's prayers and breaks down into gibberish.

Fourth shálako house: Here there were two shálako, two attendants, and two Mudheads all dancing together. It was a big two-story affair. Adair says that when one of the more pretentious Zuñis builds a two-story house, he leaves the upper story empty because he doesn't know what to do with it—it is simply an example of "conspicuous waste." I couldn't get into the room here, but had a very good view of a corner of it from one of the inside windows. It was the corner where the shálako impersonators changed. The creature would squat in the corner while attendants held up black blankets and one man got out and another got in. When it was firm on its feet again, it would snap its beak, all ready to go.

I met the Bunkers here. Bob was taking Priscilla and the children home and I went along—back about 4. The dances had upon me so hypnotic and obsessive an effect (and I had been drinking a lot of coffee) that I was glad

to have my mind taken off the monstrous beloved birds
with their possessed attendants and the bibbling babbling
Mudheads by something that had come in the mail that
made me angry so that I partly forgot them.

All the strength of the Zuñi community can be ap-
preciated in watching this festival. The motorcars and up-
to-date houses—Sáyatasha's new house was one of the
most modern in the pueblo—do not detract from its power,
but seem a part of the communal solidity that the dancers
are affirming. You quite forget the rather drab exterior of
the pueblo in the clean and brilliant interiors. The ban-
queting did not strike me as barbaric: they are seated, as
a matter of fact, at long clean tables, where they eat
mutton stew in white bowls and plates with ordinary
knives and forks. It still seemed highly civilized even
when I saw them cutting up quantities of meat and carrying it out on their heads (the women) to be cooked in
cauldrons over outside fires. A very handsome and vigorous people: some of them, of all ages, wonderful. Children
(except babies) always quiet and good. Red, green, blue
blankets and shawls, usually black for the men—they wear
them wrapped around them and folded over the bottom
parts of their faces. This community is probably the most
integrated that I have ever seen.

Call with Adair in the course of the evening at the
house of a woman, part Cherokee, part Louisiana Cajun,
who had known several of the anthropological researchers
of the past. To my astonishment, the walls were covered,
along with many feather rosettes and photographs, with
colored plates of masks out of Mrs. Stevenson's book on
Zuñi.[12] Pieces of mahogany furniture that did not go with
the rest of it; but the whole place had the bareness, the

---

[12] Matilda Stevenson, ethnologist who compiled a compre-
hensive study, *The Zuñi Indians* (1905). See *RBBO*, pp. 19–23.

starkness of furniture, so different from the Negro disorder, characteristic of Indian houses. —There was a stove
in the middle of the room, but they were all sitting at a
considerable distance from it, and we were sitting at a
considerable distance from them. The conversation was
full of the long silences which Adair tells me you have
to get used to in calling on Indians; but the head of the
family, the woman, talked quite naturally, without an
accent, and if she had not been so dark, could easily have
been mistaken for the best type of western farmer's wife.
Her daughter, however, was round, dark, black-eyed, and
altogether Zuñi. A youngish man came in, in good modern clothes, with a small mustache, and there was a pretty
plump young woman, nearly white, who might have been
mulatto. A very curious family, with, Adair tells me, a
complicated mixture of blood. The old lady has to live at
the edge of the pueblo—this was really her daughter's
house—because she is not of Zuñi blood. She told us that
the house had been a shálako house when it was new.
They always have to have ceilings high enough for the
great bird to dance. Sometimes they built temporary ones
just for the dedication, and afterwards put on a lower roof.

—Hungry and slightly sinking when we stopped for the
last time at the Adairs' just before driving home. They
had been stewing the meat bone with lentils, which made
a hot soup that everybody was delighted to get.

Piñon—smoke like roasting chestnuts
electric light from Delco plants
shower baths and Coca-Cola—stuffed deer and antelope
heads
plane overhead, while waiting—winking green and red
lights—
Indian boys on lean horses lancing across the river
Amor Brujo—Spanish motif?
drop and revival of chant—hypnotic effect

When the sun left Tóyalane: a gray-green streak came
out in it

bringing out ashes—touching the gods

children, in Margaret Lewis' house, had been hiding
from the shálako birds

the Navahos came to get a good dinner

On Tóyalane: figures on top, supposed to be Zuñi in-
siders who had been thrown off. Below, halfway up the
cliff, long-necked thing like a mountain lion—stripe
around neck and stripe around lower body

Later, at the club, I heard some bird at night, and it
might easily have been an Indian.

Casey Adair's uneasiness when little Peter began to talk
about owls—who had been talking to him about owls?

They kept the corn on the second floor of one of the
new houses.

The house where the Santo was kept—see E.
Fergusson.[13]

December 17. Slept till 11. Went over to Bunkers': he
was telephoning about accident of night before—the Gov-
ernor's nephew, driving a truck, drunk, had driven off the
road into an arroyo near Gallup, with a load of Navahos
and Zuñis, including two children, twins—three or four
killed and several injured.

The Girofalos, who had spent the night at the Adairs',
came in and told me about seeing the race of the shálako
in the morning: it had been wonderful—they had glided
back and forth like birds, dropping prayer feathers at
either end of the course. (Later, they are hunted like deer
as they are returning to the hills—nobody sees this.)
—Bob said that by early morning the attendants were

[13] Erna Fergusson's book, *Dancing Gods* (1931), had aroused
EW's interest in the shálako. See *RBBO*, p. 3.

plainly dead with fatigue—the dance declines into comedy, with the shálako snapping at the Mudheads.

Vogt told me later that he had met a drunk Zuñi at
dawn, who had behaved in a threatening way—had said,
"When we go to your dances, you make us pay—then you
come and watch our dances!" —Vogt had answered: "I
live right over at Ramah and next time I have a party I'll
invite you." —When the Zuñi found he lived at Ramah,
his attitude had changed.

Judge Denman of California and his wife, who had
often come to the dances, were friends of the faction of
the Adairs' landlady. The opposite faction had spread the
rumor that the old lady was going to take down the
prayers in shorthand, so that, when she had taken a front
seat, she was requested to leave.

Dinner at the Adairs', which Mercedes cooked in her
amiable easy way—she turned out something light with a
Mexican touch, with eggs and a can of tuna. Everybody
dead with sleep.

December 18. Walked down to the pueblo in the afternoon—windy but not so bad as the Cape—bridle path
strewn with bottles. —At Adairs', M. Lewis' son (half
Zuñi, half Cajun—Cherokee, probably an element of
white)—talked about his painting, the Zuñis wouldn't let
him sketch—he and his mother were off on a trip to
Chicago, California, and the South to advertize the Santa
Fe Railroad. —He said that we hadn't seen anything just
going shálako night—you just see a lot of Navahos. On
Monday they paid off the Mudheads—piled up provisions
for them: "I haven't got words to describe it—you have to
see it." The Mudheads made up their jokes new every
year, and the singers and musicians made up their music,
which was also more or less different every year. —I asked
him whether they still ate wood-rat paste, as Cushing had

described, and he said that there had been lately only one clan whose head had to eat it on some occasion—but that the head of the clan had died and the clan was now extinct. —He spoke of the Zuñi grapevine and said that, as soon as the police had begun stopping the bootleggers on the road, the word had been sent back to Gallup, and the bootleggers had come around another way. He told us, grinning, that some local politician had referred to the Indians as "aliens."

Adair and I went over to Vanderwagon's Trading Post; then to Kelley's. We went in back to the "Curio Room," where we found gray-haired, lean-faced, bespectacled, virulent old lady Kelley sitting at her desk. She announced to poor Adair, with portentous and venomous restraint, that a photograph of the racing shálako had appeared that morning in the Gallup paper: "These Zuñis are sincere in their religion—there's very few people that are as sincere as they are—and it's a shame that they should be bothered!" etc. She harped on this in a long lecture. The Adairs don't trade there, and Adair had taken me first to the other place. —Everybody who was told about this said it was nothing but hypocrisy on her part, as the Kelleys made their living out of fleecing the Zuñis; but I thought it wasn't a good idea to stay to dinner with the Adairs, as they asked me to, and go to the dance that night.

I had bought a few supplies at the trading post and ate a dinner of tomato juice, canned Vienna sausage, bread with peanut butter, and cookies. Spent the evening correcting John Bishop's proofs[14] (the book of his prose that I edited).

December 19.[15] Spent the day with Evon Vogt going

---

[14] *The Collected Essays of John Peale Bishop* (1948), edited with an introduction by EW.

[15] See *RBBO*, pp. 43–51.

around the Navaho country. His mother's family came to Pennsylvania in the early eighteenth century—Pennsylvania Dutch; his father's came over after '48. Blue-eyed, intelligent, good-natured. Whole day a great relief after the atmosphere of the reservation—so much easier to talk to him—not an academic anthropologist (would explain anthropological "jargon words," as he called them, when he used them), not a nervous outsider. Father had come out for his health, and they had been living on their ranch there ever since. It seemed to me absolutely exhilarating, after the pueblo and the government center, to be in a small American town again. Everything seemed so light and bright—beautiful day—rows of dry cottonwoods and poplars—village trading post: long room with high ceiling, enormous tall old stove that heated the whole room, high piled shelves of canned goods and white pasteboard boxes. Tall man in big hat and on crutches who had once been Indian supervisor—he and the narrow-eyed man who ran the store were all against John Collier—if he had only died before he had had a chance to become Indian Commissioner, everything would have been all right. They had represented the non-Indian interests who were getting their lands away from them. The town was a Mormon community. When the government had shut down on polygamy, a group of polygamous families had first gone to Mexico, then come up here. The Mormon Church forbade liquor, tobacco, coffee, or tea, but there were "jack Mormons," who didn't obey these regulations. They held the dances and movies, though, in the church.

Vogt said that John Collier hadn't quite understood how large a part their sheep played in the lives of the Navahos, they should have had them reduce their stock more gradually. They not only depended on the sheep for a living, but ate mutton and slept on sheepskins, and it was like losing part of the family.

The missionaries were against the anthropologists because they thought that the latter wanted to encourage the native religions. The Nazarenes played on the superstitions of the Navahos by telling them that unless they became converted, their flocks would die and other disasters would occur—the missionary told one man who had lost three wives that it was because he had not come to Christ.

Navaho veterans: one young man, who had never been further than Texas and California, boasted of having been overseas and killed Germans. He convinced himself of this, and they held a ceremony over him to exorcise the ghosts of the men he had killed—as well as some other returned soldiers who had actually fought in Europe. Almost all their ceremonies are intended to exorcise or to cure: the main participants are the medicine man and the patient. The veterans had been blackened all over with charcoal to keep the ghosts away; but one of them had taken a bath because he wanted to sleep with a girl. Another of the returned soldiers took no stock in the whole thing—called both Christianity and the native cult "superstition."

Lunch at the Vogts': pleasant little one-story ranch house—nice old large black dog with tan face-markings named Burdlo—trees, cabins, and animals strewing light irregular dried-leaf-like shadows on the dry bare earth—like the mountains of southern California—mild climate and sparkling day, traces of snow on the ground—plains and mild hills, with the eroded columns called giants, etc. —the notch—the curious red mesas (airplane signal)— dark blue-grays with a kind of steely iridescence.

Pleasant to be in the ranch house—so open with its low windows—informality and ease—so different from the Cape houses—Navaho rugs, white and red or gray and red, on the floors—fire burning, long room, whole shelf of

Smithsonian reports, not-bad little watercolor of landscape painted by one of the family. Mother, wife (from Kansas, round-faced midwestern blonde), married sister, and several little children, running to blue eyes, belonging to Vogt and his sister—general pleasant informality, good nature, and ease. Excellent lunch of cheese soufflé of the characteristic light local kind, string beans, lettuce salad, jelly (apple?), coffee, huckleberry pie with whipped cream (something else I have forgotten)—after lunch, they produced a large box of candy which they had made themselves and were much pleased with, because they had produced—what I have never seen before—a variety of different kinds of chocolates and bonbons—they were delighted with the names: Kentucky Colonels (Kernels) had pecans soaked in Bourbon, embedded in a white cream and covered with chocolate—there were also, I think, "Mexican Mints," which I didn't try.

—Climbed up to cliff dwellings: one window left that looked out on snowy hillside opposite, grown with piñon and juniper; smoke-covered domed ceilings; in places the walls had been replastered to cover up the smoke—Vogt said that the pueblo Indians constantly did this. Now "the pack rats had taken over" (so called because they would carry off everything, even a pair of shoes)—we saw their nests, and the floors were covered with their dung.

—El Morro: taken around by custodian—seemed to me a typical soft young man of the kind who allows himself to become marooned out here. Handsome, tanned, hazel eyes; dandiacally well-dressed in fawn-colored clothes that matched the great background of the sheer El Morro rocks —high-heeled sharp-pointed black boots. The families of both him and his wife had come from Philadelphia (her father had "come out for his health"—I wonder whether this is always true)—had been before in a national park in southern Arizona but it had been too hot down there and he had asked to be transferred. Called one "sir," pronounced Spanish well, referred to the Spaniards, etc., as "the old boy." Had spent five years at Lawrenceville but not graduated. —Attractive little house: his good-looking wife appeared with, of course, a recently born baby. I said that everybody out here had new babies, and she replied: "It's because the nights are so long and dull." Oval gold-framed Philadelphia portrait of her grandmother—a few pieces of old eastern furniture; that long set of books on the making of America, two of them placed neatly on the table. —He told me that Vogt's father was the person who had had El Morro preserved as a national monument. —Vogt said, after we left, that he had wondered why Wilson (Bates) stayed out there and did not seem to care about advancement—he had once had one of those jobs himself when he was very young—and had found it intolerably boring and lonely—had had to climb up and down ladders dozens of times a day showing the cliff-dwellers' caves, and delivering phonograph lectures. —He had worked two years in the Nevada mines getting money to go through college—hadn't liked Nevada at first, but had later, after the first two months, gotten to like it. —Thought he ought to do his anthropological work elsewhere, because he knew the locality and the people so well that he couldn't be objective.

—Very pretty Navaho girl in long blue skirt on horseback tending her flock. —Less Mongoloid, more Aryan-looking than Zuñis. —First hogan we visited. You are supposed to pause awhile outside (though you don't knock) to give them a chance to get dressed or prepare for you. They are extremely modest, unlike Zuñis—go far away and conceal themselves when performing their natural functions. —Good-looking woman and cunning little black-eyed girl—woman held fingers in front of her mouth, which Vogt told me was a "patterned gesture" of shyness—I did the handkerchief mouse for the little girl, which made quite a hit. Vogt talked Navaho to the woman. Her husband had gone to take his sweat bath (sounds like the Finnish steam baths). The hogans are unexpectedly cozy—never sordid or dirty, like Negro or poor-white cabins. You sit cross-legged on sheepskins on the floor (though the larger ones sometimes have chairs and beds)—once my legs went to sleep and I had to stretch them out. Usual Indian silences. When you shake hands, they give you a queer light stiff hand—only the most "acculturated" ones shake hands in the American way. —Women nurse the children sometimes for two or three years—till the next one comes. Vogt wondered whether man with two wives (sisters) slept with one while the other was having a baby. —They are touching and attractive—more touching because they seem less strong than the Zuñis; more sympathetic because more adaptable. —Old man who spoke Spanish and had been to Washington thirty years ago—one eye, mustache, rather fine-looking—Vogt said that he and his daughter were very strong-minded and completely dominated the family, of whom we saw a number of members. They thought I looked like Vogt's father. They had gray cats (*mossi*—a Spanish word) with rather long fur. Hogans (there were also small houses) hexagonal or octagonal, roofs built up to a dome by laying the logs in a peculiar way—roofed and cracks filled in with mud, with hole in roof through which a stovepipe passes—evaporates rain or snow. Food, utensils, and other things stowed on a shelf that runs all the way around—sometimes colored religious pictures supplied by the missionaries. Never smelt badly—everything clean and dry. Slept like the spokes of a wheel raying out from the central stove, heads toward the wall. —One woman had started a blanket in a big loom: a red-and-white strip, with its diagonal lines, had been started on the upright cords of the frame—rolls of wool ready for carding—she was twisting the thread and winding it in a spindle. —In first hogan, there was also a baby strapped to a baby-board—I sat down beside it without knowing what it was, because it was covered with a small gray blanket. She took the cover off to show it—it was sound asleep. When they are awake, they set them up against the hogan wall. Vogt says that the children are well brought up—gradually and gently trained. —There was a mass of donated Christmas candy lying on a paper on the floor, but the little girl made no attempt to grab it.

Distribution at the schoolhouse: Bob Bunker said that they had been laughing hysterically the day before—the white man had never done anything like this before and they didn't know what to make of it—and today there was a general air of cheerfulness—the women seemed to be wearing their brightest shawls—purple plaids, red and yellow stripes—and their best silver and turquoise necklaces. Bob and an Indian stenographer who couldn't spell were making out endless forms at their typewriters—two people would sometimes create difficulties by applying for the same family.

—Curious relationships: a married man cannot look at his mother-in-law or even be around where she is. He will leave the trading post if she comes in. One returned soldier had stopped doing this, thereby making the mother-in-law angry. —With your "parallel cousins," you were on terms of the utmost respect—had to use a special form of the verb. With your "cross cousins," you had a "joking relationship," as did also a man with his paternal uncles. The paternal uncle, not the father, was the disciplinarian for the boys. —The grandmothers, as with us, were indulgent—young men back from the war had begun using condoms a little, one had tried a diaphragm—the girl hadn't liked it.

—Harvard had just had a big endowment for the study of Russian anthropology. He hoped to get a job there. Ruth Benedict had advised MacArthur on handling the Japanese Emperor and anthropologists had been consulted in preparing leaflets to be dropped on Japan—same purpose with Russia?

December 20.[16] Strain seemed to have abated at pueblo. Ate waffles in evening with Adairs. They left their two children at Flora Zuñi's while we went around to the dances, which, after shálako night, begin early. Flora Zuñi household—wonderfully equipped kitchen—large house—they compete with the rich family of the other faction. Flora and her daughter and her little granddaughter all incredibly robust and handsome. She and the little girl were working over pinto beans.

Not much crowded tonight—in some houses the women and children were sitting patiently waiting for the dancers to come around. Complete silence except for the occasional popping of bubble gum—women with their green or red or flowered shawls over their heads—sometimes wore beautiful silk back-aprons. Much oilcloth and linoleum in the biggest of the new houses—on the walls, hangings with elongated ritualistic figures—fried bread: huge browned pancakes of the consistency and taste of unsugared doughnuts. While we were waiting, Adair got into conversation with a pale-skinned and handsome young Hopi woman, who came from Hanno and had married a Zuñi—she spoke three Indian languages, had traveled in Europe and the East, evidently in service—said it was hard to come back to the reservation and adapt oneself to it—narrowed eyes in a way that I haven't noticed

[16] See *RBBO*, pp. 51–64.

with Zuñis or Navahos. —Purple Heart citation on wall along with Katchina dolls—and I saw a man in a Marine's uniform.

Mudheads dance without masks, giving a kind of war cry at intervals and sometimes laughing—some were old men with bony arms. —Later, dancers with bows had three long-nosed dancing with them (different-colored eyes and snouts, fox furs and feathers) and the rear was brought up by an unmasked man with his face painted gray and a large bundle on his back (Newekwe?—other order of clowns) (fillets—also plumes down back). Everywhere a very handsome set of men came in with bows, prayer plumes, and yucca wands, long black hair down to their waists (horsehair wigs?), two feathers of eagle's down, one red, one white, one at each side of head. To them enters a black-faced bugaboo—bowing in rhythm as he walks to the head of the line—black bearskin feet, speckled legs, black mask with wide mouth ferociously showing teeth and long red tongue, eyes like crescent moons, coarse black bearskin-like wig—he dances at the end of the line, making a series of dips from time to time, and the dancers dip with him, sometimes first to one side, then to the other. The dancers keep turning about, to face in the opposite direction, the whole line turning at once. No orchestra: they sing and keep time with rattles, always perfectly in unison.

December 21. Wonderful evening: stayed in Mudhead house and saw five different numbers. Mudheads themselves were all in (had been fasting, we were told, for days), sitting against the wall, unmasked, wrapped in their blankets, their heads sunk forward, sound asleep.

(1) Gorgeous number of men with purple, blue, and red velvet cloaks, hung with turquoise and silver dollars —silk ribbons over their shoulders and hanging from poles —very strange Katchina on the side with two long purple

ribbons hanging from his two head feathers—queer gestures—two other charming Katchinas, with orange snouts, not double like beaks, and artificial pink and white roses in their headdresses—great ruffs or beards of spruce boughs—spruce sticking out from belt and armpits. —Katchina kilts. Red and white beadwork. Deer with heads hanging on wall—tapestries with square-headed elongated figures.

(2) Five broad stout men, who danced mostly with their backs to the audience—the two at the ends wore masks, with butterflies on the backs of the heads—one (on right) black-white, one (on left) red, white, and green. At intervals, they would turn around, uttering a bird cry, showing turquoise faces with slender bent beaks—orange with a streak of black over the bridge—turning all the way and back.

(3) Group, including five of the mask-faced set, black, gray, pepper-and-salt, white, and brown beards—two with ducks on their heads, bill pointing forward, tied up in red Christmas ribbon, two feathers of tail pointing out like arrow behind—black tongues—eyes and teeth plainer than in last night's red-tongued mask. Entered with gruff bugaboo sounds—more formidable chant. Bob Bunker almost walked into the red-tongued blackface passing the mission church yesterday afternoon: the Katchina gave out a roar—he thought, "I can do that, too," but smiled and stepped aside. The Indian agent shouldn't roar at the Katchinas. (Glossier black masks, no bearskin boots.) —A pseudo-Mudhead entered with them, but with protruding eyes and lips and gray feathers here and there—knelt down and pounded a sack for the drum. Was all out of time for the dancers—stage manager came forward twice to correct him, without much success—simply walloped a thing like a sack of flour with a thing like an old-fashioned policeman's club—a terrific lot of work and the

sound not so satisfactory as a drum. Also, a handsome turquoise-faced Katchina with small red ears, shálako crest.

(4) Same as last night but not so good, because the dancers were tired—all that dipping first to one side then to the other must be very exhausting. The blackface with them had the red tongue, but seemed to have a newer mask.

(5) The bear. John Adair got a turn at the door, because he was just coming in and turned around to see the bear posing at the doorway and holding up his great hairy arms and long claws. They had evidently picked all basses for this—they entered making snarling growling animal noises—the bear always faces the audience, dancing by himself outside the line—lifting first one paw, then the other, in a menacing way—he has two long black things like knitting needles stuck through his black mane so that they stick out like chopsticks in front—his eyes are made to look small and bestial (or he has been carefully chosen for the part), the bottom of his face is white with a grisly beard or chin that sticks out, and in this white part his nostrils are black with the nostrils of a beast—his bear-mitts reach halfway up the upper arm—the actor felt his part and was one of the high spots of the evening, in spite of the fact that at one point his shoe became untied or something and he had to stop to have the manager attend to it, while the chorus was momentarily silent. Their chant was a threatening growl but resembled something familiar—I think, from *Carmen.* —At the end, when the chorus had left, the bear remained on the floor and did a short act by himself, keeping time without the music like Paul Draper[17]—he would go up to the audience and look

[17] Paul Draper (b. 1911), American dancer who developed his own "ballet-tap" style.

into them, like a bear who has heard a noise and stands up and peers into the forest. Very good—in a theater it would have brought down the house, but the audience remained, as usual, silent.

—We left then. It was the first night that Priscilla had had a chance to see anything, and she enjoyed it and was in better spirits, but sat down where she could (was once put out of a chair by a Zuñi) and finally had to go—had been out of bed only two weeks since her baby. She and Casey had sat on a box in a corner, and she said it was the first chance she had to have any real conversation with Casey. Casey was feeling better, too, and made one or two cracks of the kind that they said was characteristic of her. —Hot pea soup, whiskey, and canned ravioli at the Bunkers'—everybody in good humor—though Priscilla had just found a message to call New York and found out that her mother was in bad shape—thought that she ought to go on (her agate-green eyes, cross look about forehead that I didn't quite like—moment of temper that other night with Bob). Both families are uncomfortable and worried: I commiserated with each of them about the other. —Everybody coming down with colds.

—Bob noticed that one of the Katchinas in (3) had the name of a U.S. destroyer tattooed on one arm.

—Reading Stevenson tonight at the Adairs', I discovered, to my disgust, the excrement-eating and dog-killing practices of the Newekwes, which Adair says he understands they still go in for although the disapproval of the whites has driven them underground (initiation into the order).

—Conversation about implications for religion in general. Priscilla had been brought up as a Catholic by her mother—the Zuñi religion wasn't true but the mass was —you knew it was because you had faith to know it was. I said that I had thought at first: How can they believe all this when they are surrounded by a world that doesn't? Bob said, "They see a great many more people who do believe it than who don't." I said that I was torn between admiration and the feeling that it ought to be explained to them that the whole thing was really nonsense. —Bob brought up Transubstantiation, and I had already thought about it that evening as I was reading about the excrement-eating rites. —Bob had been brought up a Unitarian —when the minister had asked him why he didn't go to Sunday school, he had said he stayed home to study—the minister had asked him what he was studying, and he had said economics. —Well, said the minister, that's about the same thing. This had puzzled him at first, but had made an impression on him as an example of Unitarian latitudinarianism.

—I left "the club" as I found it. Except for the few days of shálako, when a few people had been staying here, not a soul, except once some giggling girls that I had heard going to the ladies' room, had ever been in the place. Nobody except Bob and Adair had ever entered my room. It was comfortable and rather pleasant to be completely let alone, but in the long run rather peculiar. Rubber mats in the halls with gray and tan not-un-Indianlike designs; compact bedroom with closets and drawers of unpainted wood. All the lights were left on night and day. When I called Bob's attention to this, he said that the reservoir plant supplied more power than anybody could use—they also left all the lights on in their house.

WELLFLEET, 1948

January 19, '48. Wellfleet: I went out for a walk back of the house with the dogs—they looked quite handsome against the sheet of snow, in which there were only a few animal tracks. Beyond the hill, where you go down to the road from the Walkers', the scrub pine were all powdered with snow, so that they looked like some kind of white and green filigree. Coming back, I saw the marsh wide, blond and yellow under the graying Cape Cod sky that was yet full of bright cheering light where the sun was going down toward the bay. —I had had a good day's work on Zuñi, had taken two straight drinks of good scotch, stood in the house enjoying its brightness and pleasantness—bow window in the dining room, gleam of candlesticks, comfortable pink and blue of Elena's middle room—before starting out with the dogs, who were in a state of joyful excitement. I let them out, then came back for another drink, and enjoyed the look of the house some more. They returned, not finding me with them, and scratched at the front door.

May 10: In the gray May afternoon, between 5 and 6, the Wellfleet houses, in the dim distance, looked like white ghosts, across the dry brown marsh running to pink, on the hither side of which the shadbushes, late blooming, looked whiter.

May 11: Walking with dogs: Bambi's fur had a golden fringe from the sun, and then little gnats came flying around my head, a lighter straw-colored gold—I waved them away with my stick.

Horseshoe crabs: At the bay, in July, I found many of them lying on their backs and bent at an angle, with their sharp tails sticking up in the air, still alive but unable to get back to the water, because, except in the water, they could not turn themselves over. I would pick them up by the tail and throw them back. Their heavy bronze carapaces, six spider legs with small claws, thick laminations (?) and their [illegible]. One could see how they had been able to survive from before the days of the mammals—practically indestructible. The dead ones were making a stink.

Then I saw what I thought was a small crab pushing a large one, which had been stranded, out to sea. I picked him up by the tail, and he hung on to the one in front with his two front claws, so that this one was dangling, too. Then I saw others of these pairs. In one case, the big one (always in front) was buried in the sand, and I assumed that the small one was digging it out—I tried to help. Later, when I looked them up, I discovered that the big ones were the females and smaller ones the males. This was the mating season, when the females would drag the males in and lay their eggs at the line of the surf, burrowing into the sand. Then they would pull the male along, and he would fertilize them. At other times of year they lived in the deeper water (eating sea worms). Those who were left on their backs by the surf in the sun had no chance of getting back. It was extraordinary to think of the creatures perpetuating themselves in their present form through all those thousands of years. It inspired one with a certain respect for them. I remembered that John Bishop had also been struck by them: *Colloquy of a King Crab*. He seems to have found in them a symbol for his own later life: crawling but never destroyed. I thought rather of the superficial differences, but underlying identity, between their sexual life and ours—driven to carry on the species, resisting any attempts to interfere with it (as when I picked one up by the tail). Amount of thought one gives to sex, even at my age, when one no longer needs to. This doesn't have the effect, for me, of degrading human life (though it makes me realize that we waste time and energy on these primitive impulses), but of making me respect the animals.

Spectacle Ponds, early July '48: I went there for the first time with Reuel; then with Elena, not long afterward. I had expected to find them interesting, from what I had heard, and they enchanted me when I found them, after several futile expeditions, and had on me an emotional effect.

One sees the big one first, coming down the sandy road: its dark blue hill-and-tree-locked water. At the bottom of the road, on the left, are the gray boards of some old shack, of unrecognizable shape and purpose, and in the little clearing that leads to it, the white shriveled-up splinters of turtle eggs that lay about the holes for the nests—Reuel took them for the bones of crabs. (When I first came, however, I made my way down through the bushes.)

There is a flat stretch of ground between the two ponds, a sort of wild cranberry bog covered with little cranberry blossoms and with marvelous pogonia and

adder's mouth, larger than at Higgins Pond, and inten-
sified to vivider tinges. The colors vary in proportion to
whether they have sprung up in places where they got
more or little sun—the adder's mouth from a fainter to
a flamelike mauve (?), startling as it rises against the
green of cranberry shoots and bog grass—with the fine
little wings of its flowers and its bearded crazy flap that,
in this exceptional orchid, rises at the top like a crest instead of hanging down like a tongue. There is something
snakelike about these pogonia blossoms while the adder's
mouth, with its colubrine name, is shyer and less defiant.

On the left is the smaller and muddy pond, with both
the white bowl-like and the yellow ball-like water lilies.
If you wade in, you sink through a layer of goo but find
firm ground underneath. The clay is absolutely red, as
if the soil had a lot of iron.

On the other side, the larger pond lies, half enclosed
by a hilly bank, solitary, deep, wild, and mysterious. A
zone of some water plant with tiny white flowers runs all
the way around a little out from the shore. Between the
shore and this is white sand, where great pollywogs lie;
but the stems of the waterweeds make a forest where it
is black below. On the hither side, the bottom drops
steeply, and the middle is deep and dark. But inshore it
is limpid and still, a contrast, full of dignity and distinction, to its muddy probably shallow neighbor. Jack Phil-
lips once saw under the water what he thought was a
fabulous monster but turned out to be an enormous snapping turtle wrestling with an enormous eel. We found a
painted turtle's shell, with the red markings very bright,
completely cleaned out. The bullfrogs had the finest
voices that I ever remember to have heard: they were
really musical, tuneful. I felt about the place a wildness
unlike anything one finds at the ponds we frequent. It
was as if it existed for itself, as if the frogs and the orchids

Elena Wilson

Edmund and Helen Miranda Wilson, 1948

flourished and perfected themselves, had their lives, for their own satisfaction. Nobody came to see them. They did not have to be on their guard against being picked or caught (the frogs were not troubled by our presence but, after a moment, went on with their singing). There it was, walled in, complete in itself, absorbing its summer days, lying open from sun to sun, with the ponds bending water lilies and water grass, frogs and turtles, pickerel and perch, in their unplumbed unfished-in depths.

The emotional effect of this spot was due, I suppose, to some affinity that I felt between it and my life at this time—and a darkness into which I sink and a clear round single lens, well guarded and hidden away. Many things nourished and lurking at the bottom that have not yet been brought to light.

Elena, when she swam across it, said that it was a little stagnant.

Dos, July 28, '48: He said that he had had a pretty heavy day, packing up books and things to leave his house and going to Susan [Glaspell]'s funeral; was eager for a drink, and I poured the glass about two thirds full of Usher's. We had a conversation before dinner in my study. He seemed to have picked himself up and recovered his old enthusiasm and his excitement about travel and discovery—was very much steamed up about going to Brazil, wanted to see something of an expedition to explore the Amazon. He had just seen a cousin from Madeira, from which the Portuguese end of the family came—a man he had never met before. He had come to New York on business—D. had hoped he was a wine manufacturer, but he had turned out to be a lace manufacturer. He learned for the first time that the name, adopted, apparently, in the eighteenth century, had been Passos di (?) Christo, Steps of Christ, and that the family

crest was a crown of thorns and three nails. This had
amused him and made him feel better, as he had been
"feeling rather sorry for himself." He seemed to feel that
he had neglected his Portuguese tradition—Unamuno[1]
had told him that in Spain. He thought of studying Portuguese at the Berlitz School for a few weeks before he
left. They had some very good lyric poetry. —He had
been in Iowa and talked enthusiastically about corn hy-
bridization.

[1] Miguel Unamuno (1864–1936), Spanish philosopher and
poet.

TANGLEWOOD, 1948

[During the summer of 1948, EW and Elena went as usual to Tanglewood for the annual music festival. This time EW planned to write a piece, "Koussevitsky at Tanglewood," which appeared in *The New Yorker*, September 4 issue. His notes, however, deal less with the music than with his recent readings of Gogol and his renewed interest in Henry James, aroused by the appearance of James's *Notebooks* in 1947, edited by Matthiessen and Murdock, and the 1946 reprint of *The American Scene*, for which W. H. Auden had supplied an introduction. Wilson reviewed both volumes in *The New Yorker*. He seems also to have read two of James's plays in anticipation of Leon Edel's edition of the *Complete Plays* which was forthcoming. His reading of James led him to explore the Qu'Acre Circle of friends, of which Henry James and Edith Wharton had been the central figures— Qu'Acre being the country house in England of the expatriate Howard Sturgis, whose novel *Belchamber* EW read with some bewilderment and amusement. He does not seem to grasp in these ruminations the homosexual nature of Sturgis (who is fully described in Santayana's memoirs) and the manner in which this influenced the character of Sainty in *Belchamber*, who marries an Englishwoman, never consummates the marriage, but "mothers" her child by another man. EW's remark about "the lack of virility" of the Qu'Acre males seems to miss the deeper sources of the kind of sexual freedom espoused there and both Henry James's and Edith Wharton's acceptance of these gay friends—they having long before laid aside their residual puritanical scruples. EW seems also to have read Henry Adams' novel *Esther* for the first time.]

Tanglewood, '48: Rosenbaum, owner of drugstores, who made a trip from Cleveland by plane every weekend, to come to Tanglewood.

Crowd on lawn outside shed during Sunday concert: one group had a little sign on a pole stuck in the ground: Wanted, a hitch to N.Y.C.

Bernstein, conducting Mahler, was better than I have ever seen him—showed delicacy as well as intensity, and there were only moments when he seemed to be doing an interpretive dance to the music rather than leading the orchestra. Everything in the symphony but the kitchen stove—horns had to keep going offstage and coming back again; at one moment it sounded as if there were supposed to be a cabaret next door while more solemn developments were taking place in the orchestra.

Grechaninov, 84,[1] beaming and bowing, his hair still faintly yellow—next morning sat out in front of the an-

---

[1] Aleksander Grechaninov (1864–1956), Russian composer noted for his religious music and music for children.

tique store on a bench between the two crouching iron dogs, with his panama hat at the angle of an old master.

From the shed you look out on either side into walls of summer leafage.

Beings of sentiment and eloquence, Gogol and *Vechera Mirgorod*. Thick and rich as some Ukrainian soup full of vegetables and pieces of meat or fish—the salted and spiced dishes that the old couple are always eating in *Starosvetskiye Pomeshchiki*. The Ukrainian breads and *perozhki*—the tangled forests and overgrown gardens, where sudden transformations occur. Hobgoblins and treasures appear (extraordinary reality of these hobgoblins even in *Strashraya Mest*)—words and phrases in homely but luscious lumps—nutritious long paragraphs that flow thickly, like jam poured into a jar, or are stirred round like dough in a bowl—or words and phrases like poppy seeds or nuts in some of their solid breads. Influence of Sterne—tears.

—Naturalness and unexpectedness of the rustic or grotesque symbols: the cat in *Starosvetskiye Pomeshchiki* that is lured into joining the wild cats through a hole in the bottom of the barn and will not come back to the house again; the breakdown, the escape, of the old lady's life from the comfortable close in which she does all the work and takes care of, constantly feeding, the husband. Characteristic combination in Gogol of the stagnant and the stifling with the passionate and the *détraqué*. He nourishes himself, reposes, in this loose and easygoing and messy, rubbishy and dirty and run-down world: yet he undermines and derides it: endures chagrin, disgust—*skuchno na etom svete, gospoda*—2nd part of *Mertvye Dushi* and Gogol can't get out: the visionary characters turn out to be just as [illegible] as the others, the whole atmosphere remains provincial and vulgar—general prevalence of *poshlost*—smelly and littered and stuffy (cluttered) lady and clogged and rank—overeaten and drunken-boorish and coarsely genial.

> *Comic name: Max Korureich*
> *Father's language:* Zounds! (only person I ever heard
> say this)
> It don't matter, or, It makes no matter.
> A land office business
> Besotted with egoism

General problem of viscous prose writing in early nineteenth century: Lamb (De Quincey art), Melville—even first popular writers like Balzac and Scott—hadn't anything to do with poetry? Milton, Keats?—return to Renaissance prose? Romantic revival? Paragraphs do not move —sentences full of plums, like a fruitcake—metaphors and anecdotes that are whole little compositions in themselves: Gogol in this respect like Scott's preliminaries. Hawthorne also a form of this: difficulty of hearing something that does not move: cadences for their own sake: Sir Thomas Browne.

Reuel's limerick—*(spring of 1947)*. I had been reading him Edward Lear in the Carlyle, and he presently produced the following:

> There was an old man of Kiel.
> Who made people feel like a heel.
> When they said, You're abrupt.
> He only said, Yup—
> That consistent old man of Kiel.

When I asked him to repeat it for Elena, he threw himself around from bed to bed as he did so.

Edmund and Reuel Wilson, as photographed by
Henri Cartier-Bresson, *ca.* 1948

At Wellfleet movie: There's a huge moth on the screen.

When we were playing the adverb game (summer '48), and he had to look out the door *romantically,* he said: "Yon weather!—'Tis misty!" —Of the fishermen, lying on their wooden beds, when he went out with them in the morning, he said, "They look suspiciously characteristic."

Mark Twain's *Roughing It:* A good deal of the first volume good—but Virginia City part unsatisfactory, because you get so little idea of how he lived there. Labored tall tales and funny stories, often boring, though a few are good. Ambivalence about Indians (are they worthless or to be pitied?—check Volume I); missionaries (had they done the Hawaiians good or bad in Christianizing them?); sour picture of mining in Nevada and glowing picture of California miners. —And what is the reason for the last of the Appendices? The unfortunate journalist, "half-witted" though he may have been, obviously behaved very well in standing up to those two men, one of whom had threatened to kill him (and M.T. has told you in no uncertain terms that killing was easy and frequent), and refusing to sign a retraction. Why does M.T. hold him up to ridicule, jeering at him between the paragraphs? He had probably been punished, too, for the personalities he had published (story told us by Clark about the Welsh miners whom he had made fun of taking him up to the top of Mount Davis, stripping him, rubbing him with linseed oil, and leaving him to come back naked just at the time in the morning when everybody was going to work). Had he ever himself resented the big interests and had to knuckle under to them?

Henry James: The Author of Beltraffio:[2] on the whole, a decidedly bitter book [of tales] and unusually cruel for James—"Georgina's Reasons" contains a picture of a remorseless American bitch which is, so far as I remember, unique in James. She is also some kind of abnormal case, like Oliver Chancellor in *The Bostonians* (also of the 80s), well described but not deeply explored by James. "The Path of Duty" involves the same theme as several other stories—including, as I believe, "The Turn of the Screw," of the character—in this case the woman who is telling the story—who acts mischievously to other people's detriment, while persuaded that she is acting from the highest motives. Like the governess in "The T. of the Screw," she doesn't admit to the reader or herself that she was in love with the beautiful young Englishman. —Renunciation—the word is used and emphasized at the end—is here shown as the result of moral scruples which are the result of the hero's weakness; but the woman is made the villain in a way that is rare with James: the young navy man's impotent predicament is something that *she* has done to him.

Henry James's Theatricals: sterile little devices, the only really bad things he wrote—the false motivations: English pursuit of inheritances not necessarily implausible but ridiculous situations of men feeling compelled to marry women who propose to them—too much getting people in and out of doors (going for a walk, going to

---

[2] This was a volume of tales published by Henry James in 1885. "Georgina's Reasons" describes a New York woman who secretly marries a naval officer, has a child by him, and still secretly gives it away, as if it were illegitimate. She then marries again, thus becoming a bigamist and putting her husband in a quandary. *The Awkward Age* was not, as EW suggests, of this period; it was written thirteen years later and published in 1899.

the garden, going to one's room, going to write letters—
he takes up so much time getting them on and off the
stage that he hardly gives himself time for character and
real situation)—strange preface to second volume, in
which he talks about how almost everything has to be
thrown overboard in order to write a play: thus you gain
the "intensity" of the theater, which is just what he never,
here, comes near. It is really, I think, one of his ways of
trying to conceal from his reader and himself the thinness
and poorness of his material at this period—for he carried the mechanics on into *The Awkward Age* (like the
messengering in *The Wings of the Dove*). —The mannerism that became automatic of having someone mistake
someone else—as to whom or what was being referred to
—how did he manage to do this again and again, not
only in these plays but in his fiction, without ever becoming aware how tiresome and pointless it was.

The American Scene—in the review, I left out two of
the most important things: the fact that H.J. hadn't a
drop of Yankee blood in his veins and didn't know certain things from the inside and far back: see the passage about the Concord Bridge. If he had come from New
England, he wouldn't have thought that the embattled
farmers were unconscious of the historical importance of
their act: they were perhaps more conscious than the
Americans of the 1900s. —The way he uses here his
method of starting on the surface of a subject as if with
timidity and deference, then begins probing beneath the
conventional aspects, and finally, as it were, whisks the
covering veil away and pounces on the hidden and fundamental reality: chapter on Philadelphia—the old families,
the clubs, with the political corruption only adumbrated
(shows how the best people manage to live in a world of
horses and sport in order not to recognize it), then finally

the prison, where he finds that the prisoners seem inter-changeable with the people in the clubs.

Belchamber:[3] Same theme as H. James's short story "The Solution" and his comedy *Disengaged*; innocent and upright man induced to marry girl by being con-vinced he has compromised her. (James, Edith Whar-ton, Santayana, L. P. Smith, Howard Sturgis—Henry Adams, George Cabot Lodge, T. Stickney—all more or less the same group.) The kind of book about the English upper classes that perhaps nobody but an American could have written: it gives them away from the inside, and shows a peer letting down his position. No wonder the English public didn't like it when it first came out. It is also perhaps American of the period and the group in the lack of virility, the defeatism of its hero: H. James and H. Adams.

The homosexuality of [Henry Blake] Fuller at least kept him from the comfortable domesticity of Howells.[4]

Esther:[5] Situation seems rather improbable. If the girl had had such strong views on religion at that period, she would have been a conspicuous bluestocking, and an am-bitious young clergyman would not have dallied with her long. If she were merely reflecting her father's views, she might have adapted them if she had cared for the man. She might have had a father tie-up like Henry Adams'

[3] *Belchamber* (1904), by Howard O. Sturgis (1855–1920). Sainty is its principal character.

[4] Henry Blake Fuller (1857–1929), the Chicago novelist. See "Henry Blake Fuller: The Art of Making It Flat" in EW's posthumous *The Devils and Canon Barham* (1973).

[5] Henry Adams' pseudonymous novel *Esther* was published in 1884.

wife, which would have accounted for her not wanting to marry—he makes the father talk about murdering a successful writer—but that is not sufficiently brought out, and the situation is left as a deadlock between love and principle. The love part is hardly convincing; the principle is the kind of thing that Adams sincerely strongly felt, and the upshot—"But I don't love you, George; I love him"—is only intelligible as a parable of Adams' own dilemma between the scientific and the religious points of view. [*Belchamber*] Elena says that it follows somewhat the formula of English novels of the period about sensitive little boys such as Mrs. Humphry Ward's misunderstanding. Sainty's sex life completely unaccounted for. Also, why didn't he try to do something with his allegedly brilliant intellectual ability? —Is it a book about English society or a book about a feminine male? —Mother love for the baby. —Book quite tight and intense—liveliness which is almost vital, natural storytelling gift. —British types perhaps a little too typical.

VISIT TO EDNA MILLAY

[EW's emotional visit to Edna Millay, in the Berkshires, mentioned in the Introduction to this volume, was
recorded in the journals shortly afterwards. Millay died
two years later and EW wrote a long memoir published
in *The Nation* and then reprinted in *The Shores of Light*
(1952). The journal record gives certain literary references he did not later use and differs in a number of other
ways in the comments EW makes to himself but did not
choose to utilize in the public record. The first literary
reference is to Millay's poem "The Poet and His Book"
from *Second April,* a sustained cry for recognition of the
artist after death. The second reference was to their talk
of the translation of a poem by Catullus from which EW
quotes in his memoir the lines:

> Ipse valere, opto et taetrum hunc deponere morbum.
> O di, reddite mi hoc pro pietate mea!

This is No. lxxvi in the *Carmina* and is not always capi-
talized or punctuated as above. The James Michie translation (1969) renders the lines as follows:

> But, gods, if I have served you, grant my prayer:
> Health, and an end to this diseased despair.

The poem deals, characteristically, with the death of love.

[The third literary allusion, not incorporated in the memoir, deals with the waning of strength and the desire to be remembered as in Millay's poem. EW speaks of the passage in Proust where the narrator recounts how the writer Bergotte rationalized (when his talent was failing and he wrote something inferior) that even if what he was writing was not up to his best, it should be published nevertheless because it could still be "useful." The passage occurs in *A l'ombre des jeunes filles en fleur* and in the Scott-Moncrieff translation (*Within a Budding Grove*) reads:

> Only many years later, when he no longer had any talent, whenever he wrote anything with which he was not satisfied, so as not to have to suppress it, as he ought to have done, so as to be able to publish it with a clear conscience he would repeat, but to himself this time: "After all, it is more or less accurate, it must be of some value to the country."

EW's recall of Bergotte in Proust in relation to Millay illustrates the powerful effect her dream of posthumous recognition had on him. In another passage (in *The Guermantes Way,* Part Two) Proust writes of Bergotte's suffering from the "strain" of his diminished powers pitted against the reputation he had established. Millay had achieved a large popular reputation in her time: but she suffered now from the burning out of her talent. Proust writes: "A dead writer can at least be illustrious without any strain on himself. The effulgence of his name is stopped short by the stone upon his grave. In the deaf-

ness of the eternal sleep he is not importuned by Glory."
What is clear in EW's journal entry is the extent to
which he identified himself with Millay and thought of
himself as having survived a crisis in his own recent self-
rehabilitation.]

Visit to Edna [Millay] Boissevain,[1] *August 6 [1948].*
It was nineteen years since I had seen her. We drove
through the long tunnel of greenery that leads to their
place, and it made me feel how much she had been
buried there—passed the path that leads to the house
and came to the barns, then realized we had to go back.
Old big black farm dog came out of the path. Gene appeared from the house in his working clothes. He had
aged—was somewhat gray and stooped; shuffled in his
leather moccasin-shoes, his eyes looked rather cowed,
ashamed of his life. "I'll go and get my child." The black
bust of Sappho with its white eyes, on its big pedestal; the
black Javanese things, with their pale birds, hung on the
wall. The two couches were badly worn. It was as if the
time when two people set up keeping house together were
now so long past that it had been years since they looked
at the room, since they had tried to bring to bear on it
any creative imagination. Beyond the window were three
old rusty tin oil barrels, upended, so that they could put
food on them for the birds without having the squirrels,
who couldn't [climb] up the sides [to] get it. In the
corner, a litter of papers, copybooks and poetry books, on
the couch, the chair, the table, the floor.

Edna came in. I didn't recognize her as she was coming
around the things in the middle of the room. She had on
slacks and a white working shirt open at the neck. She

[1] Edna St. Vincent Millay Boissevain (1892–1950). See *The
Shores of Light,* pp. 744–93, and *The Twenties, passim.*

had changed terribly: her cheeks were fat and red, and she had flabby jowls—resembled her mother for the first time that I had noticed it. Her eyes looked quite different: Irish lids, like her mother's without the spectacles. Eyes bright green with a frightened expression. She was terribly nervous: her old tension had turned into a form of the shakes. I thought that she showed badly the effects of drinking. Her hands shook and her mouth and chin flapped like an old woman's. There was a martini on the little table, and Gene brought us martinis. Gene kept drinking up about two thirds of her drink, on the pretext of giving her a fresh one. At moments he would baby her in a way that had undoubtedly become habitual (just as I used to do with Mary [McCarthy]), and at moments she would show signs of bursting into tears, becoming hysterical about not being able to find a poem or something. She said she was so *excited!* about writing again during the last two months after not having done so for two years. Elena said that, from where she had been sitting, Edna's profile looked like a child's; but I saw mostly her full face, and it disconcerted me. Her hair was still red and hung, cut short, down her neck. There were moments when she sounded like a good-natured healthy laughing elderly woman, but even this seemed to cause a strain of effort, punctuating the reading of poetry, the pressure that she put upon you for assurance, approval, praise. As it went on, she became less nervous, did not tremble and gabble so, and, in proportion, we became more involved in her emotion, and I felt, just as I had when she was young, that I was being sucked into her narrow and noble world, where all that mattered was herself and her poetry, and I felt the need to break away from it—when I made the move to go—so I had, when I had been in love with her, and experienced such relief, at one point, at putting her out of my mind and returning to my old intellectual life by starting a play of Sophocles, even before she had gone to Europe.

I was surprised that she should say she had read John Bishop's elegy on Scott,[2] and that she should talk with enthusiasm of J.'s poetry—said it had more overtones than that of anybody else: like a row of poplars on a river, with another row reflected in the river. When I talked about my not having realized, at the time that he was alive, that the gloomy side of his writing was real and mortal, she said, yes, he had been despairing. Much of her own new work was of an unrelieved darkness, and she was translating the poem of Catullus in which he prays to have his early *pietas* restored, which was very much in her own present mood. In judging the Guggenheim candidates, she had gagged at Horace Gregory's[3] Catullus and didn't want to give him a fellowship in spite of a long list of names supporting him.

I got her to read "The Poet and His Book" and, having by that time had three or four martinis, was almost in tears before she had finished it. —Elena said that Gene was shaking me at her as if I had been a new toy. —I was depressed at her complaints about the critics—this continual complaining and having to be comforted is one of the most annoying traits of women writers: Elinor Wylie, Louise Bogan, Anaïs Nin (Dawn Powell the only woman I know, I think, who doesn't have it)—especially when it turned out that the subversive mockers of one of her sonnets were simply the writers of unfavorable reviews.

Gene talked about his family in Holland. A cousin had been tortured and killed, others had had hairbreadth escapes in hiding. Partly explains E.'s war hysteria. She

---

[2] Bishop's elegy on F. Scott Fitzgerald appeared in *The Crack-Up* (1945), edited by EW.

[3] Horace Gregory, the poet, essayist, and translator.

Edna St. Vincent Millay and Eugen Boissevain

talked about his family as "our relatives" and had been furiously sending them packages. Had learned Dutch and written a poem in Dutch, which she read to Elena.

I felt a certain satisfaction in the idea that I was out-lasting her, but at the same time was troubled and de-pressed at finding the metamorphosis she had undergone. She seemed to have ceased to care about her looks—one of the things that happens to the drinker, and I decided that the reason she did not like to go out was that she did not want to be seen. I kept looking away and out the window. —At the same time, the strength of her char-acter and her genius overcame me, as the visit went on, just as it always had. One could not make any impression upon her—except occasionally by criticizing her poetry—any more now than in her youth. —I reflected in dismay, but not without some satisfaction, at my own relative competence and health, on the tendency of the writers of my generation to burn themselves out or break down: Scott and Zelda, John, Phelps Putnam (just dead),[4] Paul Rosenfeld, Elinor Wylie, Edna. One didn't really believe till one saw it demonstrated that giving oneself up com-pletely to art, to emotion, to enjoyment, without planning for the future or counting the cost, produced dreadful disabilities and bankruptcies later. How could I have imagined the later fate of either Phelps or Edna even at the time I wrote my sonnet about them, when I saw them as merely hung up or becalmed.

—Gene said that he would ask us to dinner, but that he was the only thing in the house. I made a little joke based on the assumption that he meant he was the only thing to eat, in which Edna merrily joined—then it oc-curred to me that he *was* the only thing to eat, and that

[4] Phelps Putnam (1894–1948), American poet befriended by EW.

E. had more or less eaten him. I'm the cook and bottle washer and maid—he went on to explain. —And the crew of the *Nancy Brig!* cried Edna. —What would she do if he died first?

—She said that she had been dismayed when *Make Bright the Arrows* had been issued in the same format as her other books as if it had been meant to be on a plane with them. She had intended it to be a pamphlet in paper, to be read and thrown away. And then the reviewers had said about it that Miss Millay had used to be a conscientious artist, but had now apparently given up the effort—dreadful things like that! —When she began talking about whether it wasn't better that the public should get Catullus even in an imperfect translation, Gene pulled her up—said, Remember that was what you thought about your war poetry: that it was important to rouse the country. I thought this was very shrewd of him and showed excellent judgment—I agreed and said that it was dangerous to let yourself down, giving the excuse that you were benefiting other people: you could never do people good by giving them inferior work. I thought of the passage in Proust where he tells how Bergotte believed, when his talent was failing, and he wrote something he knew to be inferior, that it ought to be published because it was "useful."

—A few days afterwards (August 10), the whole thing had come to seem like one of my recurrent dreams about her (though in these she would be still small, though rather wrinkled, never at all stout)—a little obsessively nightmarish: going back into that early state of mind, intense, imprisonedly, desperately personal. The intervening eighteen years made so long a stretch that I couldn't really imagine or contemplate it; I had found them just as I had left them when I had gone to call there with the Holdens [Louise Bogan], except for the physical changes, their apparently constantly increasing isolation, and the signs of the wear and tear of their reciprocal relation—so that, connecting itself only with the past, with nothing that had happened in between either to me or to the world, the visit was like the desires and fears, the revived emotions, of sleep: old images exaggerated, deformed, swollen with longing and horror. She was there, though in a somewhat different way, almost as disconcerting as she had ever been in the twenties, to which she had completely belonged—for she was not a part of the present, and my relation to her, taking place now, did not belong to the present and exerted on me a sort of pressure as if to gouge me out, extirpate me, from my present personality and point of view and all that, during the intervening years, had made it.

Lenox. We walked along the back road at night and went into the driveway of a deserted place, where the path was growing weedy and long and the pines were massed in the darkness. At last we came to an angle of low outbuildings—one couldn't tell what they had been before—and, beyond them, what Elena took for a swimming pool, but what turned out to be the enormous cellar of a house demolished for taxes, pale and untidy in the night. It had not been entirely cleaned and there were large chunks of debris—ceilings? walls?—of which one could not tell the use. The whole effect was desolate and spooky.

—And so was the immense mansion of Mrs. Henry White,[5] now turned into a hotel called Elm Court, which

[5] Mrs. Henry White, the former Margaret Stuyvesant Rutherford, had been a friend of Edith Wharton's in Newport. She was the wife of the American diplomat and later ambassador, and lived in England for many years.

was $25 a day. $15 for a servant's room. Overgrown imitation of an Elizabethan (?) cottage, a super-witch's house, painted a brownish yellow and with carved black wooden fringe around the gables (made in the Sloane workshops?) —Mrs. W. had been a Miss Rutherford: nineteenth-century romantic busts and a painting of a Puritan youth and maiden praying in a field, big Chinese jars with dragons, a clock inlaid with wood and mother-of-pearl. In the front a reproduction of the turtle fountain in Rome; behind, the gardens, a cloister with dolphin drinking founts, bright red and yellow geraniums planted in pots, a sundial of bronze hoops held by a mythological figure. Inside, enormous couches.

Edith Wharton's place.[6] It had been painted white with green blinds since the summer before when we had seen it. Also desolating, but in a different style. You went upstairs to the second floor, as in a French château. Pale green walls, white molded ceilings; dark and rather unimaginative Dutch panels of flowers and fruit; bronze linings to the fireplaces, with bas-relief figures of cooks, etc. Dining room, living room, library—house looks large from outside, but not so many rooms. Whole wings of servants' quarters and presumably first floor. Formal furniture, perhaps not hers—did not seem to have been adopted as a school building, though now used for the seniors of Fox Hollow School. Strange to see cheap standardized tables and chairs (like the pieces I bought at Hyannis) and the little dormitory beds in the high and stately bedrooms. Porch roof, from which you look down on the terrace: conical cypresses (?), hemlocks and hemlock hedges; wide steps lead down from the terrace (Clyde Fitch and Henry James must have been enter-

[6] Edith Wharton's house, The Mount, was built by her at Lenox in 1901.

tained out there): bleak and false effect of imitation of
an Italian villa—lake in a picturesque distance. Gardens
blooming now only meagerly: a few small long-stemmed
yellow lilies—she must have known all the names of the
flowers. Semi-rough wall with ogival apertures, now covered with vines but not quite like a ruin, that she built
from the proceeds of *The House of Mirth.* —The whole
place characteristic: deliberate dignity; France and Italy
Americanized; but good style, no bad taste. —All these
places, which represent a kind of thing that I used to see
in my youth, now belong to an obsolete period. You leave
them with a depressing feeling of emptiness, of expen-
diture and grandeur of living that did not procure satisfaction, the achievement of human values. They did not
last, they should not have lasted. They are today only
good for schools, for the activities of Tanglewood, and
they are not well adapted for these. —Summer in the
1900s.

WELLFLEET AND STAMFORD, 1949

January 18, '49. Spectacle Ponds: Walked there with Elena—she in her gray coat that she said was old-fashioned, with the hood around her head. The big pond a wonderful deep dark green that reflected the pines of the banks in a deeper green than they were—it lay there embedded in the ground, a solid substance, absolutely smooth, absolutely motionless, with no watery vibration, not exactly vitreous, not exactly gelatinous, but like an unheard-of clear and rich mineral. The little oaks had lost all their leaves and scratched the dark background around it with slight gray skeletons that looked like the pale tracings of trees on photographic negatives. —The dogs plunged around after rabbits and deer—we would hear them excitedly shrieking from up the further slope, as if they thought they had treed something, and on the way back, Pal would be heard beagling-beagling, and they would dash off after him, eventually catching up with us again. No animals—only the dogs knew their presence. —It had been an evenly gray January day, but on the way home, as twilight came on, the gray of the west seemed translucent—brighter and clearer and fresher

than any light one had had that day. This cheerful late
clearness and the quietness of evening in the winter coun-
tryside. Satisfaction, while looking at the pond, where
George C.'s[1] cigarette package and paper cups still lay, of
feeling that one remained with the things of the Cape
and saw them as vacationers never did.

Stamford from February 14, '49. Hillcrest Park, with
its big and ugly and not well-designed houses, built in the
early 1900s. The Eitingon "casias" had originally been a
big stable and was still hardly filled with stalls, in the
back a big door at the top of an incline, where the hay
wagons had been brought in. They had added a few
flimsy rooms, decorated in very bad taste—which are supposed to have cost $2,000 apiece (I think)—to the big
"studio," where Franz [Höllering] had written his novel
and Marc Blitzstein one of his operas. Lamps in the
living room, with stands of some green material which
worried one both by their clumsiness and by the impossibility of making out whether they represented dolphins
or human figures—actually they represented neither, but
were merely rough twists that meant nothing, two busts
of Negroes, done by Bess, a man and a woman, the latter
with rouge on the mouth and nails and the upper arms
too short; also, two abominable paintings: one a still-life,
one a green and black abstract affair that involved
patches of leopardskin and pink and suggested a sexual
entanglement (interlacing?) that was difficult to work
out. In the corner, a big double bed covered, including
the headboard, with green and pink chintz patterned with
enormous blossoms. Dark-stained bookcases above the radiators, dried up and warped miscellaneous books: a
cheap old series of the English romantic poets mixed up

[1] George Cram Cook.

with odds and ends of Soviet Marxist publications.
—Nevertheless, I liked the room—reminded me pleas-
antly of my best days at Trees: some warmish days, then
some snow that for a short time snowed us in, then languid sleepy blurry days, a heavy mist from the sound, a
clump of yellow crocuses, then bright and clear days of
earliest spring, with the grass between the house and the
lake already very green. I found a little brown tree toad
on the threshold of the door from the garage to one bedroom.

—Staleness and bad taste of all this aspect of Stamford
—but there is something about it I rather like, has something in common with Red Bank and Rumson. Elena can
hardly be expected to like it much, though. Old lumpy
stone porte cocheres that shadow the cavernous portals of
those uncomfortable somber expensive houses that nobody much wants any longer or that people can no longer
keep up. The Japanese place next door.

—Reckie, who has never before been anywhere but the
Cape, very homesick and depressed at finding himself in
a community where he was no longer supreme but obliged
to contend with other dogs: red setters, Dalmatians,
Marta H.'s Kerry blue—that did not recognize his position. There were also several spaniels—most of the dogs
rather ratty like everything else in Hillcrest Park. Reckie
and Bambi would return from their forays with muzzle
and ears chewed up.

—When I walked into town with Reckie, we attracted
the attention of a pack of dogs, dirty mongrel tramps that
seemed in some cases to have a chow strain, that reminded
me of the dogs of Zuñi, and when I arrived at the Rip-
powan River, I was surprised and disgusted to find that
there was a kind of reef in the middle, the gray skeleton
of a Flexible Flyer lying on its back like a dead horseshoe

crab—sand flats matted with long dead grass, on which were stranded tin cans, an old mattress and an old umbrella—and this reminded me of the Zuñi River. How messy, after all, a good deal of America is! I was told that the Democrats and Republicans were always displacing one another in Stamford, so that they cared nothing about improving the city but only about getting for themselves what they could while they were in office. Greenwich—it was a man from Greenwich, who had picked me up on my way into town—was better run, he said—they had some kind of permanent board (probably not all politicians) who were responsible for things.

Edith Verrell: Her conversation at dinner: had been put upon and exploited, it seemed, by everybody she had ever worked for. She had been employed as a nanny by a cousin who occupied a higher station in life and who had apparently been merciless with her; also, by a family with a title in London. They made the servants work so hard: there'd be a day when they'd polish all the brasses, etc. When she'd broken a vase or something, they took it out of her wages, which meant she didn't [have] any for weeks.

—English food: shells, cockles, winkles, fish and chips, bubble and squeak, suet pudding—her unfeigned enthusiasm for them all—Oh, it's wonderful!—never seemed to her ignoble or unappetizing—kidney pie, veal and ham pie.

—I sent her to the movie of *Hamlet*—thought she'd seen it on the stage. After she had seen the film, she said that "the tragedy was a little overdone."

—Came from the country near Brighton (where Arthur Verrall, the Greek scholar, was born: this pleased her immensely when I told her). Dropped her *g*'s, did

not say *wahnderful* or *aao*. Had always been deaf and
that was why she was so backward. They had not thought
it worthwhile or possible to have her taught anything.

—The Höllerings said that she gave the impression of
being one of the Brontë sisters who didn't write, she had
just had a hysterectomy or something.

February 21, '49. Louise C.:[2] When she had come on
two winters ago, she had been much too fat; now she was
rather too thin—with an effect, such as I had never
known her to have, of gauntness: her face was sallow and
seemed almost leathery—so different from her old straw-
berry-and-cream lusciousness, with its flushing of high
color, and the lines in it might have been cut [with]
knives. She had a look of having suffered and of suffering, and she talked on and on, never asking us about ourselves and not always hearing our questions, slowly, em-
phatically, rather raspingly—Elena said she was getting
an old voice—about Henri[3] (of whose freedom in New
York she seemed to be somewhat jealous, complaining of
her sponging on people, of her taking home from restaurants bread and even desserts that she couldn't eat—she
had said that L. was "too aristocratic" when L. had objected to this—had her room at the Van Rensselaer full of
milk bottles, cracker boxes, and other odds and ends of
food, which she more or less lived on—even Elizabeth
Holding had stopped writing and given herself up to
drink, living on her former profits—and Henri had made
L. leave off her glasses because they made her look so
old, so she had difficulty reading the menu, and had
bought her on 14th St. the little hat she was wearing,
of which she wanted to know our opinion—I admired

[2] Louise Fort Connor.
[3] Henrietta Fort, Louise's sister, referred to as Henri.

her new bronzy mottled dress, which was characteristic
of her better taste); about her father (now 85 and living
in a club in Boston that had many other old men, one of
whom told indecent stories—her father would say, Now,
don't begin telling that story: I've heard it one thousand
times!); about her work as a nurse's aide (her hours were
11 p.m. to 7—she slept during the day—the other people
in the apartment house made so much noise that the only
way she could sleep was by keeping the radio on—she
was so good at handling relatives and friends of the pa-
tients that people thought she was the head nurse). The
only thing that she said that was amusing and characteristic was when I had thought the Three Cities were
Rock Island, Davenport, and Des Moines (should be
Moline), she said, laughing, "Don't be so eastern!" I
couldn't make any contact with her. It was probably
partly her deafness and partly the same kind of prattling
—she told us at merciless and unnecessary length about
the circumstances of her meeting Rosalind at the Ven-
dôme Hotel—that she and Henri had always done; but
it seemed to me that there was something wrong and I
even wondered whether, working at the hospital, she
hadn't been taking drugs—though, as she told us that
she drank in the evenings, this could hardly be possible.
Rosalind later reported that she took quantities of sleeping pills. She drank coffee at other times, and this would
have made her jittery and strain-worn. The Wymans had
given Pete[4] a job at their works: Bill W. was dull;
Dwight had been out once for a directors' meeting and
stayed about two minutes. You think you are going to
Chicago, which is about three and a half hours away, but
actually you don't get there. Couldn't understand how
Elena could drop her job at *Town and Country* to get

[4] Pete Connor, Louise's husband.

married and go and live in the country. Had the bitter-
ness—which I note also in Marta Höllering—of the
aging woman who hasn't had what she wanted in life and
becomes disagreeable about other people (Dorothy, Aunt
Laura[5]): spoke slightingly of our being "suburban," apropos of our consulting the timetable and arranging to meet
at the 4:30 and of my producing my briefcase. —All very
depressing, and one of the transformations that one hadn't
expected of life. What happened to Louise and Henrietta,
Ted Paramore, the Fitzgeralds, the Amens, Phelps
Putnam, John Bishop, Edna, Jean Gorman,[6] Berenice
Dewey[7] (Cummings is tougher), all the "glamorous" personalities of that period? John Amen's inadequate competence and [there] not being another job in Germany, as
reported by Miss Glover—it had all been a holiday for
him—a chance to make a new kind of whoopee—buz-
zing down to the Riviera on a plane, touring the Scandi-
navian countries, taking a week off in Paris. —When I
asked about Henri's elderly Irish admirer, L. said that he
was dead—adding, I can't help laughing when I hear
that somebody is dead. —I remembered, when I heard
about the sleeping pills, that, at the time she was on before, she made me drive her to a doctor so that she could
get the kind of pill that had been prescribed for her,
which she couldn't get without a prescription.

February 26. —She came to the Princeton Club at
4:15 and we sat in the deserted room for an hour. I got
quite a different impression this time. The room was
darker, so that she looked better. Evidently suffering a

[5] Dorothy Kimball, EW's cousin, and his aunt Laura Kimball.
[6] Wife of Herbert Gorman, the journalist and critic and first
biographer of James Joyce.
[7] See *The Thirties*, p. 354.

revulsion from N.Y. in the direction of Rock Island and her family. Obviously much better for them than California: Pete had a job in the Export Department of the Wymans' agricultural implement business—had learned all about tractors, etc., and they had some sort of position —were expected to entertain foreign buyers, though they couldn't speak any foreign language. After all, she said, P. had been better to her than anybody else, and she had been "unjust" to him in some ways. She showed me letters from her children. Talked herself the whole time. I simply sat there and asked her a question from time to time which she sometimes answered, sometimes not. Did I tell you about the Herbert Tareyton—man at cigar counter who had wanted to buy her cigarettes—attempted flirtation with which she would have nothing to do—had done it too many times, and they were awful. Amens: didn't like having mistresses around, especially upper-class mistresses. Mrs. —— was a friend of Marion's, John's mistress (a gratuitous assumption), and he made M. have her to dinner—had tried to fix up L. with his business associate. She had been rude to J., and didn't think he had liked it. Had left after dinner, saying he had a business conference. She had talked till 1:20 with M. —Depressing account of Henri and her poison-pen letters against Louise and her patrons. At her sessions with Elizabeth Holding, the latter, at a certain point of drinking, would thrust at Henri with a home truth. —When she was out West, she thought she wanted to come to New York, but when she did, it was disappointing. —She made much more sense than the time before, and I ceased to be worried about her. —Only at the end did she say anything about me or my affairs—said that Elena was "real"—J. and Mr. Amen were not real—but El. was the real McCoy. Only question she asked was what El. had thought of her.

Visit of MacInneses. March '49: Cady told me that Jim
had just had a case in which he had defended a Negro.
Two Negroes with their girls had been coming back to
the rooms of one of them after a night out. A scuffle had
occurred, and one of the men had been shot with his own
gun, which the two women testified they had felt in the
inside pocket of his coat while he was dancing with them.
The accused man said that it had gone off in the confusion, while they were struggling for possession of it. The
prosecution pointed out that it had been filed (what does
this mean?), so that it would have taken more effort to
cock it than would have been possible in the situation described: it would have needed both hands. When the trial
took place a month later, Jim took the gun and showed
that he could cock it with ease, then took it in the left
hand and did the same thing: he had been taking finger
exercises every day. He had spoken to me, also, of "dis-
appearing witnesses." In New York, he had been handling what he described as "a cloak and dagger affair."
This was one of those cases of women turning up and
charging that well-known movie actors were the fathers
of their children. J. was defending the actor. He and
Edith, he told me, had been out with Billie Holiday, the
black singer, who had been arrested in California for the
possession of narcotics, who was now barred from appearing in New York, and whom J. was trying to get cleared.
Halliman had just been in trouble for forging a client's
name to a document instead of getting a power of attorney from him. Just a matter of not bothering. Everybody
liked him and knew how generous he was—rich from his
real estate (that highest building) and law practice. Dis-
barred for six months, not beginning till spring. J. un-
scrupulous in resorting to trickery, probably not so in
principle. Had rigged up offices opposite the courthouse,

in imitation of Hummel and Howe—spittoons and old-fashioned furniture. He said to me, "A lawyer is a charlatan." Very boyish and San Franciscan: all good fellows together and everything good clean fun.

—They had had dinner with Dwyer in Flatbush, with his Irish friends. D. had just had to play some role in connection with the St. Patrick's Day parade.

—At home they had a beloved horse called Nuggett that the whole family seemed to ride. They brought him in the house for Christmas Eve and had him in the dining room. They left him there all night, and his stampings kept them awake. People outside the next day were surprised to see a gray horse looking out of the third-floor window. It had been easy to bring him upstairs, but they had a very hard time getting him down and had to lure him with sugar and apples. They took him to the house of friends, led him up the front steps, then rang the bell and shouted, Merry Christmas. It was one of J.'s inventions that the man had come to the door and, though a little surprised, had said unperturbedly to his wife, Shall we ask him in? —They had married young and had three children in successive years—now six, seven, and eight—she had taken care of them completely herself. Now they evidently fought like tigers—their quarrels, she said, were very bloody. One of the boys had cut the girl in the house next door throwing a tin can, and the neighbors had thought he was a menace and reported to the police instead of coming to them.

—Edith, born in Boise, Idaho, is a fine specimen of western girl, a robust well-set-up organism—very handsome, with a deep voice, and a grasp of life, but with something of the old-fashioned American (cute?) prettiness. Well-dressed.

—Their only servants were a colored couple (whose

dollar bills I had autographed). The woman was a religious fanatic and they could go out only two nights a
week, because she had to go to church constantly.

—His father and mother had died when he was small,
and he was an only child. He had been brought up as a
Catholic, but seemed rather to pride himself on his
Scotch ancestry—had advanced on the jury, at the time
of the *Hecate County* trial, having taken off his coat,
which is not usually done in the courtroom—and displayed his plaid galluses and belt and said, "This is the
plaid of my clan." —The psychology of being a Catholic
—the "dirty Irish trick": Scott Fitzgerald, Kenneth Simpson, and Mary (Kenneth not brought up as a Catholic,
though). His legal unscrupulousness may have had something to do with this.

—His enjoyment of California history: the story of the
Broderick (?) duel.

Dawn Powell in St. Luke's, March 31, 1949: She looked
fresher and younger than I think I had ever seen her:
complexion smooth and clear, no rings or pouches around
her eyes. I commented on this and said it was because she
didn't get a chance to drink. No, it wasn't that, she said:
it was that, if she "hit the jackpot," as she had called it
over the phone, she'd be out of all her difficulties—and
at the moment she had no responsibility and they fed her
constantly on beefsteak and filet mignon. Had been scared
at first but wasn't now, and was beginning to be proud of
"being a freak"—the doctors there were all excited about
her case and eager to see the operations. A tumor (?)
that was lodged between her lungs—a very rare position,
they told her—and had grown so that it prevented her
breathing to more than a third the normal extent—it was
attached to her heart, which sounded dangerous, and had
been crowding and affecting all her organs. Expected it

to come out with a high hat and a volume of Palgrave's *Golden Treasury*. She had chased all her friends away, she told me when I called her two days later, because they had exploited going to see her there as a golden opportunity for telling her about their own operations. She had a pleasant corner room that looked out on the Angel Gabriel on the top of St. John the Divine.

—In this volume, I am constantly writing about death, illness, and decay of old friends. —It has been reassuring to see Peggy Bacon[8] coming back lately to her real personality—has stopped drinking so much—which had the effect on her of putting her in a daze so that she simply became silent and didn't hear what you said and asked you to repeat everything. She says that she is more in demand socially again and goes out a good deal and enjoys it. It was actually like seeing an old friend that I hadn't seen at all for years. Had got tired of hearing about Dawn's messes, thought she was sadistic and tortured Joe —"He's around more than you think"—encouraging him to think that she went to bed with all her men friends. She had said, How touching and at the same time how horrible!, when I had told about being at Dawn's when she had received the red roses sent by Joe. They're red roses, aren't they? she had said, with her back to the door, where Louise was receiving them. They're from Joe, she explained to me. Is it your wedding anniversary? No: it's the anniversary of the day when we first had lunch together. He sends me red roses every year. —Dawn, Peggy said, had seemed to get more malicious as her personal affairs got more difficult. After a drink or two, she would become insulting—and Peggy had finally realized that she was completely finished with her. When this

---

[8] EW's artist friend. See "Peggy Bacon: Poet with Picture" in *The Shores of Light* (1952), pp. 701-4.

happened with her about a person, there was absolutely
no appeal. She didn't want to see Dawn again, though she
looked her up still about twice a year so as not to hurt
her feelings—didn't think any more she was funny. It
had been the same thing with Alec.[9] —I wish him well,
but I don't want to see him—there's nothing he could
do or say that could please me. I said that I hoped that
would never happen with me. Oh, no: it happens very
rarely, but when it does, it's complete and final. —I told
her about Allen Tate and his immediately repeating to
Mary what I had told him about having taken in one
year about $35,000. She laughed, then went on laughing
and told me that she was so glad to find somebody to
whom she could tell the following: A week before, she
had seen Cobey Gilman:[10] he had told her about Dawn's
having been seriously ill, and about his having lost his
job, through the folding up of McBride and *Travel*, so
that he was now on relief, and then asked her to marry
him . . . I think, the sequence! . . . I told him that he
just wanted to marry for a home—thought he could creep
in with me . . . It had pleased her a little, though, I
thought. I said that I supposed a number of people had
asked her to marry them. All ineligibles! Old people, she
had added, come up with the most extraordinary things.
Her cousin who had studied French for years without
ever being able either to speak it or read it—her daughter
had married an Italian who spoke English perfectly, but
she had announced that she was learning Italian in order
to make him feel more at home.

—It was pleasant to see her her old self—well-bred,
deliberate, dignified, dry, quietly and a little cruelly amus-

[9] Alexander Brook, an artist, was married to Peggy Bacon.
They divorced in 1940.
[10] Coborn Gilman, mutual friend of EW, Dawn Powell, and
Peggy Bacon. See *The Thirties*, p. 627.

ing. A genre entirely different from anybody else in that set.

—She had been in bed when I had called her, and I had taken her out to a late breakfast. She had been to a big party the night before, the first she had been to in years. I asked if she had had a good time. No. The Reggie Marshes: they gave one every year to discharge their social debts, invited everybody, no fun, crowded into three rooms. She had stayed away for several years, but this had hurt their feelings. Horrid results and insulting to the people invited.

—After Longchamps, we went to her apartment and played her new album of Cole Porter's *Kiss Me, Kate*. She had found it disappointing, and I thought myself that some of the songs sounded both vulgar and labored—the risqué side seemed distinctly senile—imitations of his earlier songs. That era was certainly over. Cole Porter would never glitter again in the way that he had done in the 20s and 30s, because the atmosphere now was so different.

—I noticed for the first time that her acrid dissent from any enthusiastic opinion that I tried to thrust upon her was involuntary and habitual: Betjeman, eggs Benedict.

Mrs. Rosen's apartment house at 111 Riverside Drive: The Russians, of whom there are many up here, have found something in New York that is congenial and somehow seems typically Russian. The entrance a great expanse of plate glass framed in fancy ironwork with a pattern something like a Greek key. Inside, a little waiting room with a fireplace of green tiles with a gas log, a mainly green colored-glass window with atrophied fleur-de-lys (word for limbs that are no longer used), faded maroon carpet, a velocipede. Space, tasteless bourgeois grandeur, lack of sharp corners and narrow rooms not

characteristic of New York, only found here on Riverside
Drive, left over from the lavishness of the early 1900s.

May 13, '49. Spectacle Ponds: First seen through the
trees of mid-May, the gray and brittle-looking stems just
yellowing with the early leaves the dullness of which, if
it had been autumn, one would have described as rusty.
The big pond looked unexpectedly dark and even a little
muddy. A tiny butterfly, itself mud-dark and orange, flit-
ted along the sand-pale sun before me, never rising high
and settling at very short intervals. No animals or birds—
except, in the distance, crows; only flowers a few little
white violets, the little coral-pink flowers of the bear-
berries, and the pale Dutchman's-breeches—like waxen
clusters on bushes (what are these?). The big pond, when
I got down to it, was unexpectedly clear—more so than in
summer, when it is forested with water plants and somewhat clouded by decaying vegetation—a few polliwogs.
A broken wine bottle in a clearing that I didn't remember
to have seen there. In the sand beside the road, going
back, a few indentations of what seemed to be nests for
turtle eggs—in the woods it was cool, with warmish sun.
—Last act of *Little Blue Light*:[11] on the way there, walking quickly, I was as stimulated as if I were drunk and
wrote down a lot of notes on a little office pad. First long
walk of spring: when I got back, I was suddenly and completely exhausted.

June 7. —Pond pale slate among greenery—laurel growing bright with purplish pink, first pale adder's mouths,
water-lily buds bobbing up (on stalks) like the yolks of
hard-boiled eggs. The roads of soft sand.

[11] EW's play, produced in Cambridge in 1950 and published
in *Five Plays* (1954).

while I am playing Schubert's Quintet, and reflect that nobody today could imagine that the shaking of the leaves had anything to do with the music—if he were composing music: either that it represented the music or that the music represented it. —Wonderful sunrises and sunsets and cloudscapes, seen while flying in plane—well described in the little magazines by some English aviators during the war (also by Dos [Passos] in his account of his trip to the Philippines)—but nobody ever thinks of giving them an apocalyptic significance or even of drawing a lesson from them. The light refractions and clouds are unduly atmospheric phenomena that one encounters in skimming around the globe. It's a question of getting through them and past them. —It's hard to imagine anyone today apostrophizing them in the old way—[seven words illegible] step is not to step up our morale in an impulse from the cloudbanks or the incarnadined sea of light, but to fly away from the earth altogether and find out what there is beyond.

Felix Frankfurter, summer of 1949. With what Dos called his police captain's sense of where people are going to be and at what time (Dos says that F. called up Archie MacLeish in Washington the moment he had arrived at his house, to find out how he was taking *The Irresponsibles*),[1] he got hold of me at Lenox by calling the hotel and having me paged when Elena and I were having lunch there. I'll fly over, Frankfurter said— I thought he was actually going to fly, and accounted for his non-arrival at the time he had said to afternoon thunderstorms. But when he finally did arrive, late, he told me I was very

[1] *The Irresponsibles* (1940), Archibald MacLeish's polemical essay accusing American writers of the Left and Right of having failed to take an unequivocal stand for democracy.

literal-minded, that he had meant merely that he was coming right over. He now said that, due to the fact that Marion's[2] niece was visiting them and that he had to get her home or something of the kind, he could not stay to pay a visit just then. He was hurried, seemed embarrassed; I walked with him up the street to his car. He began: "It has come to my ears—by what we call in the law *hearsay*, and we have a legal principle—which I'm sure you agree with—that hearsay is not admitted as valid evidence"—I cut in and asked him what he had heard. Well, not precisely that you don't have any use for me. I gently deprecated that. But he wanted to talk to me, he said. Then we arrived at the car—I greeted Marion, we made an engagement, and he hastily departed.

On the day we had lunch together, he told me that he approved of *Hecate County,* thought my improprieties were justified by the social points I wanted to make— really didn't know what he would have decided if he had had to sit on the case, but couldn't have thought of doing so, because he was a friend of mine—though his [word missing], he made a point of mentioning, had never appeared in print. I reminded him that he had not disqualified himself, on the ground that he was a friend of Lovett's, in connection with the Virgin Islands affair. This had never come into his head, and he was silent for a long moment (equivalent, as John Biggs said, when I told him about it, to a cataleptic fit on the part of another man), reflecting and mustering an answer. Then I should have disqualified myself, he said—adding as justification that he had thought of Lovett as a historical figure. He then quickly left this behind and explained that he had re-

[2] Marion Loundes (b. 1906). She and her husband, Floyd, were Dos Passos' longtime friends with whom he lived after Katy's death.

cently disqualified himself in the case of some property or
other in which some relation of Marion's had a very tiny
interest. He turned to Elena and asked whether she found
these problems of law very difficult to understand. She
replied that she didn't find them difficult at all. Later, he
began complaining about the intolerance of the Catholics.
I pointed out that the Catholics had been involved in the
suppression of *Hecate County*. —At lunch, I had said, in
the Lovett connection, that I was sorry he had not begun
deciding to disqualify himself in cases where his friends
were involved just after, rather than just before, the case
of *H.C.* had come up. I've said I was wrong, he repeated,
not to have disqualified myself in the Lovett case. —My
liberal friends expect me to defend their interests in the
Court—but they don't understand that I'm there to do
something altogether different—to decide on the legality
of statements and opinions. My own opinions are liberal
—I'm opposed to all kinds of intolerance. —I reminded
him that he had been on the other side when the police
magazines were cleared by his colleagues. Did I realize
that they caused juvenile delinquency?

—Later on in the summer, the F. Biddles and the
Gardner Jacksons[3] came to dinner in Wellfleet. Before
the B[iddle]s came, Pat [Jackson] and I discussed Felix:
he said that it had been a calamity that he had ever been
appointed to the Supreme Court—that he had said so at
the time. We agreed that he had been much better off
mildly liberalizing the students at Harvard Law and
lightly influencing politics by remote control. But don't
talk against him to Francis, Paddy said: Francis is devoted
to him. —Nevertheless, when the B.'s came, I mentioned
the *Hecate County* matter to F. He told me—agreeing

---

[3] Gardner Jackson, nicknamed Pat or Paddy, journalist and
fighter for liberal causes. See *The Thirties*, pp. 319–20.

with John Biggs and Charley Curtis—that he thought it had been unnecessary for Felix to disqualify himself. I said that I had the impression that, instead of deciding cases on principle, he was always thinking of the impression that it would be politic to make on the public. Felix hasn't any principles, Francis said. Later in the evening, I said to Mrs. B. that Felix was an old faker and that I never wanted to see him again. She seemed a little horrified by this and took a more kindly line. We mentioned Felix again when the B.'s were leaving and I was easing them off outside, when the Jacksons, who had not gone yet, were in the middle room. Mrs. B., explaining her loyalty when we had talked of him before, said, You know, Gardner Jackson adores him. —When I went back, I told Paddy about this, and he roared.

—Isaiah Berlin[4] called Felix a [illegible Russian word] and the 2nd violin in a Vienna orchestra. —Felix told me that, according to Arthur Krock, he (F.) should have been a journalist, whereas Krock should have been a judge. I think that there is something in this, so far as F. is concerned: he is always full of ideas for newspapers and magazines, and he has an instinctive news sense of what is going on at the moment, who the key people are, etc.

[4] Sir Isaiah Berlin (b. 1909), British social historian and philosopher, eminent authority on Russian letters.

HAITI, 1949

[EW traveled to Haiti late in 1949 to write a series of articles on that new republic for *The Reporter* magazine. He saw Haiti during the last days of the shaky regime of President Dumarsais Estimé. Eight years of further unstable regimes would follow before the setting up of the Duvalier dictatorship.

[EW was in Haiti from the end of November to December 20. The articles appeared in *The Reporter* on May 9 and 23 and June 6, 1950. Six years later EW revised them into the more rounded account he gives in *Red, Black, Blond and Olive* (1956), pp. 71–146. His manuscript notes of this trip are given textually here; they are among the scrappiest of all the journal notes, often illegible because written on the run in situations when he could only scribble impressions or information briefly. They have been decoded for inclusion with the aid of his letters to Elena Wilson, which EW asked her to keep since they were in effect the equivalent of journal entries. The correspondence may be read in *Letters on Literature and Politics* (1977), pp. 461–70.]

Trip to Miami. —Go to sleep in the black winter darkness and wake up to dazzling golden light and green palms and little pines dripping with the moss—great flat plains full of birds—white egret and gray heron and other long-winged birds that I couldn't identify—as well as a variety of smaller ones that look as if they had flown right out of Audubon—he must have gone crazy when he came here. They are all flying close to the ground and it gave me the greatest pleasure to watch their contrasting tempos and the different rhythms of the movement of their wings. It is wonderful to see a white egret drifting and folding its wings from the flying position with deliberate dignity and grace.

It is all a great pageant of wildlife that goes past the window—they are flying close to the ground and very near the train. —Flew in flocks, several kinds with quick wingbeat, two beige or bluish herons.

Déclaration Paysanne [by Emile Roumer[1]]

> Marabout de mon coeur, aux seins de mandarine,
> tu m'es plus savoureux que crabe en aubergine,
> tu es mon afiba dedans mon calalou,
> le doumbreuil de mon pois, mon thé de zerbe à clou.
> Tu es le boeuf salé dont mon coeur es la douane,
>
> L'accasan au sirop qui coule en ma gargoine.
> Tu es un plat fumant, diondion avec du riz,
> des acras croustillants et des thazars bien frits . . .
> Ma fringale d'amour te suit où que tu ailles.
> Ta fesse est un boumba chargé de victuailles.

Movie in Miami. —When I sat down in seat, it proved to be one of those that swings back to let people pass you

---

[1] Emile Roumer, Haitian poet. See *RBBO*, pp. 112–13.

and having some kind of cushioning *that* lets you down with unexpected softness. Theater modern-designed and indirect-lighted—ribbed above like the inside of the carapace of a turtle; forward, two great pseudo-mythological figures with hounds framed in conventionalized seashells, like caricatures of the monstrous brass warehouses by Paul Manship and others in the Rockefeller Center buildings. —Back part of house gray, forward part shrimp pink and on either side of the proscenium arch great white plaster bas-reliefs like the sea crawfish of the Miami aquarium with two out-claws, but with long defensive antennae— pink imitation loops above the proscenium to give a suggestion of the old theater curtain. —The show [*Oh You Great*] *Big Beautiful Doll,* exploiting the nostalgia for the immediate American past (enlarge on this). —Technicolor, enormous screen—shorts consisted of hunting, bantam cock playing baseball, some good [illegible] in this, whippet racing (the grooms have to work harder than the greyhounds!). Animals more interesting than people— Americans used to be attractive at the beach—Red Bank, etc.

Miami is not so attractive—it is, in fact, of an unimaginable awfulness—much like other American seaside resorts but on an unprecedented scale: acres of cheap white shops, mountain ranges of white hotels. After lunch, I had a taxi drive me over to Miami Beach. It goes on for miles —thousands of hotels and houses and monotonous lines of palms. I can't imagine how people live here or why so many of them come: it all seems a great insipid vacuum —less amusing than southern California, because there is no touch of fantasy about anything.

All these attempts to exploit the immediate past show the rapidity of the bankruptcy of the movies as purveyors of popular entertainment, but the Miami audience showed that there is a public that enjoys their product. They were

the characterless devitalized drove that seems to popula..
Miami, and they sat in a muffled atmosphere that smelled
like scented face powder—I couldn't tell whether the
theater was perfumed or whether it was due to the fact
that the women all used the same kind of cosmetics. The
characters in the picture represented the same kind of
insipid people, brightly colored and gigantically magni-
fied. The three shorts all dealt with animals: a hunting
number, an animated cartoon, and a picture about racing
whippets. I felt that the human beings were no good as
animal organisms any more, and that we had had to fall
back on the lower animals, who were at least good examples of their various species.

I don't think it had been brought home to me before
how all this side of America had been developing, and
how it looks today to foreigners who come here. It is only
when you go to the airfield and see them handling these
big planes that you are made to feel better as you become
aware that the personal deterioration has been offset by
these mechanical creations—which somewhat restores
your pride.

Hotel Oloffson, Port-au-Prince, Haiti, Nov. 28. —I am
very much impressed with the Haitians. You have only
to see them to realize what a wretched life we have made
for the Negroes in the States. The Haitians with whom I
traveled on the plane and the officials who handled the
passengers at the airport were entirely different from our
Negroes. It is not merely that they are quick and polite
but that they have no consciousness of inferiority—so that
their faces and bearing are different. I went out for a walk
yesterday afternoon and got the same impression from the
ordinary people on the streets. They are extremely good-
looking, and to see the children playing and the older
people taking their Sunday afternoon walks made me

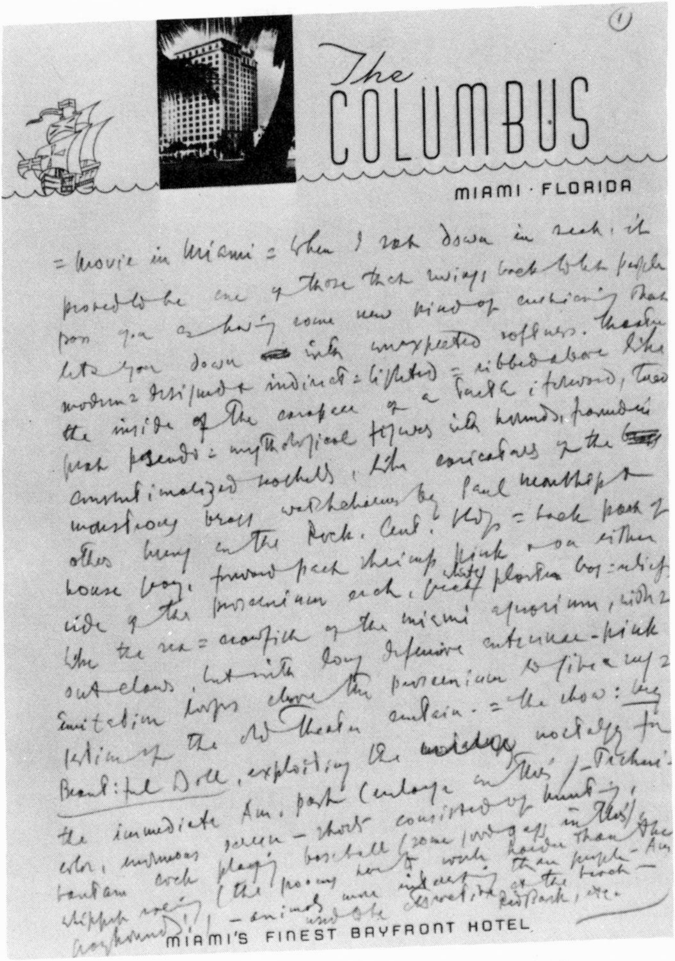
The COLUMBUS
MIAMI · FLORIDA
MIAMI'S FINEST BAYFRONT HOTEL

From Edmund Wilson's notes of his trip to Haiti, 1949

realize that our Negroes are never at home. There is no squalor (in this part of town, but, driving in from the airport, I went through a more African-looking quarter), though most of the houses seem rickety or flimsy—many of them are decorated with this wooden lace. They were all wearing their best Sunday clothes—not stylish, but very clean. What is fascinating is to see people of a different race really (as they don't seem to be in the U.S.) at their physical best. They seemed quick, sober, and gentle.

On the plane an amiable Belgian ex-consul said that the people were "a little slow." They like to write but were perhaps a little too *"lyrique."* He seemed to feel that the production of poetry was one of the main industries of Haiti. He told me that the climate was "delicious"—which seems to be true—quite warm, but in the morning and at night there is a cool little breeze. There is an agreeable fragrance of cooking and coffee in the air. The only thing it reminds me of is a little of New Orleans.

I had dinner on the verandah, which corresponds to the balcony on the second floor and has a good view of the town and the harbor. The food here is not fancy but it is all right. I went to bed after dinner and read Aimé Césaire's[2] long Surrealist poem and the book that Waldo [Frank] lent me on Toussaint L'Ouverture.[3] They are both extremely painful. Césaire's poem—*Cahier d'un retour au pays natal*—seems to me about the best thing I have read in the school of Rimbaud and Lautréamont. It is infinitely superior to the Surrealist stuff because it is about something important: Césaire's situation as a Negro from Martinique who has been civilizing himself in Paris.

[2] Aimé Césaire (b. 1913). See *RBBO*, pp. 74–78.
[3] Pierre François Dominique Toussaint L'Ouverture (1743–1803), Haitian soldier and freedom fighter.

The account of the slave trade in the other book almost made me sick. You are closer to all that out here. Our idea of it is blurred in the States, where, bad though the situation was, the slaves must have been treated somewhat better.

November 29.[4] Looking down from my balcony over Port-au-Prince is a little like looking out on Athens—but Athens is twinkling and drily alive, very much organized —the view of Port-au-Prince is muffled in palm and banana trees and there are not many lights. A French honking of taxis, but otherwise quiet (except, later, for the fighting cocks and dogs). —There seems to be no actual squalor. (It seems that there is—though I didn't see it. Ella Griffin told me that she had never seen anything here like Nashville, Tenn., in the early '40s, when she was a social worker there.) The arcades of the main business streets make one think of an Italian town, but there is no filth, no bad smells, no disgusting sights—I saw no repulsive objects sold in the popular market and the only two beggars who accosted me looked in very good condition—a *chétive* woman with a tin cup, a smiling man who seemed quite well dressed but said that he was hungry. —On the other hand, it is monotonous, dreary—the goods are all cheap: no better-class shops, no gay trinkets for tourists, no good restaurants, no fancy cafés. The Haitians dislike the U.S. Negroes for their loud laughter and talk, their flashy clothes and their habitual playing the clown. They are quite right, but they themselves have rather too meager a life—of course, at least, at the present time, they don't have any access to the abundance of food, clothes, musical entertainment, and other things that our Negroes can get if they work it that way. (Envy of office-

4 *RBBO*, pp. 135–38.

holders.) Incomparably better off than people in the poor
quarters of the southern Italian cities—or than the people
in the poor part of Athens themselves. Unless I haven't
seen that part of Port-au-Prince yet.

—*Au clair de lune* on auto horn—also sung in the
street.

—Mixture of black and white fascinating but disconcerting—extreme difference of types—a coffee-colored
woman who looks completely French and is handsome in
a sharp-faced way, but other mulattos that are anomalous-
looking, as well as the wonderful completely black African
types, who seem to turn up among the "elite" as well as
among the common people.

—No debris in the street, though I found a small dead
dog at the ridge of the wide road beside the cemetery. No
chaussées to the streets, except where there are arcades in
town—I suppose because they were built at a time when
everybody who was anybody was able to ride in a carriage
or on horseback, and there were no cars to make it de-
sirable to have separate pavement for pedestrians.

These expeditions of mine are beginning to fall into a
pattern: the principal writer whose books I make a point
of reading, the dowdy Jewish girl—archaeologist or social
worker—who has been in the country a long time, who
is slightly at a tangent to everything (that she originally
perhaps thought would solve her problem) but who gives
you the most intelligent and accurate information, the
Embassy people and the cultural attaché here correspond
to the British Council people and the Italian cultural liaison man in Italy—has impressed me equally by speaking
good French and showing considerable knowledge of cultural activities in Haiti, while at the same time coming
from Alabama and showing no trace of color prejudice—
the 11 o'clock coffee in the First Secretary's office, he, too,

apparently from the South: the local writers whom I meet; finding my way among the various newspapers; the excursion with UNRRA or UNESCO field workers.

I don't know whether I shall ever be able to do another [expedition]—I suffer sleepless lonely nights (and my reading matter here: Aimé Césaire and this English book on Toussaint L'Ouverture must be among the most painful in the world); stiffness of the knees and ankles, which today made me hobble around; and a certain political cynicism that makes me tend to discount the Left.

—Prevalence of La Fontaine—three attempts to translate it into Creole—first rather sophisticated—*La Cigale dansait le calinda*[5]—then, as done by Ella Griffin, very simple, seriously intended to teach the illiterate to read Creole—I even saw Taine's book on La Fontaine in a *vitrage,* perhaps a new edition—the meeting point of French culture and African folklore.

—Césaire and his debt to Rimbaud and Lautréamont —perhaps Lautréamont, who seems to me rather a second-rate adolescent writer, has a value that a foreigner doesn't appreciate. Coming as a boy from Montevideo, he had the effect, if not the intention, of blowing up the classical French forms. This is probably what he means to Césaire, who, according to [André] Breton, enormously admires him.

—Submission or adaptation of the Americans to other peoples, so that they don't [illegible] themselves in the same way and don't have the same sharp outlines. Something quite new, that I've never seen before—quite dif-

[5] Translation into Creole of the Jean de La Fontaine (1621–95) fable *La Cigale et la fourmi.* See *RBBO,* p. 100.

ferent from the old-fashioned highly educated international people. —Very interesting how this differs from the English method—the officials govern them firmly and with a well-thought-out system, a few fanatics agitate for the natives without (I'm not sure of this) accomplishing so much as our old Buells and people did. The English don't get out till they're driven out; the Americans are soon shamed into withdrawal—in Haiti, ten years.

—What it means for the Negroes to have been Americanized—some things more brilliant, which are not at all brilliant here (music, etc.)—greater individual successes, but not many of them—dreariness of Harlem, dreariness of Port-au-Prince.

A shoeshine boy drumming with a stick, as he walks, on the wooden box he uses for shining.

Dantès Bellegarde:[6] Looks rather like an American: tall, graying hair *en brosse* and toothbrush mustache, spectacles. Conventional, old-fashioned, conscientious, and good. They all—men and women both—called him Bellegarde. I called him M. de Bellegarde once by mistake. —Dropping his eyes when we first began talking. I said he was *sorti du peuple* and educated at the popular expense, because all grades of education are free in Haiti. Thought Creole ought to be taught, not phonetically, but spelled like French, so that they could easily go on to learn French—otherwise, have difficulty with words like *suwa,* into which an English letter has been introduced. Almost no African in Creole. Explained about the language lucidly, at length and a little repetitiously and bor-

[6] A Haitian who wrote about the American occupation of Haiti. See *RBBO*, pp. 74–78.

ingly. —The pity was that, when agents of the big American interests came here, they found *gens à tout faire* to do their work. —Two friends were there, one with his almost-white wife, who must once have been a round pretty little woman. One of the friends was black, wearing dark glasses; the other a dumpy little man, very pale, who made speeches in typical French fashion. —Large house in a great nest of large houses all rather close together and producing, like everything else, an impression of untidiness and carelessness (along with dryness and cleanness), as if they had been built at random—(just as the public buildings seem) scattered in a completely unplanned way about the central park. —They served little goblets of rum, with tall glasses of some amber-colored syrup (I had a delicious pink lemonade in Higgins Bar, with a slice of lime on the edge of the glass). Better houses, with all their neatness and comfortable modern furniture, do not show much actual taste.

More like young French poet than newspaper editor. Valéry on table, Haitian paintings on walls. Very polished, fine hands holding cigarette—with his dark glasses, he seemed to me a little like a Japanese. —Very young, would giggle like a boy. Had graduated from Columbia —something like eighteen months in the States, but never in France. Came from Jacmel, told of flood at Marbial,[7] where 1,000 had been drowned, others came crying for help—body of 18-year-old girl, whom they buried— but they said they preferred the flood to the drought. Trouble with the Haitian end of the administration of the UNESCO experiment was that they were always chang-

---

[7] Jacmel, coastal town, 24 miles southwest of Port-au-Prince, pop. 8,545, and Marbial, chosen as the site for the UNESCO educational experiment. See *RBBO*, pp. 95–103.

ing the Minister of Education—now had an absent-
minded professor of the type who boiled his watch and
wound up the egg—made frightful errors in statistics.
The papers always attacked the ministers. —Why? —Because they "weren't good"—when public dissatisfaction
reached a certain point, the President would get a new
ministry. When somebody from the outside had asked him
why a given ministry had fallen, he said, because it had
slipped on a banana peel. He never attacked the Minister
of Education though—that was his own field and I understood that he would like the job himself. He had to attack
the Minister of the Interior—after all, he was a journalist
and could not accept the suppression of the papers.
—Very good judgment, I thought, about literature.
—Barbancourt three-star rum served with soda by a cute
houseboy to whom he gave orders rather in the oriental
style. We talked about the local rum. He was going to say
something that people often said in the U.S.: that their
rum was the best in the world. Not made from molasses
like Jamaica, Puerto Rico, and Virgin Islands rum, but
directly from the juice of the sugarcane. No hangover.
Clairin is the same thing, without the caramel coloring
and not aged—much cheaper. You did get a hangover
from it and visiting Americans sometimes preferred [it]
because they would rather have a hangover than a really
good drink. *"Notre nectare nationale,"* as the paper called
it in the controversy the other day. No harshness, no bit-
terness, no sickening molasses taste.

He [unidentified] said that Bellegarde was really "not
honest" in his opposition to having Creole taught phonetically—the truth was that he didn't want it taught at all.
Actually, it was more like English than French—simple
structure, few inflections—and his implication was, I
think, it would be easy to pass from Creole to English.

—The government's plans for roads were on such a grandiose scale that they had never yet come near to carrying them out, and he had been over the whole subject and couldn't possibly see how U.S. capital could be induced to invest in them the requisite amount. In the meantime, nothing whatever was done and the roads were getting into worse and worse repair. —Pétionville an agreeable suburb.

Climbing to the Citadelle,[8] setting out about 8. (Breakfast looking out the window at the bright gold, through the big-leaved plants with window box and the lace-leaved plants by the tennis court.) Climbing up on horseback among those wonderful morning hills with the fresh and strong light on top of them, saturating the small unmoving clouds—the hills green with so many leaves and fruits but not a jungle, still quite natural to a North American —how fresh and rich it must have looked to the planters! —You mount and get to the top: it is as if you embrace the morning—on a level with the peaks of those solid and self-assertive (this is not quite it) non-undulating hills, like illustrative hills/peaks plucked up by a [illegible] in a newly laundered tablecloth (King Christophe's Tomb not unlike one)—also have a military look—"mamelous and ravelous"—in the courtyard of the Citadel by Christophe's Tomb[9] (limestone mound beside it), greenery with red hibiscus flowers, two hours before noon, the full-lit sky overhead—tranquillity, the fury like Christophe, are sleeping: *le roi soleil, Dieu et mon Droit—honi soit qui mal y pense*—fruit—dolphin-handled (English and

[8] See letter to Elena Wilson, *Letters on Literature and Politics*, pp. 465–67, and *RBBO*, pp. 80–83.
[9] Henri Christophe (1767–1820), Negro general and King of Haiti, 1811–20.

French both)—these engraved and elegant guns of bronze—Napoleon, too. —The gun dropped in *michemin* (was it being taken up to the Citadel when Christophe shot himself with silver bullet—O'Neill's *Emperor Jones*). He is God of the Heavens and our God of the *Terre*—pride they all take in this.

Bananas, mangoes, breadfruit, cocoanut, yams, coffee—beans, cocoa beans, some kind of custard apple and citronella, mahogany trees (morning glories), calabashes (*raquette*). —All these trees are giving out like mad, but it seems that they don't know what they're for (use them for various illnesses)—haven't discovered the use of marijuana, the whole thing open not junglelike (green and free)—cocoanut, oranges, red bananas, avocados, bamboo, pomegranates, sugarcane.

—The great expanse below, which is now too big, the plain, the white town of Cap-Haïtien[10] that borders the bay in a curving strip, a white old-fashioned strip of buildings, from that distance above just a little slice, the blue water that is not so different from green that it makes a sharp contrast with it—the flat, but not too flat expanse, so that, where nobody else can meddle, where you think you can command all approaches, you can sit pretty and exult over the scene. —The stronger part, the great brick and lime wedge, the "prow"—the weak part the Sans Souci Palace, with its staircase that imitates Versailles, the Appartement de la Reine, of which nothing now remains but stripped arches and walls as ruined as Rome (and for the same reasons)—one great feminine head set out of doors near the justice-dispensing oak, as to which it is impossible to tell whether it represents a bust or a statue. Everything was stolen—what was left by the native plunderers was bought up by the Americans during

[10] Coastal town, 85 miles northeast of Port-au-Prince.

the occupation. —Bared bricks and decayed plastics—a shell even more hollow than the Colosseum. —Bring [illegible] of wife and children back for the Exposition (a nice surprise). —Old French gates of deserted plantations, where the wonderful greenery is growing yet.

Gabriel[11] said that they said in France that Haitians talked like books.

Seabrook[12] said that it was strange to go to a party for politicians and find everybody talking about poetry. Gabriel said that at that time, when the Americans were running everything, the politicals had a great deal of leisure to cultivate literature.

Trip to Cap-Haïtien—Dec. 3–4. Edith Bogat said that, when they went out into the town, Fortuné[13] would sometimes have the appearance of looking out for *bagarres* —he explained that it was probably a heritage from slave days, when they were always hoping that things were going badly, that there was going to be trouble—which would give the slaves a break.

He is touching with her—evidently proud to have an able intelligent modern white woman—probably only partly understands how spoiled, egocentric, and vulgar she is. She says that he has taught her to be brave and to control herself and that there is such a thing as evil. He said to her, while I was with them and she was speaking with indignation about not being able to get the people here to do something, that when you had a problem,

[11] Emmanuel Gabriel, interim UNESCO director who suggested the project to educate the Haitians.

[12] William Seabrook wrote *The Magic Island* (1928), a book on Haitian voodoo rites, zombies, and charms.

[13] Fortuné Bogat, a businessman in Haiti.

you must think of some way of solving it, then try to put
your plan into execution—and if you fail, if you are "very
religious," you can pray; if you're not, there's nothing to
do. I said that they ought to make him President, and she
said that they were already kidding her about being Mme.
Perón. When she and I had been talking about the bad
marital relations in the U.S.—she venomously on the
women's side, excoriating the "flabby" American men who
only wanted to be "mothered"—he said, at the end of the
discussion, that his grandfather had had sixteen wives and
his [great-]grandfather he didn't know how many, and
that he was glad to have only one. When I came up to the
room in the hotel, they were kissing outside their door,
and at the house of the Italian businessman and somewhere else they had public embraces. As he had perfect
manners and tact, I imagine the public clinches were her
doing: exhibitionism and affirmation of her choice before
an audience.

While we were having lemonades in the bar of the
Hôtellerie du Roi Christophe, she and I had discussed the
Nazis. I had told her she oughtn't to perpetuate her bit-
terness, not refuse to shake hands with Germans, etc.;
talked about fatal facility of race and class prejudice. She
declared that there was a great difference between de-
clining to meet people socially and killing them in gas
ovens. He said that he didn't agree: he would much
rather that somebody frankly called him a *bête* (animal)
—took him out and shot him than that there should be
"so many doors through which he could not go" because
his skin was black. (If I behave the way you expect me
to behave, etc.) *Russians, Poles*. She had spoken to me of
the hysterical outbursts against her as a white on the part
of people with whom she thought she knew where she
was.

Aquiline, though perfectly black, so that, with his tall-ness and broad shoulders, he looked rather like an American. American businessmen often came to him, and he told the Haitians that if they would only study the American point of view they would get along with Americans much better. But was evidently not pro-American—was silent when I asked him whether the pressure that the U.S. still exercised was a bad thing. He said that in his relations with the people of the South American and West Indian countries, who accepted him, he thought, as one of themselves, he had never heard them say anything good about the U.S.

He works for a Haitian company which acts as dealers for a variety of foreign products—the only enterprise of the kind that has ever lasted here. He handles cars— (Buick Dynaflows—the people in the little towns would yell "Dynaflow" after us)—and radios. He has none of the overcultivation and *fin de race* one finds in the mulatto elite, and is the only man I have met who seemed to me to have something of the qualities of the heroic Roman figures of the revolutionary time.

On the way back, wanting to make time, he discarded the one-eyed falsetto-voiced driver who had brought us there and about whom she had rather naggingly complained, and made it in five hours—running over a pig. In the meantime, she talked to me, from the front seat, incessantly through the whole trip: E. M. Forster, Evelyn Waugh, Joyce; she didn't understand why these people like Eliot, who had gone in for religion, weren't happier than they seemed to be. If *she* were a Catholic, she would be perfectly happy, would never worry about anything again—attitude of moral superiority: *she* would be a saint. I explained to her that religious people, like anybody else, often fell below their best lights—she did that,

didn't she? She tried her best not to, evidently didn't
think she did. —Winston Churchill, whom she thought
I resembled, and our foreign policy. —Backwardness of
the Haitians and social conventionality (she had pre-
viously told me at the hotel that she had no Haitian
women friends); Cap-Haïtien apparently "a very queer
place"—the wife of the Italian had said to her that if a
woman [did] anything whatever outside her home, she
was talked about for not attending to her household. A
girl who had come there from somewhere else had created
scandal by playing tennis. Though Edith Bogat had
spoken to me before of the complexity of the social organism, she rather stupidly tended to talk as if she didn't
understand the stratification determined by the various
degrees of black and white blood, and I am sure that is a
negative reaction, of which she is completely unaware,
against her aggressiveness and vulgarity—wrinkling of
her nose between her spectacles when she wants to express disgusted disapproval. —But, apropos of St. Francis,
she thought she could be a saint—was teaching herself
not to hate people and thought that she had succeeded,
had compelled herself not to hate cockroaches and not to
kill them, didn't see why we couldn't follow St. Francis.
How about the three rules of the Franciscan order: poverty, chastity, obedience—did she think that she could
accept them, chastity by itself would bring the race to an
end. Well, not chastity, perhaps. I couldn't see her as ab-
bess of a nunnery. Well, perhaps at some later phase that
she hadn't arrived at yet. —The Jewish family—her parents Russian Jews, all intellectuals, her father a high-
school teacher, who had brought her up with the idea that
she must be different from "all the little imbeciles on the
block"—had had such a wonderful time in childhood
(had been to school in Switz.) that it had been hard for
her to grow up. —Maturity and childhood—I gave her a

sententious little lecture—she antagonized me, as well as
being so dreadfully unattractive, and I was sometimes
rather short with her—yet I have a certain respect for her
and wish her well—she has chosen a hard role and I hope
she continues to take it seriously. She has evidently—
married three years—just got to the point now where the
gesture, the dramatic role, the impression on another people, the conflict with her family, no longer sustain her
ego, and she is having to settle down to the conditions of
living in Haiti. She is never quite boring, and there is
something first-rate in her good French, her mastery of
Creole, her grasp of Haitian affairs, and her desire to do
the appropriate things, in a hostess role, for visitors. (She
told me, having asked me, in the car, whether I remembered, from the *Vita Nuova,* any of Dante's sonnets by
heart, that she had learned classical Italian at school so
thoroughly that she could read it and write it fluently,
without being able to manage the modern variety.)
—Her brother was very brilliant, was studying brain
problems at Harvard. They had "hazed" him when he
had gone to apply, had said, you know, they don't like
Jews at Harvard—apparently to test his reaction. He had
said that there were good Jews and bad Jews. As soon as
he had got back to New York, he had had word that he
was accepted. Afterwards, they had joked about it.
—Tendency to think that all the whites are suffering
from feelings of guilt about the race problem, which they
want to expiate—transference from Jewish situation.

Why wouldn't it be a good idea to have photoelectric
eyes that set off lights along the road, so you wouldn't
have to honk your horn?—or something that would play
back—had to wrap a handkerchief around her head so
she wouldn't hear noises—I know what I don't like! she
exclaimed, with an air of discovery: it's irrational noises!

I can listen to a symphony of Beethoven with all the noise in the world!

He had never noticed the poverty. The New York Jews' lack of interest in nature—Waldo [Frank] is the same way.

She said, after her dinner party, that Hibbert was a wise apple.

Bogat's remark that the Oloffson, about whose disrepair I had been complaining, was probably kept in just bad enough shape so that the customers would leave when they had heard all De Young's stories.

Cap-Haïtien: You get an idea of what the luxurious planters' life was like. In town, several planters' *manoirs,* with the old walls around them, over which purple bougainvilleas spill, used for various purposes. The hotel is one of these, with beautifully kept grounds and garden. In the country, the old broken gateless portals open on wild fields. A fine old solid grand white Spanish church built in the eighteenth century. The white mulatto woman who ran the hotel—I took her for a white Frenchwoman—the tongue-lashing she gave my poor guide, who had asked me for "five bucks"—not excessive, if the price was $2.50, since he had had the one-eyed driver as well as me—poor fellow was very crestfallen after his expansiveness over King Christophe—everybody who comes here says it is *incroyable,* nobody can understand it!—driver, who had never been up there before, gleefully repeated several times in his high voice Christophe's statement that God might be the God of the Heavens but he was God of the Earth.

—Our walk after dinner in the moonlight—the blue

and clement sky with its small clouds—the town looked
Latin and attractive—sordidness and dilapidation were no
longer visible at night—tranquillity, at this season, of
nature in this part of the world.

Bogat said: *les têtes magistrals des palms royales.* I
said it sounded like Chateaubriand, but it was simply a
remark of his own.

Marbial, trip there Dec. 6—They had at first found
the people so miserable that they had had to set up *can-
tines* and give the people work on roads and buildings
before they could undertake to teach them anything. The
question was even now whether, even assuming that the
region was thoroughly irrigated, their subsistence level
could ever be raised to the point where they could develop much. They had been chosen, though, because
they wanted improvement—the people in the even more
backward regions were unable to conceive anything different from the kind of lives they had. But it would be a
pity, I thought, to drop it and let them down. Most of
the instructors came from outside, but one or two from
Marbial.

There was *toute une histoire* about the Catholics having passed the project because they thought it was the
commune of Marbial, where the Catholics were in the
majority, whereas actually it was the parish of Marbial.

Bonhomme, a fanatical Protestant, had been the government representative for Marbial. This had aroused the
opposition of the priest. School had been started in the
Protestant church, but afterwards moved on account of
this opposition. The population of 30,000 are about half
and half Catholic and Protestant. Bonhomme was then
removed in order not to antagonize the people, leaving
no government representative. Gabriel is an interim

UNESCO director, while they are waiting for some Britisher to be sent. Money has all run out, teachers' salaries have not been paid for weeks; but they are supposed to start with a budget Jan. 1—UNESCO puts up part of the money and Haitian government part. The director at the center is the doctor.

To Jacmel by plane, 2 minutes. Command car (old and rickety, had been sold to the people here after not being able to negotiate the road to Jérémie, where it had half fallen over a precipice) out of commission, had to borrow the hospital truck, while it was supposed to be being put into shape. Hospital, I thought, very clean—better than that Odessa hospital[14]—additions were being made.

Road to Marbial—terrible, full of great holes. Gosseline [river] on left all the way—shallow, pale stones, pale mud—seems to be, with the road, the center of their life: purple-black men bathing in it, little naked children with swollen bellies due to malnutrition, women washing clothes, cattle and horses being watered. Along the road little stands selling things, sometimes on the ground, sometimes in little shelters covered with dried palm and banana leaves: syrup in bottles, bananas, little phalliform leaves, some confection like pralines or peanut brittle. Children holding on their heads oranges or calabashes, women balancing baskets and trays, with tinware, bottles, fruit, a cow's head with one ear wagging, donkeys that balk in the middle of the road and hold up the car—in one case being pulled by a girl with a big flat straw hat; in another case by a woman puffing/smoking a pipe, as a good many of them do, assisted by a daughter—men and women both carrying chickens under their arms; they handily fold them up, as if they were parasols, tying the

---

[14] EW had scarlet fever in 1935 when in Odessa and was confined to a children's hospital. See *The Thirties*, pp. 586–90.

legs together and holding them by the legs while the rest of the bird is tucked under their arm. One boy had a very handsome gamecock in a special fancy basket: their pastime and their luxury, and their only aesthetic objects. Two men sawing logs on a high improvised sawhorse, one man standing on the horse with the top end of the saw and the other working the lower end from below; dogs, lean black pigs led on ropes. Yaws sores—donkey with ears cut off.

The Center. The Creole signs—the little white building, hardly more than a shelter—schoolrooms with maps (Etazini) and charts in Creole. McConnell tried the children out after class and said that no attempt had [been] made to arrange a transition from Creole to French—had simply been taught in the old way to memorize passages in French, so that they couldn't read anything on sight— one boy that he asked to read began with the last word of a sentence. —Weaving mats of sisal, beautifully white, making ceramics from the pale local clay, horn combs, basketry, woodwork. Reservoir and Delco plant. They are trying to teach erosion control and administration, etc., cooperative marketing (a little vague).

In all Haiti (rural districts) 60,000 children in school out of 300,000 of school age (seven to fourteen).

Out of Marbial population of 30,000, with 3,000 children of school age, from 600 to 700 in school—200 in UNESCO school. At this center there were four teachers for the primary school, one for adults, five for the crafts— but there were 27 UNESCO centers, where reading, writing, simple arithmetic, and fundamental hygiene were taught, and 16 volunteer centers.

Small dispensary, where doctor came once a week, and in the meantime a nurse and a man assistant gave *piqûres et pansements.* They got about 600 cases a week—60 percent of them yaws, 20 percent syphilis. This was their first free clinic, hitherto the doctor had only come when they called, and they paid him. They gave us *chadégur* juice to drink.

Nursery: pistachio, eggplant, tobacco, divi-divi for tanning, to save mahogany which had been being used up for this purpose.

—Difficulties of getting back. Had first been promised airplane, for $35, if we needed it, then told it couldn't be done till tomorrow, weather too bad. Local man who received us didn't want to drive us back—car in garage with about seven people—waited around for hours—local man and mechanic from garage coming and going at intervals, while we waited at the hotel, everybody always missing one another. Gabriel's morale began to get rather undermined, feared they were sabotaging our trip as a protest against Bonhomme's removal, since the whole thing had originally been organized by him. Local man said he was going to change his clothes and never reappeared; mechanic changed clothes and undertook to drive us, etc. When I saw the road, I could quite understand anybody would be reluctant to start out on it at night in that car, but Gabriel told me that they had been notified of our coming and they should have provided a conveyance in good order. The command car had been stuck in the river and left there for several days. Gabriel in his blue buttoned-down shirt, his gray felt with the brim smartly cocked, and his knee breeches with some kind of puttees —a "field worker's" roughing-it costume—had not perhaps gone over very well with them. —Running over yellow dog as we finally started out in the bus from Jacmel—the driver [exclaimed] "Ha ha."

I was roused out of bed this morning [Dec. 7] by the arrival at eleven of the Marcelin brothers. They had breakfast with me and then came up here and talked till after two. I was very much interested in them. Pierre, who writes the novels with Phito,[15] was different from what I had expected . . . He is in some ways much more attractive than Phito, has an almost feminine good looks, sensitiveness, and charm (without giving a pansy impression). I think that he is probably the more important of the two in their literary collaboration. My guess is that their collaboration is very close and I imagine that what will happen is that Pierre will join Phito in Washington and that they will write another novel together. Pierre speaks even more indistinctly than Phito, and when he is talking about anything at all delicate, absolutely whispers, so that the things I most want to hear are completely unintelligible to me. The other brother [Milo] attends the voodoo ceremonies and commits them all to memory without writing them down. He is publishing texts of all their rites. They talked about voodoo mythology. I think that they are rather *fin de race* and at the same time rather *déséquilibrés* between their French tradition and their African heritage. They have all three made a cult of *"le peuple"*—these two told me, as Phito had, that the peasants represented *"le meilleur de l'Haïti,"* and that their life is really richer than that of the bourgeoisie because they think they are surrounded by the spirits of the voodoo mythology and in constant communication with and possession by them. The Marcelin family is very distinguished here—there are a *rue* Marcelin and a *pont* Marcelin—but I am told that, with their considerable Negro admixture, they don't belong to the very top layer, which, it seems, consists entirely of people who are almost entirely white, who marry only whites or each other and who only engage in business, never politics.

[15] Philippe Thoby-Marcelin and his brother Pierre collaborated on novels of Haiti dealing with the influence of ancestral African religions.

The only example of this I have seen is the woman who runs the wonderful hotel at Cap-Haïtien and whom I took for a white Frenchwoman. She gave my black guide a horrible tongue-lashing, which made me feel sorry for him. He had expounded the Citadel with much eloquence. This guide, though a little of a fraud, I found rather sympathetic. He was full of misinformation. In the forest, I asked him what the bird was which was giving a harsh cachinating cry. *"C'est le rossignol, monsieur,"* he said. Was it really, I asked, the nightingale that was celebrated for its song? *"C'est le même oiseau, monsieur,"* he answered. They told me afterwards that it was some kind of woodpecker.

The big layer of political and professional people, to which the Marcelins belong, has a sort of social equality with these, but does not intermarry with them. Below is a third stratum of government employees, which continually takes in black blood.

Embassy party: I became involved in a conversation with the younger Embassy and State Department people, who finally rather disgusted me by their plugging of the beneficent purposes of the U.S. in respect to the rest of the world. I suppose that what we are doing in the West Indies and South America is all right, but I react unfavorably against attempts to represent it as disinterested. The First Secretary's house is in a section of large and handsome residences that I hadn't yet seen. Life must be rather agreeable here. I found a former cultural attaché who had been superseded but was just staying on. No Negroes except a Negro agricultural expert, an American, attached to the Embassy, with his wife.

Opening of Exposition, Dec. 8: They had set the date of opening for the 8th and, in spite of the fact that almost nothing was finished and many things hardly begun, they had the ceremonies then, with services by the clergy and speeches by officials. Masses in the morning—church bells, the sound of ringing, and few cannon firing salutes —officials in silk hats around the Exposition and the Palais National—a few fireworks in the evening (a brief and feeble exhibition compared to Wellfleet's on 4th of July). The Exposition almost nonexistent: the only places where people were milling were the post office, which was open but hardly functioning, and the Palace of Tourism, which was empty and closed, but where people stood looking through the windows at the mural: grotesque and horrible wood carvings in the post office that were attracting some quiet attention—perfectly dreadful murals, evidently all by the same man, squashed hideous two-dimensional symbolic figures—the Negro breaking his chains, etc.—formless caricatures, if that, no drawing, no composition, no sense of color.

In the evening, I visited the carnival—almost nothing going but the American attractions—Ferris wheel, merry-go-round, airplane wing, sideshow, souvenir stand; cafés open; center with tall lighted palms—in the midst of it a high platform, where people danced—artificial lake with abstract half-reclining statues. Might be gay and all right when they get it started. Disappointment of great posters advertizing girl shows (cooch) and snake charmer with only scaffolding and darkness behind them. Seats being built for some sort of outdoor theater. Cockfighting place with electric sign of fighting cocks outside, but apparently nothing going on inside. Lack of makeup or bright clothes for the women, except in the case of very pale pretty girls, likely to be [illegible] looking, accompanied by obviously well-to-do men. Everybody slow and quiet—murmur only rising to chatter where the crowd around the amusements was very dense. People in considerable numbers would walk through empty buildings that happened to be open, though they were so far from

being finished that you couldn't tell what they were going
to be. —But they are going to have another opening in
February.

—Statue of Maréchal Ney stolen from some ship
—nose changed and set up as Dessalines
—Bogat's story of the haunted house—soft step on the
stairs: one rat on its back, with an egg in its paws, being
pulled downstairs by the tail by another rat. They also
ate the ends of his fingers one night when his hand was
hanging down from the bed. He hadn't felt it—the legend
was that their breathing on what they were gnawing acted
as an anesthetic.

Pastor [H. Ormonde] McConnell[16]—I was impressed
by Pastor McConnell, who had been so active in the
movement to teach Creole and with whom I made a trip
to Marbial. Energetic, driving car, teaching, godly household—County Cork, Yeats and Shaw, humorous, extremely competent; French and Creole uncongenial to
Haitians—since even unbelievers have a certain Catholic
position. Prosaic, clear-cut, and positive, Wesley his whole
culture. Admiration 1786—the Methodists at work in a
more clear-cut way than I had ever seen done before. He
was leery of evangelism. His somewhat isolated position
in Haiti made me understand the nature of Protestantism
more clearly than I had ever done before. I had never seen
a first-rate Methodist at work, missionary work in West
Indies, begun during the lifetime of Wesley, has always
been a specialty of Wesleyanism from the time when
1,100 Negroes were converted to that church in Antigua.
The Catholic priests in Haiti have been on a pretty low
level. The Catholic Church has long had the habit, very
annoying to Haitians, of referring to Haiti as La Bretagne

[16] See *RBBO*, pp. 95–134.

Noir, and sending them ignorant priests from Brittany. These priests have presided at an amalgamation of Catholicism with voodoo. Each of the saints is identified with one of the voodoo deities, and the Madonna in her various aspects with the various aspects of Erzilie.[17] In the museum, you see voodoo altars with Catholic chromolithographs.

Pastor McConnell, of course, will not countenance anything of this kind. He will not compromise with the voodoo cult, and he admits having had very little success in converting the natives from it. In the whole of his years in Haiti, he has effected only one conversion. There had been a man at Cap-Haïtien whose wife was always ill, and who believed they were bedeviled with a *loa*.[18] He had made an impression on this man. I asked him whether he told them that the *loa* did not exist. There would be no use telling them that, he said: the *loa* were just as real to them as anything else in their lives. He told them that the *loa* were evil spirits. They already sometimes called them Satan, having no doubt been taught to do so by the Catholic priest. He would ask them which they thought was stronger; the spirits or J.C. The man in question had been persuaded to burn up all this paraphernalia, which he had brought out of hiding places in the ceiling and the floor: fetishes, bottles, gowns. His wife had then recovered.

In all this, the fundamental difference between the Catholic point of view and the Protestant was brought out

[17] Grande Erzilie, a Haitian goddess and part of the voodoo pantheon. See *RBBO*, p. 121.

[18] *Loa* are voodoo deities described by Stanley Resor as "sparks from the divine anvil broken off when the Grande Maît[re] fashioned the universe." Resor, a Marine Corps medic, arrived in Haiti in the 1920s, and according to EW "knew more about voodoo than any other white man."

for me very plainly. The isolation of McConnell in Haiti, where there are very few Protestant ministers, threw him into conspicuous relief. In the case of the priest in Haiti, his function was to represent the Catholic Church, to go through with its prescribed rites, which meant inducing the natives to submit to them by meeting them on their own level. To the Methodist pastor, who must get results, it is quite evident that the voodoo-worshipping peasant can never understand the convictions that the pastor has derived from the Gospels, and that he cannot learn Christian morality till his cultural level has been raised. To effect this, he must be taught to read and write the language he speaks and in which he thinks. The task of the missionary, then, is primarily education; and it is one of the striking proofs of McConnell's magnanimity and common sense that he will not mix religion with his teaching, and he disapproved of La Fontaine since it encouraged various kinds of roguery. In the meantime, the only way in which positive proof may be offered of the value of Christ's teaching is by giving a good example, by illustrating this in one's own person. The Protestant must impress himself as an individual where the priest is but an atom in relation to the Church. Pastor McConnell did not explain this, but one became very strongly aware of it when one watched the precision and patience with which he taught the children in his school. The Protestant must demonstrate virtue, and this demonstration, of course, if it exceeds the internal resources, may become an odious fraud, and infinitely less sympathetic than the humble routine of a simple priest; but—since my own tradition is strongly Protestant—a really good example of it is to me far more sympathetic than the best of either Catholicism or voodoo.

—UNESCO conference in Paris, October 1946. [Emmanuel] Gabriel in office under previous government, inspector of city schools—preparatory commission—[had held] British scholarship—prompted McConnell to go to [President Dumarsais] Estimé, who asked McConnell to draft letter to Haitian minister in London to forward to UNESCO—asked Haitian government to choose suitable place for experiment (Dr. Laubach[19] was present in Paris)—who sent request on to Doret, then under secretary now Minister of Education. Difference between the commune and the parish (twice as big as the commune?). Doret got statistics from bishop referring to parish which seemed to show that some Roman Catholic centers were teaching Creole, actually it was a bigger area including Protestants—transport problems terrible and hard for people to raise subsistence level.

Arthur Bonhomme, brought up in Methodist Church, ultra-nationalistic, opposed to foreigners, asked Trumbull to preach to them, but he didn't get $100 a month, went back to old church, while Bonhomme group founded Free Methodist Church. Attack on President [Sténio] Vincent about ten years ago, Bonhomme knew about it and was imprisoned and became converted, reading the Bible in prison, and had vision in which he saw himself as John Wesley of Haiti to lead it back to Christian faith—came out after about two years preaching red-hot evangelistic gospel and got idea of putting Scriptures into Creole, became head of Haitian Bible Society and active in little group, joined up with Laubach method—became head of committee *pour la diffusion par enseignement de la Créole, Bureau de l'éducation des adultes.* January 1946, after revolution assumed position of government representative on Marbial—McConnell had kept religion out of Creole teaching, disagreeing with Bonhomme—(confidential)

[19] Frank C. Laubach, an American missionary whose reading methods are still successfully reducing adult illiteracy in Haiti.

Bonhomme removed Protestants from committee, supported Fignolé,[20] who was telling the blacks to massacre
the whites—made Minister of Education and behind
[illegible] bought by Dr. Bond, colored American sent
by State Department—later lost job and given $380 a
month as technical adviser to President—Fignolé pro-
masses against elite. Mouvement Ouvrier Populaire—
MOP—Minister of Finance said he would not sanction
giving funds for Creole while Bonhomme was head of
office for adult education.

Bonhomme had assumed position of go-between Haitian
government and UNESCO—Métraux[21] didn't want job,
an anthropologist, left—then Métraux with Spanish came
down and found Bonhomme in charge, who wouldn't cooperate, and Métraux went away—then Gabriel arrived
to prepare reading materials and a new reading method,
based on [I. A.] Richards, and put as temporary head of
project till Odden comes. —English educational expert
(confidential) Bonhomme would put in request for
$1,000, which he'd spent on teachers' back wages (having
engaged too many) though he'd asked for money for different purpose. —New method will take three months,
whereas old one takes fifteen days.

McConnell criticisms: no educational director, no reading matter. No new Creole book since 1945 and old books
out of print (because they felt they couldn't trust Bonhomme's lavishness—had spent money on large office instead of printing paper)—McConnell printed books on
$300 he got from coordinator's office (American).

—1,000 copies of three books

[20] Daniel Fignolé organized the resistance Mouvement Ouvrier
Populaire.
[21] Dr. Alfred Métraux, American anthropologist sent by
UNESCO to Marbial.

—movement for teaching Creole began in 1939

—Toward a World Literature, Frank C. Laubach (Columbia)

—Committee on World Literature for Mission Conference of N.A. Etienne Bourand, professor in Law School, worked it out with McConnell—went to Fouché, Minister of Education, whom he knew and who had just come in. Question of uplifting masses. —They showed Fouché charts and talked to him—he offered to print charts and did 1,000 copies for experiment, first experiment was made 1st May 1940 at Tupion, near Petit Goave, and other experiments not very successful. Story of Rescal. In 1940 produced first paper. Rescal produced better results—people in plains better than in mountains. McConnell took over schools without being able to pay much, promised to try to get teachers jobs. [During] 1940–1943 concentrated on Plaine de Cul-de-Sac, got influential people out, who were incredulous that they'd learned to read in two or three months, went on three years, with more school—by 1943 one thousand people had learned to read. Tremendous opposition from Roman Catholics and old-fashioned French culturists. English phonetics not French—real reason: people were easily exploited when ignorant. Laubach came in 1943; [President Elie] Lescot in 1943, but not Minister of Education, won over—committee formed, Emmanuel Gabriel as president and McConnell general secretary 1943—paper began and published two and a half years. Limiè-Fos-Progrè—3,000 copies—new chart and lessons prepared—government never gave enough for nationwide campaign planned—at present time publishes 500 or 600—government gives half money $27,000 total—school I saw volunteer Protestant affair not supported by government—30,000 people perhaps have learned to read. —Bonhomme took over committee at time of revolution when others away. —Recent law about 1947 for eliminating illiteracy by use of both French and Creole (to impress UNES-CO). Peasants not good at learning because have never used minds for anything like that.

Banana story: the Standard Fruit Company was shipping out eight million stems a year—new government took plantations away from them, mismanaged the whole thing, did not take good care of the bananas—now only about a million. —You always struck snags when you set out to make a success of anything.

The Standard Fruit Co., with its monopoly, had had everything organized. Estimé, when he took away from them all but a few private plantations, gave the various properties to his deputies, who ran them each for his own profit, underpaid the peasants, failed to take care of the trees—peasants quit and trees died (?)—also, question of getting boats to transport them.

Elite much addicted to voodoo however much they might pretend not to be. Exposé by Frenchman, in Roman Catholic paper, about 70 voodoo temples in a certain part of Port-au-Prince to which presumably the best people went. They made him leave the country.

Lescot was trying to put through a new constitution in order to succeed himself. They had arrested him, much to his surprise. —Estimé trying to do the same thing. —$8,400,000 had been appropriated for the Exposition, much of it disappeared and almost nothing built, and the foreign buildings didn't come out of this money. One official is supposed to have diverted a lot of concrete to his own new house that had been meant for a public project. When it was found there, he had said frankly: Certainly—it's our turn now.

—Voting: in the country, the people would simply hand their cards to the pastor, who would use them for his candidate. On other occasions, they would disregard the names indicated by the people and write in the names of their own candidates. The literate ones they get drunk so that they don't notice.

—Some years back, the Catholics made a campaign against the Protestants, accused them of superstition and circulated songs saying that Protestantism was worse than voodoo. One of the ministers, to stop the trouble, had finally made a *bagarre,* shooting off a gun in a Catholic church to give the gov. an excuse to proceed against the Catholics.

McConnell's patience and care with pupils. —I am certainly Protestant, as Auden said, in expecting the priest of a religion to be good. To be valid as a religious teacher you have to give an example of virtue—and this is a very difficult thing to do and rather very few people can do it, because any kind of exhibitionism, though the preacher may be Karl Marx or Woodrow Wilson, and however much power he may exert, will in the long run render him odious. If your gospel hasn't made a man of you, why should other people accept it? If McConnell got anywhere with any Haitians, it was because he set them an example—if he was able to sell them the Gospels, it was because they could see that they had made him what he was, that he embodied them. He was a man, not an institution. —But limited: strange blankness about Parnell and Wolfe Tone, Shaw and Yeats—he took my remark literally—Shaw was a freethinker! Concurred in them one by one—Protestantism—if you make any impression on one person, you are doing well.

—I thought afterwards about his role on our trip—kept the driver from driving off the road—but when we left the bus—the streets were cleared (he had asked us in to hot soup, which we declined)—he drove us all home like a demon (contrast to De Young). —Lack of animus, merely critical, in discussions of Catholics and the fanatical Bonhomme. —These stories (such as Haitian with two women) may sound sententious as I tell them, but did not sound so as McConnell told them. —The whole household was a genuinely religious one (grace at dinner). —He was very clear, self-disciplined, direct—ironically humorous in a not unkind way. Had given himself an answer to every question.

McC.'s kind of Protestantism is, after all, the form of religion that I most surely sympathize with. —On the side of his limitations didn't even have very wide connections in Haiti—self-disciplining of Scotch bumptiousness, but he was born in Co. Cork.—competence, clearness, human tact. —John Wesley obviously his hero—stopping on the steps to admire the view—Bonhomme wanted to be the Haitian Wesley—human rivalries, etc., in all this, but a moral ideal getting perceptibly close to being embodied.

Impingement of French—disequilibrium of a variety of kinds—all the complications of color—but for that very reason the remarkable individuals stand out—they are not good examples of the French or the Negro or whatever type—their dignity and distinction is that of men and women (of course, in other countries, the mixtures may be equally varied—all the class differences, difference of breeding and education, but here the difference can be read on the Negro, and this makes everybody more self-conscious). Example of Toussaint (all black).

—The result of this black and white rating is to reduce the whole breeding business to absurdity.

December 12—I was right in my idea that Haiti has a

unique importance and interest. It is the only place where you can see independent Negroes, with a tradition of victory behind them, trained in a highly developed culture. One curious thing I had noticed, that Yvonne Sylvain talked about explicitly: the Haitians make a point of not visiting and not knowing much about the other West Indian islands, where the Negroes are still kept in an inferior position. They have lately taken a little to amusing themselves in Havana, but otherwise, except for sending young ladies to learn English in Jamaica, they simply ignore the rest of the Antilles. When they make trips, they go to France or the United States. She says that the slums of Port-au-Prince are as bad as any anywhere, but that I am right in my impression that all except the poorest people in P.-au-P. are clean. Soap, she says, is one of their chief articles of consumption.

—Mme. Marcelin: *une femme de mon nuance* showing me her wrist.

Whole attitude the opposite of crouching down and writhing on the ground characteristic, from Exposition show of voodoo ceremonies.

(Introduce at this point (?) association of voodoo with Catholicism—evidence for these myths about this source —I do not get McC.'s morals out of the Gospels myself, but he has undoubtedly made it into something consistent and virile. —Better to be McC. sitting upright in his jeep than those white-robed and nightcapped crouching voodoos.)

De Young a cheap (not exactly the word) Belgian, with a certain force and charm.

The UNESCO virus versus the yaws virus.

Gentleness of people in taxis—quarrel over one or two gourds between driver, with family at Exposition and light mulatto who stammered and offered to get into front seat and drive to the police—white (or almost) girl who forgot to pay fare. *"Vous n'avez pas payé, mademoiselle."* *"Ça arrive à tout le monde."*

The voodoo is one of the things that keep the Negroes groveling . . .

Dec. 14, 3:35 p.m. Port-au-Prince: Exquisite varied shades of blue of the harbor and mountains, as seen from my verandah—not too heavily rain-saturated clouds above, stretching low and long above the long hills; shadow, in all the foreground, on the green treetops, sown with roofs, of the town; beyond, the few white spires and domes and low bulks of public buildings picked out by the sun among the greenery; then, a paler green of strips of land off the wharves; to the left, the greenish shallows, to the right, the tender blue, like the discovery of some delicate watercolorist, with a little white sail or two; then, the dim darkening blue of the mountains, which, as I watched, became faintly purplish, that charming, that delicate, water that lay below it, too—like nothing so solid as water, but a soft element, purely aesthetic, that had been provided as a pure tint—the Marcelin novels compare it to silk—this was only in the sensitive lap of the inmost part of the bay—to the left, the water was darker, with gradations of color that were never sudden. —Never so bright as southern Italy. The warm red of the Haitian flag (on a spindling white radio (?) tower) above the Exposition.

—Later, about 5 at the Savoy, I saw long clouds of a soft diluted gray hanging over a sky of a dull diluted orange—all of this like light tints laid on paper—to the left, above the hither mountains, heavier clouds full of exquisite effects of a diluted inkiness.

Pink and yellow bisque of the buildings in town—the arcades with arches that looked as if they were made of some very soft substance, like that of Necco wafers.

Performance by Dames de St. François de Sales: —Coiffures of young debutantes in front of me: reddish but crinkly, white-looking girl with brown hair, others had abundant black hair, quite straight and done up in the normal way; but one girl in a different row had a prodigious dense head of black crinkly hair; old lady with normal-looking white hair; man in the black straight glossy hair slicked back.

—Unattractiveness of young girls' dresses and general lack of taste; set was simply a big paper screen full of punctures and gashes, little picture hung ridiculously high, windows with blinds painted on, doorways a nasty yellow, curtains with brown snakelike garlands, badly designed, department store furniture, wicker and wood.

—Bad lighting, actors in *Antigone* casting shadows on one another, and front of stage not adequately lighted— horrible harsh and metallic loudspeaker that kept repeating a phonograph record of what must have been a female voice singing a Strauss waltz—whereas the performance at the Exposition is a very distinguished show, which would enchant an audience anywhere in the world.

Dec. 15. Next morning the sky pale, mountains a shadowed dim buff, hung, above, with small unmoving clouds, sea—a little before, a deep glowing blue like Elena's eyes—now a taut almost insubstantial pale blue silk, with two long strips of darker blue. —Then, a little later, these stripes got beautifully wider and bluer. Freshness and richness of the mornings.

At night the sound of the native drum, which they play with their hands, so far away one can't clearly catch its rhythms, is like the drip of eaves after rain.

Moderation of the Haitian climate and the beauties of the Haitian landscape—nothing like what one thinks of as tropical—this combined with French influence to make them restrained and quiet. —What I thought meager applause at the dance festival, they told me showed great enthusiasm for Haiti.

Voodoo forbidden by Toussaint, who wanted to please the Catholic planters—also to prevent insubordination against himself—still officially forbidden, but members of an all-black government supposed to practice it. Police get rake-off to permit it. —J. Fosset, a Catholic priest, who made charges against the upper classes in *La Phalange* and was compelled to leave the country. (The priests sell the country people images, to which they give the names of voodoo gods.)

Dr. Price-Mars, *Ainsi parle l'oncle* appeared in '25. Seabrook's book also important (1928).

Educational experts began advocating teaching of folk tales and dancing of folk dances in the schools, in order to dissociate them from religion from 1931.

Folk dances in the Champ de Mars, creating a scandal, on Flag Day (under Lescot) in May '45.

Trade union movement began in '46.

Pro-black agitation by [Daniel] Fignolé under Lescot (MOP) on radio—made Minister of Education by Estimé, but lasted only a few months—said his job was to found schools and give injections, and freely criticized his colleagues. Dismissed and since in opposition—pro-masses and anti-bourgeois. (Did he take refuge in the American Embassy?)

—Black and mulatto issue mainly a product of the American occupation—Lescot had appointed to Cabinet all his friends, who were mulattoes. —Fignolé, when he had seen a black government, renounced his racial policy, saying that the blacks in power were worse than the mulattoes.

Haiti rather like Greece.

Haitian flag the tricolor with the white knocked out.

Gabriel on Césaire: *C'est un Français—c'est un Français.* (The French take a few bright boys, educate them, and make them into Frenchmen.)

We had threatened to send Haitian officers to Martinique, after the fall of France, so that the Germans wouldn't grab it. France had given *départemental* status to Martinique, Guadeloupe, French Africa, and French Guinea.

Another sign of their dissociating themselves from the other French islands: Gabriel didn't even remember, though usually exact on Haitian history, that the final resistance to Leclerc had been aroused by the news that, by Napoleon's orders, slavery had been restored in Guadeloupe. Trujillo not invited to Exposition.

They do not overrate their own literature, because they set it up against French.

African character of the Sylvain house: moundlike, the grounds themselves are a sort of mound, swelling up from the street and the adjacent places, wide cobbled walk, front; the house swells from the grounds—blindlike latticed doors, dark hall inside with old bookcases full of confused books. A big old tree, little grass, hibiscus and other plants growing wild and tangled. —A big black-head in Yvonne's sister's ear and a large sore place where another had been removed. Her sulkiness at the night-club, which spoiled the evening for Yvonne because they had not waited for her—refused to *smile* or speak.

Fishing trip. Blond-blue and fluid silver all awash in the wake of the boat. —Exploring the coral forest with a glass mask—little blue-and-yellow fish and fish with light stripes on dark—branching coral and purple sea fans. Water too tepid for the best kind of swimming. Uncertainty about what is going to be hard and what soft.

Political situation. Students struck, would not go to classes, called out comrades (?), but at this moment the government *mit main basse* on the leaders and suppressed nine papers; some of them were party bulletins. Fignolé took refuge in Argentine Embassy, but, according to de Consay, not there now. President had said that liberated leaders were now free to do whatever they pleased, including publish their papers. Fignolé's point of view, indistinguishable from that of Estimé—apparently had no real program.

State of siege declared June or July—tinkering with the Constitution—dismissing people from the Conseil Communal, which is unconstitutional, because the municipal councils elect the deputies by registering the votes.

—The "Christian" Catholic party was in the opposition because they were against the government's encouragement of voodoo. —Choley's point of view about the Exposition—was it really that they had nothing to exhibit? —Creole not a language, you couldn't teach it. —Didn't approve of women working, carrying produce to market; a relic of the early days when the men were in hiding, also reason for houses being built among trees.

Gabriel's adoption of his mother's name—that of a man who had, on being brought from Africa, immediately escaped and never been a slave—a warrior (?).

Martinique. There were rumors in 1940 that American troops might be sent to seize Martinique, then the strongest Vichy outpost in the Western Hemisphere.

May 24, 1941, the monster German battleship *Bismarck* had a brief engagement with British ships and got away, and Roosevelt thought it might go to Martinique and take possession of that strategic outpost. Should we attack and try to sink her? The *Bismarck,* however, turned eastward and was sunk by the Royal Navy.

Special detachment of American troops had been in training in amphibious operation for the capture of Martinique in case Germany tried to take it over from the Vichy government.

Haiti ended relations with Vichy France Nov. 10, '42.

INDEX